SHIPS AND SEASCAPES

AN INTRODUCTION TO MARITIME PRINTS, DRAWINGS AND WATERCOLOURS

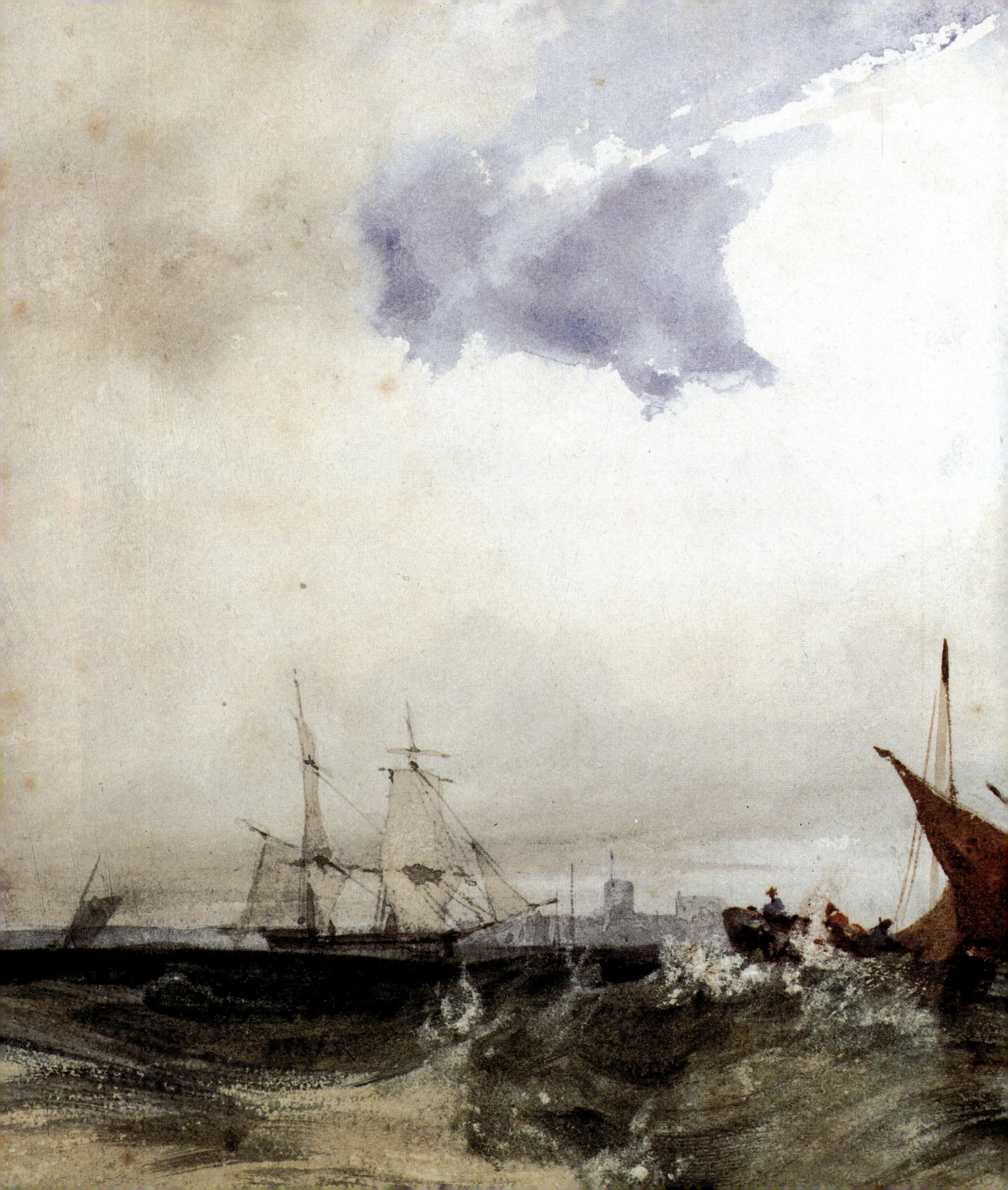

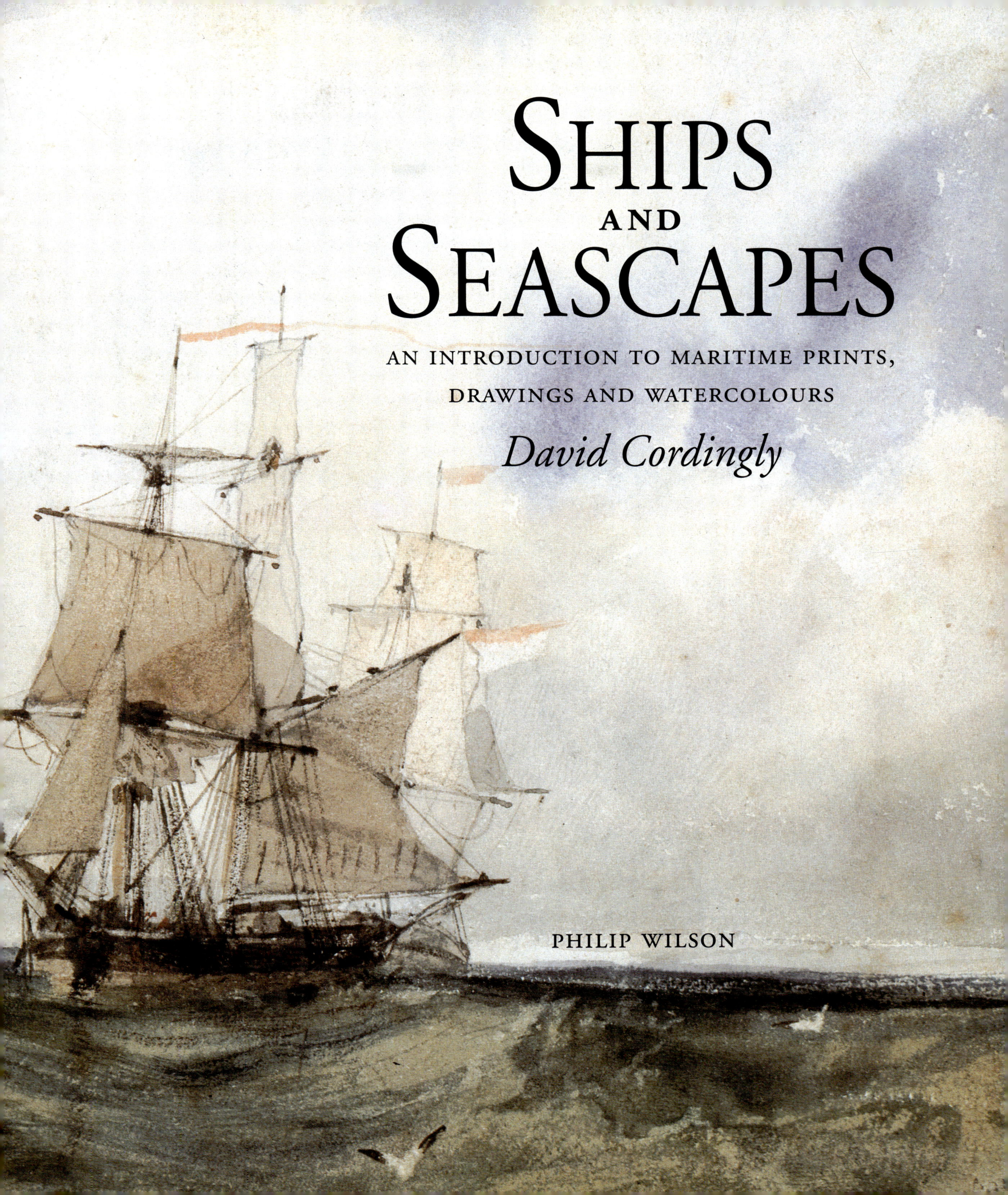

SHIPS AND SEASCAPES

AN INTRODUCTION TO MARITIME PRINTS, DRAWINGS AND WATERCOLOURS

David Cordingly

PHILIP WILSON

For my mother Mary Cordingly

Copies of pictures from the collections of the
National Maritime Museum which are reproduced in this book
may be obtained from Photo Sales, The National Maritime Museum,
Greenwich, London SEIO 9NF.

First published in 1997 by
Philip Wilson Publishers Limited
143-149 Great Portland Street
London WIN 5FB

ISBN 0 85667 484 2

Edited by Gwen Rigby
Designed by Langley Iddins

Printed and bound in Italy by
Società Editoriale Libraria per azioni, Trieste

Contents

Preface and acknowledgements

A museum colleague once remarked to me that the problem with marine paintings was that they all looked the same. He pointed out that the upper part of every picture was always taken up with sky, the lower part with sea, and somewhere in the middle there were always ships.

Of course most marine paintings are dominated by sea, sky and ships but this has not prevented artists from portraying these elements in very different ways. Some of these differences are the result of the individual vision of each artist. Others are determined by the subject matter and by the weather which invariably sets the mood of a seascape. .

One of the aims of this book is to show the variety of pictures which fall under the general heading of marine paintings or seascapes, and to demonstrate the numerous techniques which have been used over the years by artists and printmakers to portray ships and small craft. The emphasis is on watercolours and prints but as it is difficult to describe the development of marine art without reference to oil paintings I have in some instances used pictures of oil paintings to indicate the characteristic subject matter and style of artists such as Bakhuizen, Brooking, and Van de Velde the Younger.

The book is intended as an introduction to a fascinating subject and makes no pretence at being comprehensive. The selection of artists and illustrations for inclusion is personal and may seem rather arbitrary. I have concentrated on Dutch and British marine artists and am aware that I have not done justice to the artists of the French and American schools, let alone the artists from other maritime nations, or the many fine marine artists working today. The heavy charges currently imposed by many museums and art galleries for photography and reproduction fees has meant that, like many other authors of art books, I have tended to rely on pictures from commercial galleries and auction houses rather than museums, and this has inevitably limited the range of pictures available.

Fortunately my former colleagues at the National Maritime Museum, Greenwich, have been unfailingly helpful: I am particularly grateful to David Spence and Chris Gray for assistance with the photographic order which I put their way; to Roger Quarm who read the chapter on Prints and Processes and made many useful suggestions; and to James Taylor, Pieter van der Merwe, Lynsey Macfarlane,

Ros Whitford, Paul Cook and Tina Chambers who helped me in my search for suitable illustrations.

I would like to thank Jack Shirreff and his assistant at the 107 Workshop in Wiltshire for taking me through the mysteries of printmaking and demonstrating how to make aquatints, copper engravings and etchings, and lithographs. I am grateful to Duncan McNeill for the special photography required to show the various techniques of printmaking. I would like to thank Anne Jackson and the staff at Philip Wilson Publishers, and Gwen Rigby the editor, for all their help during the production of the book. I am most grateful to the designer, Langley Iddins, for his sympathetic handling of the material and for producing such a handsome looking volume.

I owe a special debt to Julia Korner who read the introductory chapter, checked my comments on the sale-rooms and tracked down numerous pictures for me. As on previous occasions Frank and Dorothea Cockett came to my rescue and helped me fill gaps with pictures from their fine collection. Mark Myers had much good advice on living marine artists and I only regret that the constraints of space prevented me from following up his many suggestions.

I am especially grateful to the owners and staff of the London galleries and sale-rooms who allowed me access to their photographic archives, and lent me colour transparencies and prints for reproduction in this book. My thanks are due to Richard Kingzett at Thomas Agnew & Sons; Roger and Jill Hadlee at the Royal Exchange Art Gallery; Oliver Swann of the Tryon & Swann Gallery; Rodney and Charles Omell of the N.R.Omell Gallery; Patrick Conner at the Martyn Gregory Gallery; the Parker Gallery for the loan of a fine mezzotint and a soft ground etching; and the staff at Bonhams, Christie's Images, Phillips and Sotheby's. I am aware that many of the pictures reproduced come from private collections and would like to thank all those who have given permission for their works to be reproduced and to apologise to all those who I have not been able to contact.

I would like to thank Peter Neill, President of South Street Seaport Museum, for many enjoyable discussions about marine art at his home in New York; and a special word of thanks to the artist and writer William Gilkerson for his generous encouragement, advice and much practical assistance from the outset of this project. And finally my thanks to my wife Shirley for her patience and constant support during yet another spell of dawn-to-dusk research and writing.

D.C.

Brighton, Sussex. July 1997

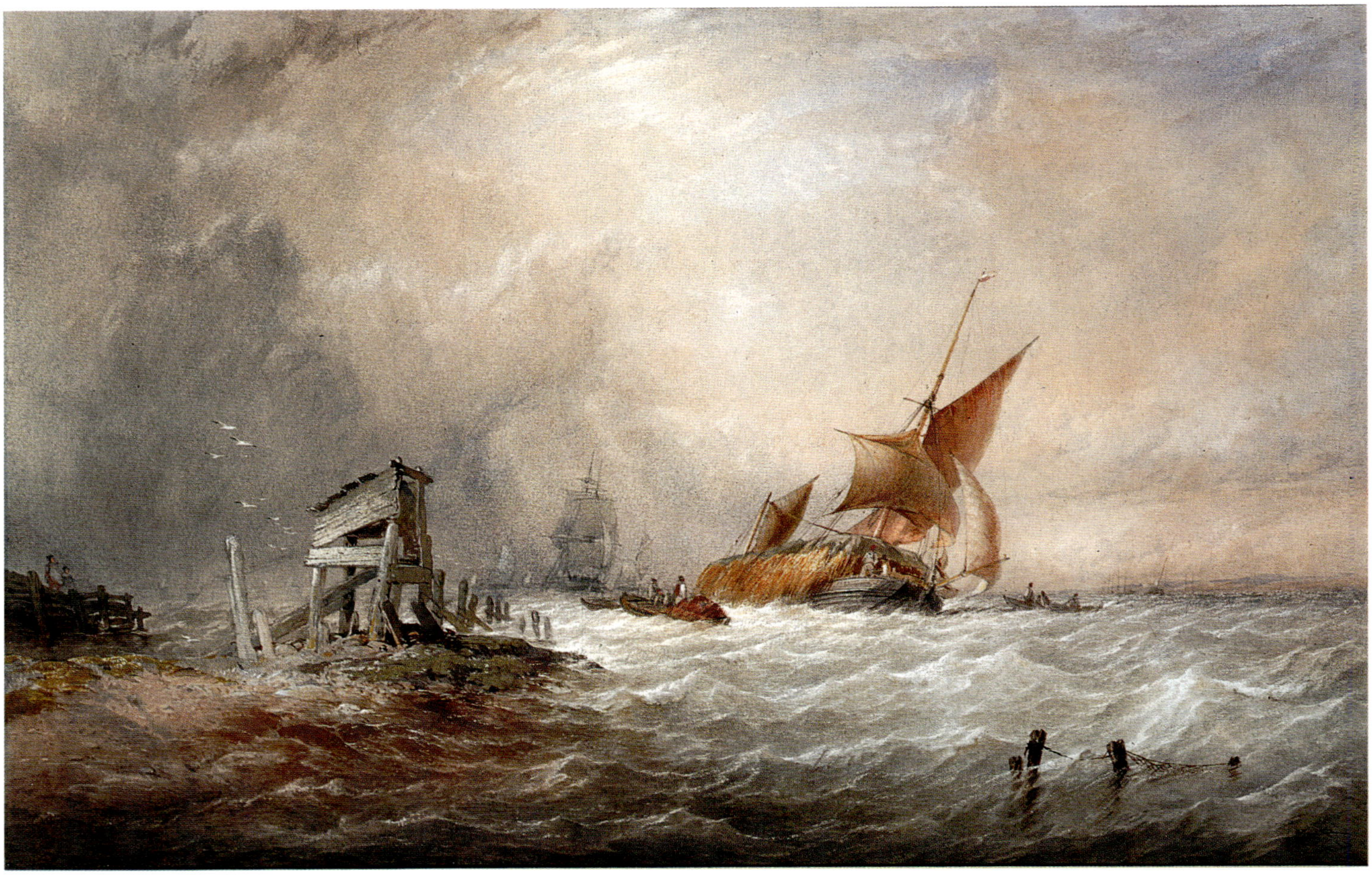

Thomas Sewell Robins

A hay barge passing close inshore

This unusually fine example of Robins' work shows a scene on the Thames estuary, with a brisk wind whipping up short, steep waves. A Thames barge, laden with hay for the horses in London, heads upstream followed by several ships.

Pencil and watercolour heightened with white. Signed with initials and dated '64. Private collection.

OPPOSITE

Sir Oswald Brierly

Allied ships lying in the Bay of Balaklava in the Black Sea during the Crimean War

On the outbreak of war between England and Russia in 1854, an allied French and British fleet was sent to the Crimea. Brierly was invited by Captain Keppel to sail on board the *St Jean d'Acre*, 100 guns, and he made a large number of drawings and watercolours of the fleets' manoeuvres.

Pencil and watercolour. Signed. 1854. Private collection.

Chapter one

INTRODUCTION

Every year several thousand marine paintings, drawings and prints pass through the sale rooms. They range from storms and sea battles to tranquil estuary scenes. They include major works by Turner, Van de Velde and Winslow Homer, as well as crude ship portraits and picturesque coastal views by amateur painters. Sometimes the pictures are given titles that describe their subject matter in detail, but often the entry in the sale catalogue will be restricted to the vaguest of descriptions, such as *Shipping off a coast* or *A harbour scene.* They tell us nothing about the ships portrayed, or the location, or what is happening in the picture.

We do not need to know the subject matter to enjoy a picture, and with a sparkling beach scene by Boudin or Monet it hardly matters. But many pictures, especially seascapes, come to life when we know what the picture is about. In 1836 John Constable gave a series of lectures on landscape painting at the Royal Institution in London. Much of his third lecture was devoted to the Dutch School, particularly to Jacob van Ruisdael, whose paintings were a source of inspiration for him. After describing a stormy river scene by Ruisdael he turned to a winter landscape.

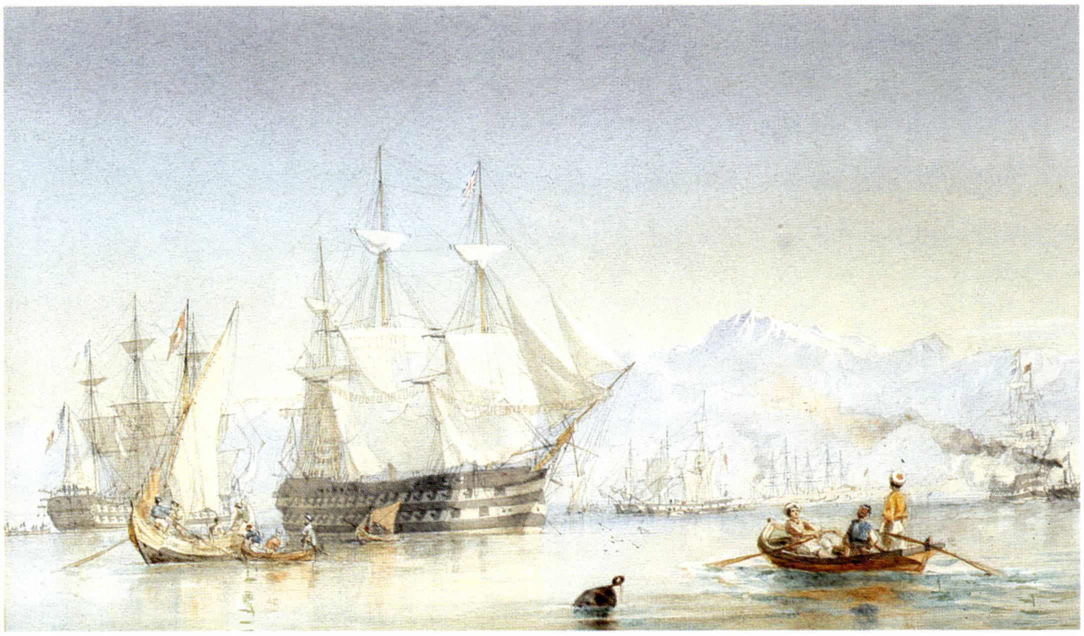

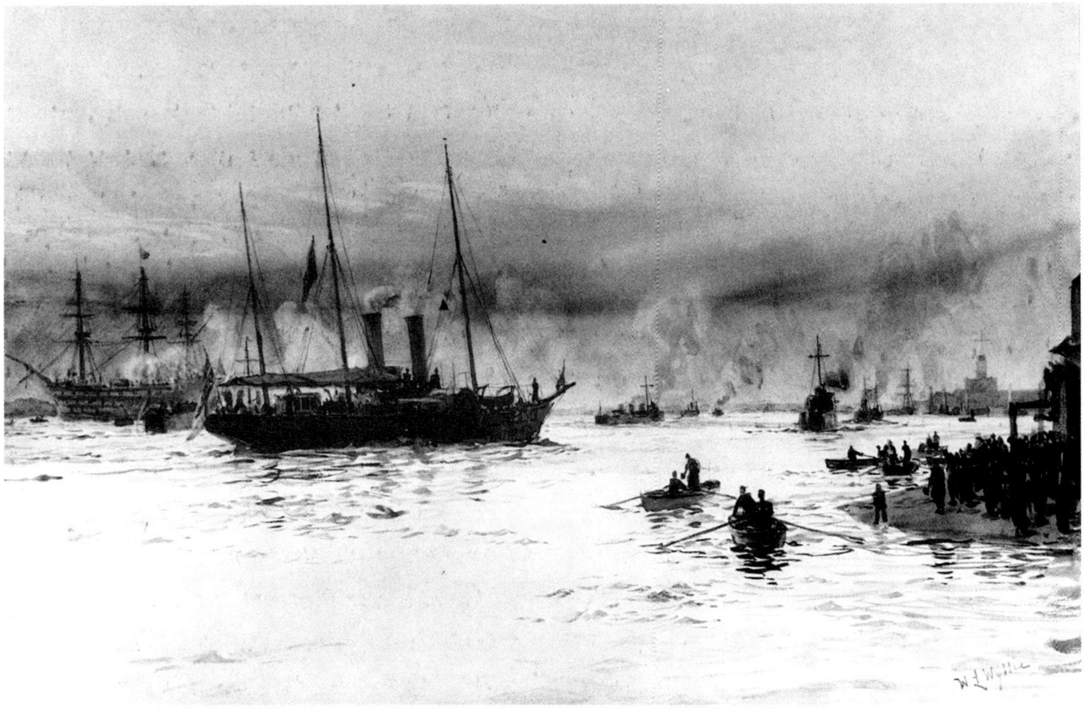

W.L.Wyllie
Queen Victoria's funeral: HMY Alberta *entering Portsmouth Harbour, February 1901*

The royal yacht *Alberta*, carrying Queen Victoria's coffin, steams slowly into Portsmouth harbour. Wyllie made nine studies of the waterborne procession of ships and subsequently exhibited them at Agnews gallery in London.

Pencil, grey wash and white heightening. National Maritime Museum, London.

'This picture,' he said, 'represents an approaching thaw. The ground is covered with snow, and the trees are still white, but there are two windmills near the centre; the one has the sails furled, and is turned in the position from which the wind blew when the mill left off work, the other has the canvas on the poles, and is turned the other way, which indicates a change in the wind; the clouds are opening in that direction, which appears by the glow in the sky to the south (the sun's winter habitation in our hemisphere), and this change will produce a thaw before the morning. The occurrence of these circumstances shows that Ruisdael *understands* what he is painting, he has here told a story.'

Constable had a countryman's eye for clouds and changes in the weather, but he also understood the workings of windmills because his father owned a mill at East Bergholt in Suffolk. This enabled him to interpret Ruisdael's picture and to appreciate the artist's accurate observation. In much the same way, it is possible to interpret the seascapes of Simon de Vlieger, Ludolf Bakhuizen and the other marine artists who were Ruisdael's contemporaries, as well as of those who followed them. If we look at the picture above, we see what appears to be a rapidly executed sketch of a steamer with smoke rising up from the funnels of several ships. This is clearly the work of an accomplished artist, but is there anything more to the picture than first meets the eye?

The signature at the bottom indicates that the drawing is by W.L. Wyllie, who was one of the most gifted and prolific of all British marine artists. In a long and active working life he painted almost every type of craft afloat. He was a keen yachtsman, and from 1907 until his death in 1931 he lived in a large house overlooking the busy waters of Portsmouth harbour.

This drawing is one of hundreds from the artist's studio bequeathed to the National Maritime Museum at Greenwich by his family. The subject is Queen Victoria's funeral, an occasion which Wyllie witnessed in February 1901. The steamer in the centre is the royal yacht *Alberta*, which is taking the coffin containing the queen's body from the Isle of Wight, where she died, to Portsmouth harbour; from there, the coffin was taken to London for the lying-in-state at Windsor Castle. The royal yacht is heading into the harbour preceded by a small warship and other vessels. The royal standard flies at half-mast from her mainmast. The three-masted sailing ship that can be seen on the left, beyond the stern of the *Alberta,* is Nelson's flagship HMS *Victory*, which was still afloat a century after the battle of Trafalgar; it was a few years later that she went into drydock for major restoration. In the far distance on the right of the picture is the tower of the Gun Wharf, which marks the entrance into the harbour, and on the shore in the foreground a large crowd has gathered to see the royal yacht and pay their respects.

Wyllie's picture is typical of a great number of seascapes that at first sight appear nothing more than a random group of ships but on examination prove to be documentary records of actual events or places. A large collection of vessels anchored off a shore may be a royal embarkation or a fleet of merchant ships at the conclusion of a successful voyage to the East. A warship firing a gun may be engaged in a naval action, or may be firing a salute as the admiral comes alongside in his barge. A carefully detailed picture showing the broadside view of one ship and two similar ships, one viewed from the bow and the other from the stern, is likely to be a portrait of a single ship shown in three positions. The picture was probably commissioned by the ship's owner or her captain, and it is often possible to identify the ship from the decoration on her stern or her figurehead, or by the flags she is flying. A picture of fishing boats drawn up on the beach usually shows a particular place at a particular time, and it may be possible to find out where it is by identifying the types of boat or looking for a landmark such as a lighthouse, a church tower or castle ruins in the distance. A knowledge of what a picture is about not only gives it added interest but can also add considerably to its value.

One of the aims of this book is to provide an introduction and a guide to the subject matter of marine prints and drawings. The book also aims to show how the pictures were produced. Most people are familiar with the materials used to make drawings and watercolours, but are at a loss when it comes to understanding the

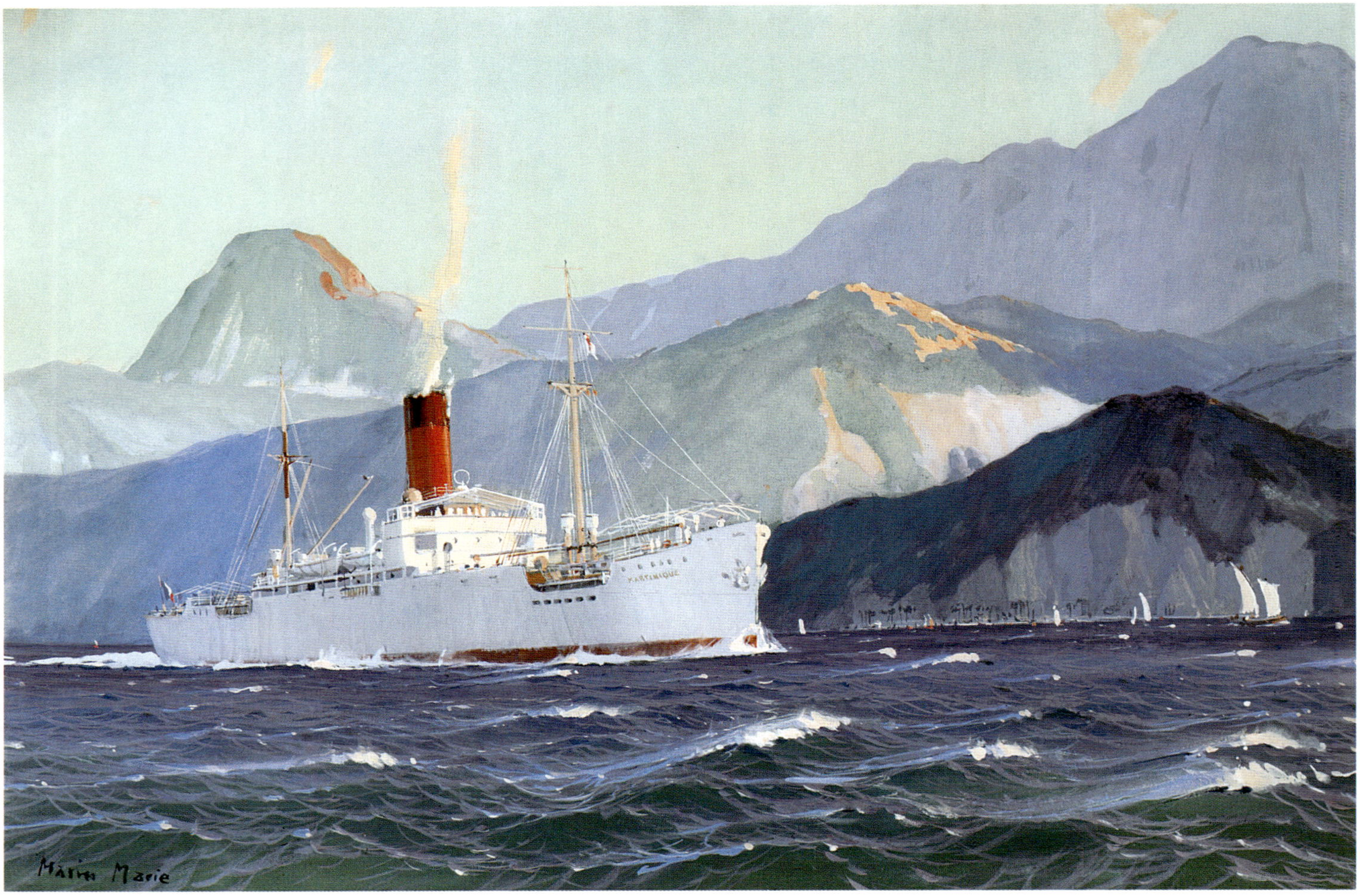

MARIN-MARIE
The French Line's steamer Martinique

The ship in this colourful picture, built for the Castle Line in 1883, was originally named the *Norham Castle*, and for many years sailed from England to Cape Town; in 1903 she was purchased by the French Line. Marin-Marie is probably the best-known French marine artist of the 20th century. He twice sailed single-handed across the Atlantic and was appointed *Peintre Officiel de la Marine* in 1935.

Bodycolour. Signed. Private collection.

Roger Chapelet
The Cutty Sark *in the English Channel*

The famous tea clipper is shown picking up the pilot, who has been rowed across from the pilot cutter in the foreground. In the distance, beyond the red buoy, can be seen a Thames barge. Roger Chapelet was born at Versailles, studied painting in Paris, and served in the French Navy during the Second World War.

Bodycolour. Signed. Private collection.

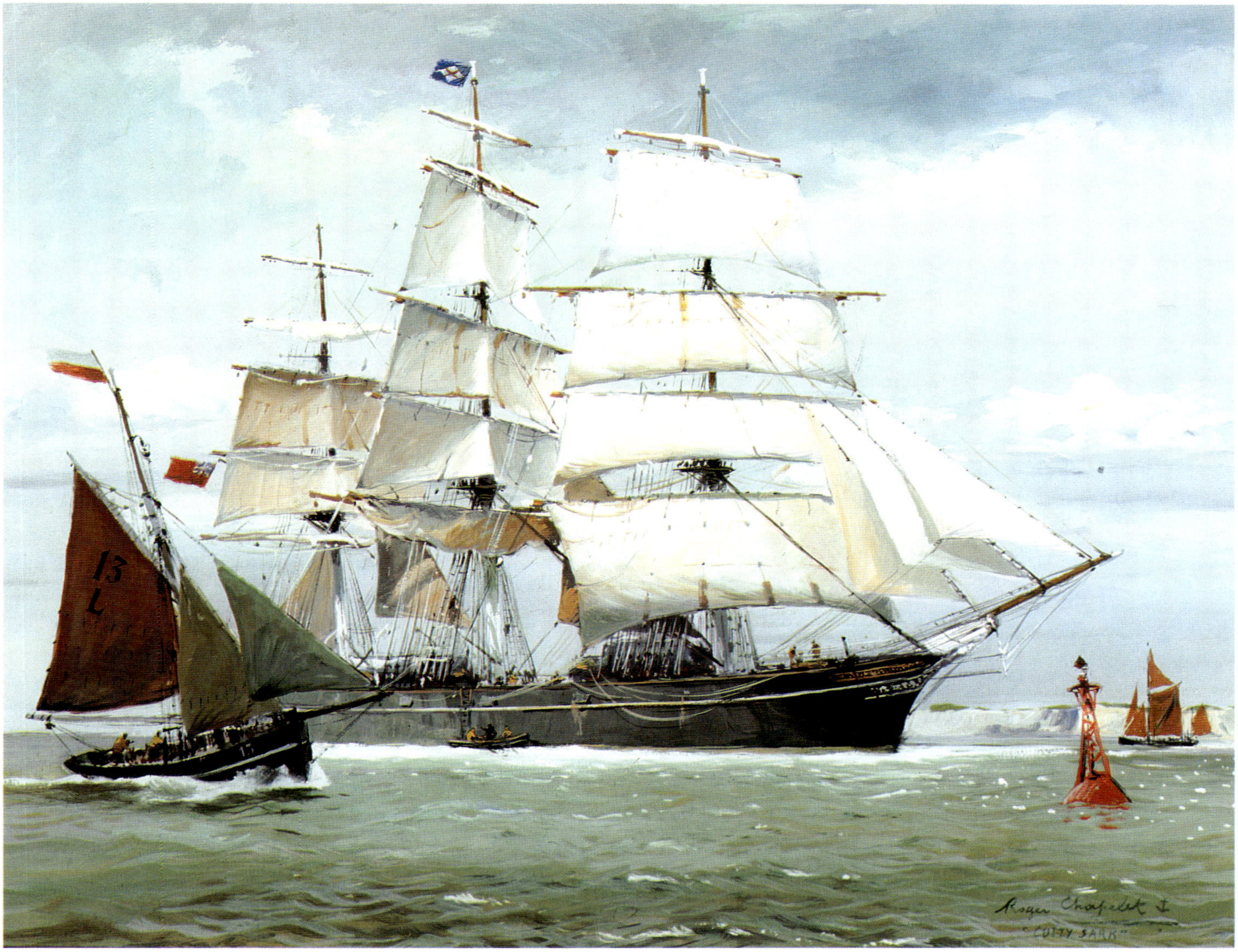

difference between an etching and an engraving, an aquatint and a lithograph. The principle methods of printmaking are discussed, and there is a reading list for those wishing to explore this interesting area in more detail.

The book has been arranged in two parts. The first four chapters deal with the technical aspects of marine prints and drawings: with methods and processes; and with ship types. The remaining chapters provide a general survey of marine artists and print-makers. They are set out in broadly chronological order, with sub-sections devoted to subjects such as Thames views, beach scenes, naval battles, yachting pictures and so on. The purpose of this is to indicate the scope and variety of the subject and to introduce some of the major and minor artists who painted seascapes. This is not intended to be a comprehensive survey. There are more than 1500 names listed in E.H.H. Archibald's *Dictionary of Sea Painters* and only a fraction of this number has been included here. The aim has been to select artists who represent particular periods or schools, such as the early Dutch School or the war artists of the Second World War; to illustrate particular types of picture, such as shipwrecks; and to demonstrate processes, such as woodcuts or hand-coloured etchings. Mention is made of marine artists in France, Germany, the Netherlands and the United States, but the emphasis is on British artists. This is partly because they have shown a special talent for painting in watercolours, and partly because the maritime history of Britain has led to an unusually flourishing tradition of marine art in this country.

No particular distinction has been drawn between landscape artists who painted occasional beach scenes and specialist marine artists who devoted their lives to recording ships because there is no clear dividing line between the two. Clarkson Stanfield, a former seaman whose paintings of shipping are remarkable for their authenticity, also painted a great number of topographical views and landscapes, while some of the greatest contributions to marine art have been made by artists such as Courbet, Monet, Turner, Whistler and Winslow Homer, for whom seascapes were only one of many subjects they portrayed. Similarly, there seems no point in being too pedantic about defining what is and what is not a marine painting. In theory, it ought to include the sea, but such a definition would rule out all those wonderful river estuary scenes by Van de Velde and Brooking, the shipyard scenes of John Cleveley the Elder and Francis Holman, and the many memorable pictures painted over the years of shipping on the Charles River at Boston, on the Seine, or along the Thames waterfront. It is usual to include such pictures in any discussion of marine paintings and they are certainly included here.

Thirty years ago, the books available on the subject of marine painting were few and far between. There were various Victorian and Edwardian monographs on marine artists that could be tracked down in the British Library, the Library of Congress or the library of the National Maritime Museum. But the only books that were readily available were *Sea and River Painters of the Netherlands* by Admiral Sir Lionel Preston; *Old Sea Paintings* by Keble Chatterton; *Sea Painters of Britain* by F. Gordon Roe; and a slim volume entitled *An Introduction to British Marine Painting* by the maritime historian Oliver Warner. These were joined in 1967 by Arnold Wilson's *Dictionary of British Marine Painters*, which provided a useful survey.

During the last 20 years, the picture has changed dramatically. There have been some impressive exhibitions of marine art in museums and galleries in Britain, Holland, Germany and the United States. A number of commercial galleries have organized annual shows of marine works, and there are several art dealers who specialize in holding stocks of marine art. Perhaps most important from the point of view of the collector are the specialist sales of marine art and artefacts that are held regularly by all the big auction houses.

Marine painting, like sporting art, has become a recognized branch of art with its own following of enthusiastic and often very knowledgeable collectors. It has also accumulated its own literature and there are now several books available. These include the catalogues of the collections of some of the major maritime museums, a number of general surveys of marine painting and several dictionaries. The list of monographs on individual marine artists continues to grow. It is headed by the magisterial volumes by Michael Robinson on the paintings of the two Willem van de Veldes, but many other artists have been the subject of specialized studies, including Arthur Briscoe, James Buttersworth, E.W. Cooke, George Chambers, Montague Dawson, Fitz Hugh Lane, Nicholas Pocock, Clarkson Stanfield, Samuel Walters and W.L. Wyllie. The one area that is not covered in most of the books is the price of pictures, and this is obviously something which is of considerable concern to anyone who is starting to collect prints and drawings.

The reason that writers are reluctant to mention prices is because the values change from year to year. Unfashionable artists suddenly become fashionable, and their works command high prices; the fashionable artists fall out of fashion; and the art market as a whole is also affected by wider economic forces.

The easiest way to find out the current price of marine pictures is to get hold of a copy of *The Art Sales Index* or Miller's *Picture Price Guide.* These are updated and issued each year. Miller's *Guide* is profusely illustrated, but because it covers a huge range of pictures the illustrations tend to be too small to give much idea of the quality of the works shown. The best way to get a feel for prices is to go along to the salerooms of the larger auction houses during the two or three days before a sale of marine pictures. You can spend as long as you like examining the pictures on show, and the auction catalogue will include the estimated price of all the works for sale. It is usual for auction houses to issue details of the prices realized for all pictures sold, so later on you can easily find out what each picture actually fetched and compare this with the estimate, which will help you to gain an idea of current prices.

BUYING PICTURES AT AUCTION

This is not nearly as alarming as might be imagined. In the first place, you can attend the auction and bid for the picture on the spot. However, you do not have to do so but can leave a bid with the staff, or even telephone a bid up to the moment the lot comes up for sale. All you need to do is to give the lot number of the picture you want to buy, the top price you are prepared to pay for it, and your name, address and telephone number. You may also be asked for details of your bank or for other suitable references. If you want to avoid this procedure each time, you can obtain a client number from the auction house, which will simplify any bidding in the future. Alternatively, you can ask an art dealer to make the bid for you and a good dealer will be able to advise you on the sort of price pictures are likely to fetch.

Most auction houses charge the buyer a premium on each sale, together with VAT at the current rate (in Britain), so you will have to allow for these additional charges when calculating how much you can afford to spend. If you have never purchased a picture at an auction, it is worth studying the small print in the catalogues. These provide full details of charges and procedures and set out the conventions that are used to describe pictures.

Finally, it always pays to have a close look at a picture before putting in a bid because it is very difficult to get an idea of its size, quality and condition from an illustration in a catalogue. Watercolours, in particular, are notoriously vulnerable to fading if exposed to strong light, and it is common to find that the fugitive blues and greens in an 18th-century seascape have been replaced by varying tones of rusty red and brown. The surest way to check on the fading is to lift the mount and see whether the area of the picture protected by it is a different colour from the area that has been exposed to the light. Obviously, this check will not be possible if the picture is framed behind glass, but you can ask for a condition report from the auction house. A skilled conservator can remove fox marks and stains from a drawing or watercolour, but there is only a limited amount that can be done to rectify the damage caused by years of exposure to sunlight.

Chapter two

DRAWINGS AND WATERCOLOURS

Images of ships have been found in Egyptian tombs dating from about 1500 BC, on Greek vases and among the decorations on the walls of houses in ancient Rome. In medieval times numerous glimpses of ships and the sea appear among the brilliantly coloured decorations of illuminated manuscripts. These are usually associated with biblical stories. Noah's ark and the Flood, Jonah and the whale, and the shipwreck of St Paul are perhaps the most common, but there are also stories associated with St Nicholas of Myra, who was the patron saint of sailors, and pictures showing Christ on the Sea of Galilee. Sea battles were occasionally illustrated in manuscripts, as well as more peaceful scenes of fishermen at work, or ships being unloaded in sea ports.

The Egyptian tomb paintings were painted with an opaque watercolour bound with egg white or gum and the illuminated manuscripts were also painted with watercolours. So, too, were the early sea charts. The earliest of these date from the 12th century and coincide with the introduction of the magnetic compass to the Western world, which made it possible to show the shape of coastlines with reasonable accuracy. These charts, known as portulans, were drawn on sheepskin or goatskin and were embellished with coloured flags, elaborate compass roses and stylized pictures of major sea ports. The heraldic appearance of these early charts gradually gave way to a more naturalistic approach. Mountains, trees and animals were shown on the land masses, and a variety of fish and sea monsters appear among the sailing ships scattered across the oceans.

Maritime images painted in watercolours frequently appear in the sketchbooks and journals made by artists who travelled abroad or accompanied voyages of discovery. Among the finest examples of these are the views of rivers, coasts and harbours painted by Wenceslaus Hollar during his travels across Europe in the 17th century. The voyages of Captain Cook were notable for the hundreds of watercolour sketches made by John Webber, William Hodges and Sydney Parkinson, who were employed as draughtsmen on board the ships.

Drawings were frequently employed for military purposes, and drawing masters were appointed at the military and naval academies in England in the 18th century.

Ange-Joseph Antoine Roux
Pages from a sketch book of studies of Mediterranean fishing boats and local trading vessels

These two pages are from an album of 24 watercolours depicting various types of local craft in the Mediterranean. The vessel on the left is a *tartan* from Nice, and on the right are fishing boats from the port of Marseille.

Pencil, pen, watercolour and bodycolour. Private collection.

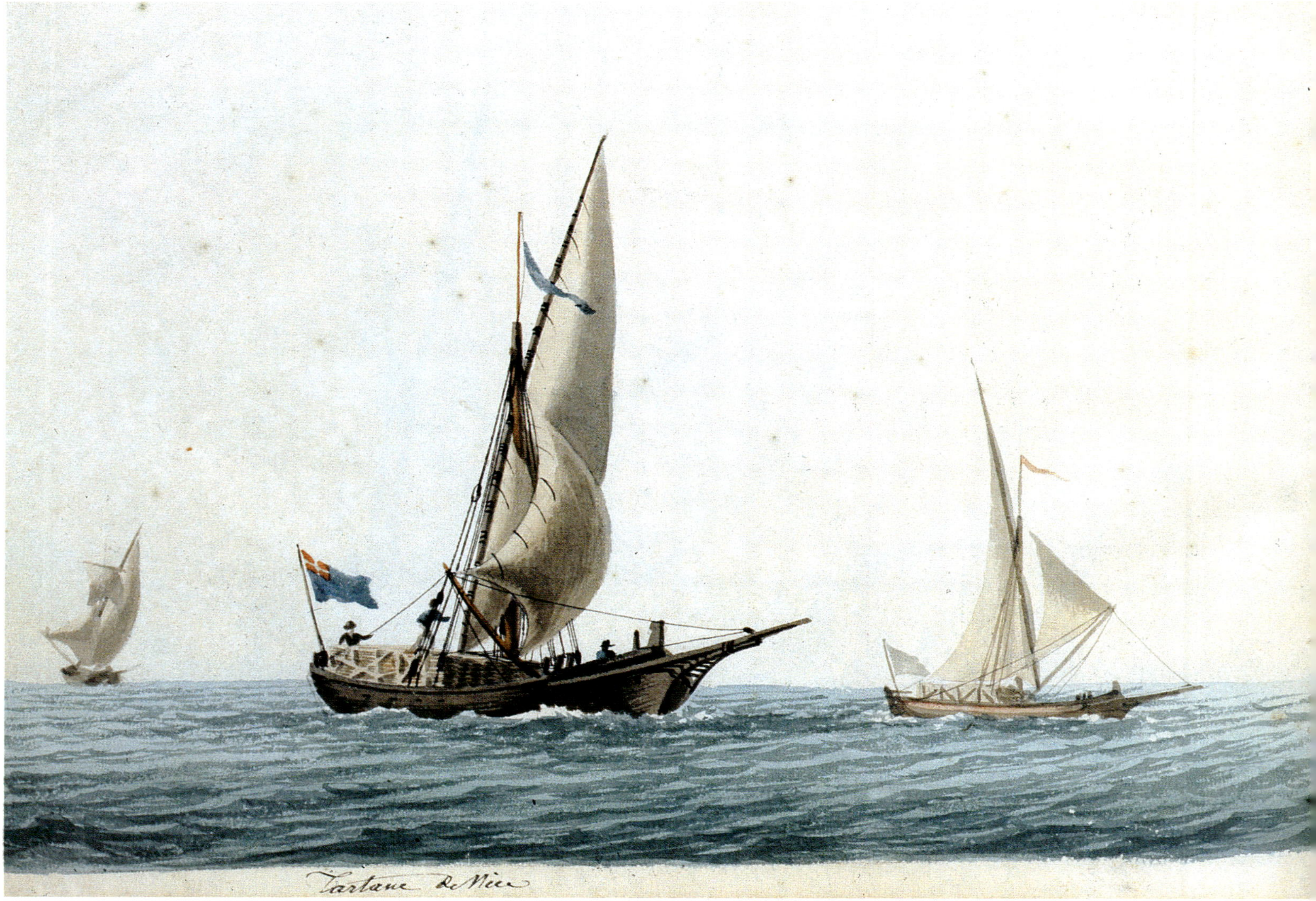

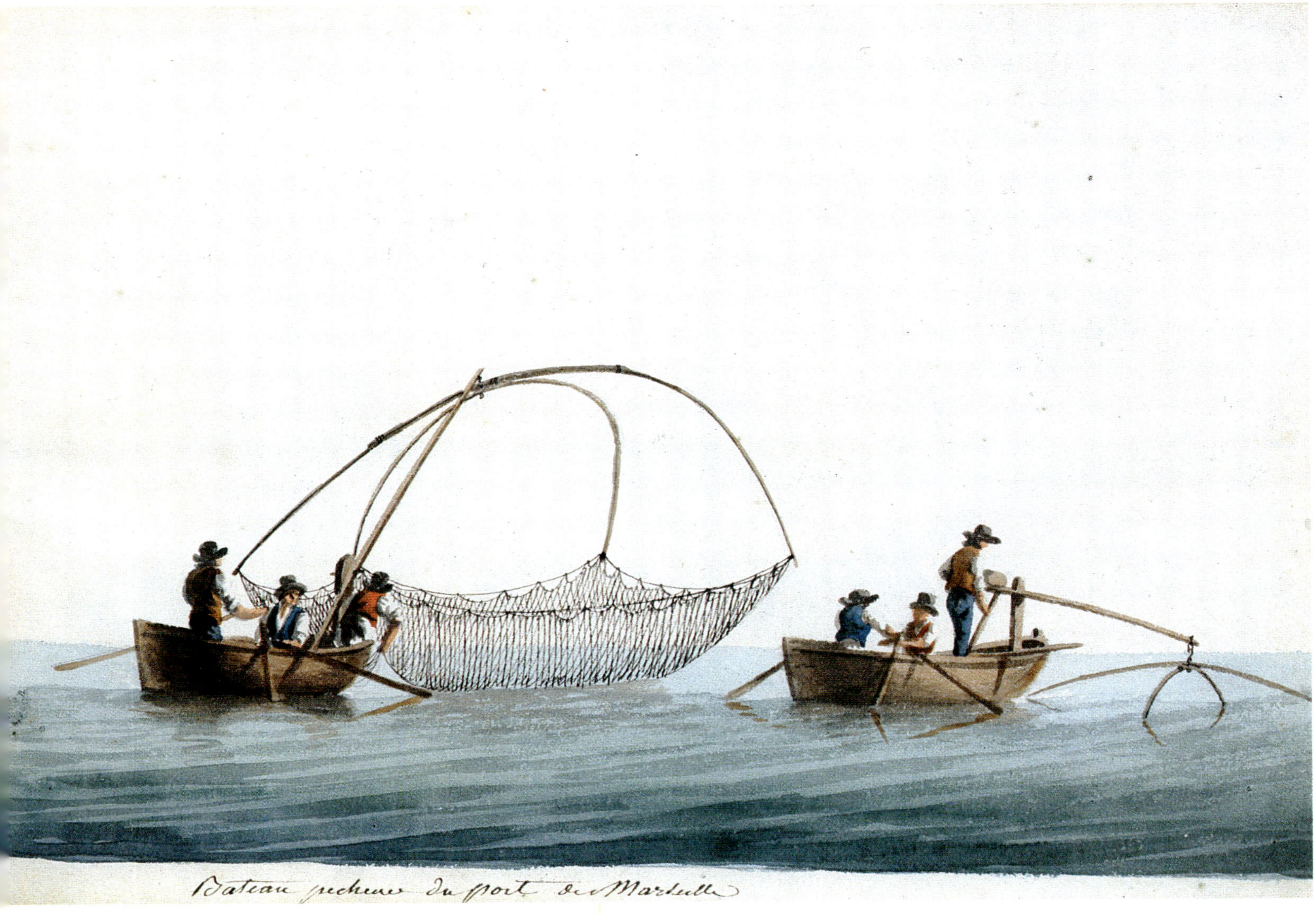
Bateau pecheur du port de Marseille

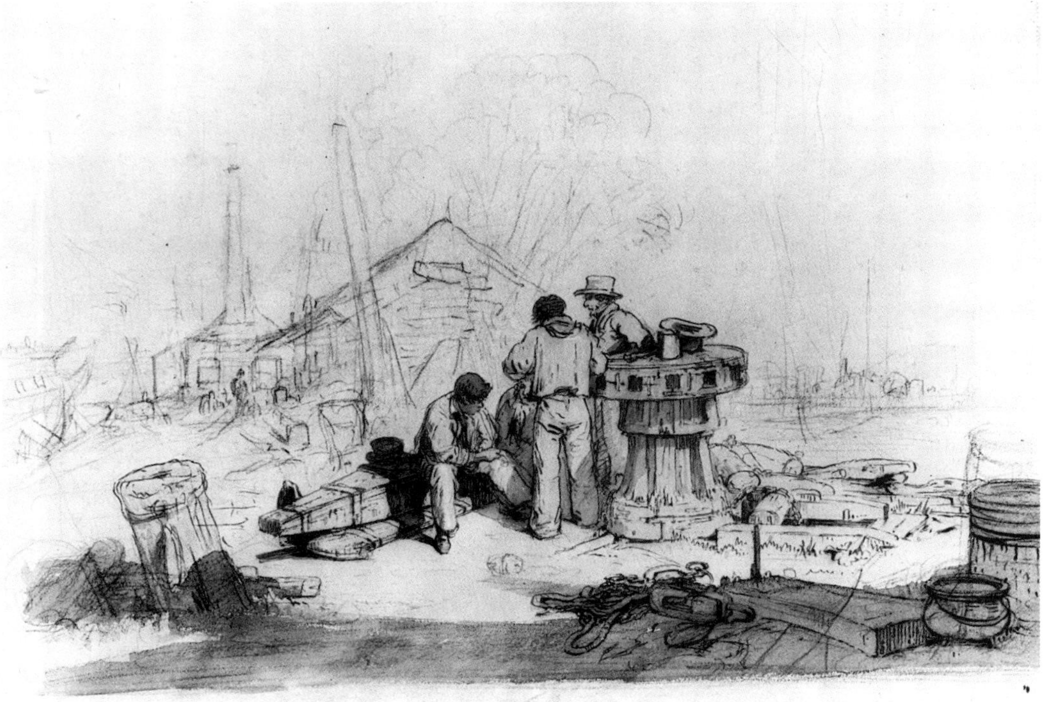

EDWARD DUNCAN
Study of a shipyard with seamen, a capstan, and ships' gear

Professional marine artists filled their sketchbooks with studies such as this, which provided the raw material for their oil paintings, watercolours and book illustrations.

Pencil, pen and grey wash. Martyn Gregory Gallery, London.

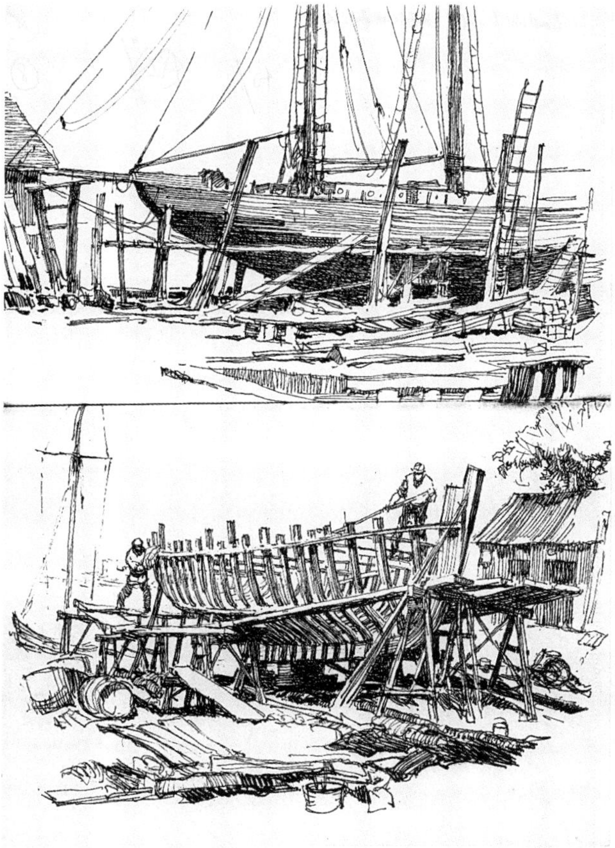

GORDON GRANT
Boatyard sketches

Grant sailed around the Horn as a young man and later became an illustrator for the *San Francisco Chronicle* and *Harper's Weekly.* He wrote and illustrated a number of books on the sea and became one of the most successful American marine artists of his day, exhibiting widely in America and at the Paris Salon. These are two pages from the artist's sketchbook.

Pen and ink drawing. *c* 1930

Naval officers were encouraged to learn how to paint in watercolours so that they could record enemy fortifications and harbour installations. Drawings were also used to record maritime events and battles. Willem van de Velde the Elder was present at most of the battles of the Anglo–Dutch wars in the 1670s. Sitting on the deck of a small sailing vessel he made dozens of rapid pen and wash drawings as the battles raged around him. A hundred years later, Nicholas Pocock made similar on-the-spot drawings from the frigate *Pegasus* during the Battle of the Glorious First of June. In this century, war artists were officially appointed to record the events of the two World Wars, which resulted in some powerful and memorable images being produced by artists such as Charles Pears, Richard Eurich, Eric Ravilious and Norman Wilkinson.

There was a great demand in the early 19th century for travel books and books of picturesque views. These were illustrated with engravings or etchings that were usually taken from watercolours specially commissioned for the purpose. Many of the highly finished watercolours by Clarkson Stanfield, Edward Duncan and Samuel Prout were originally produced as book illustrations. Watercolours were also used as the basis for many of the engraved illustrations in magazines such as the *Illustrated London News* or *Harper's Monthly Magazine* and *Harper's Weekly.*

In spite of the long tradition of watercolour painting and the splendid examples to be found in manuscripts and among the portrait miniatures of the Tudor and Stuart periods, it took a long time for watercolours to be accepted as suitable pictures for public exhibition. When the Royal Academy was founded in 1768 a number of watercolours were included in the annual exhibitions, but they were generally

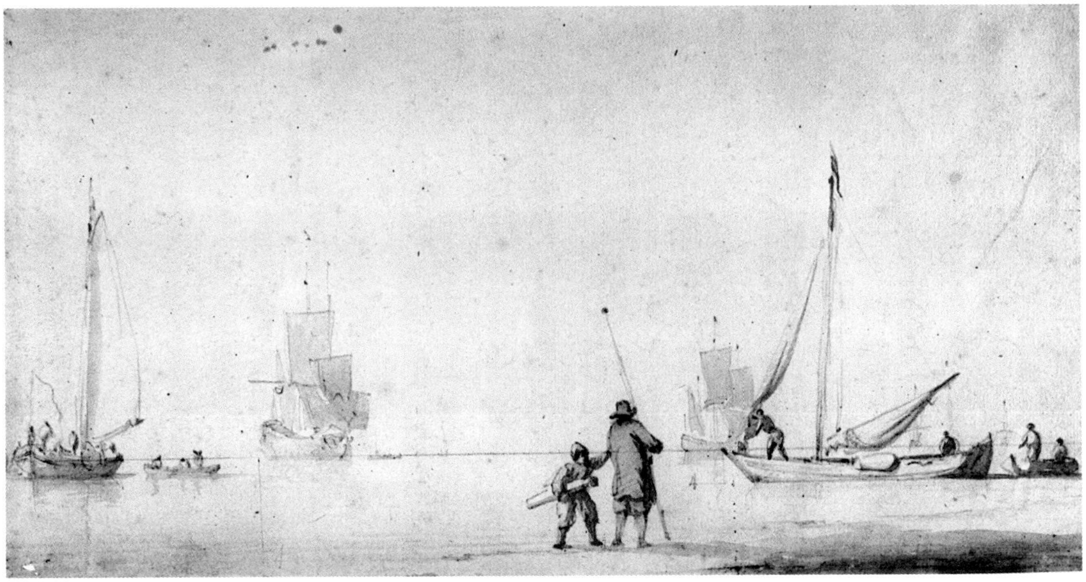

WILLEM VAN DE VELDE THE YOUNGER
A perspective study of Dutch vessels near the shore

The artist demonstrates in this sketch how to place ships in the correct perspective, depending on the onlooker's viewpoint. Here, it is 1.2m (4ft) above the foreshore, the same height as the boy standing next to the man with a pole in the foreground.

Pen and brown ink with grey wash. *c* 1675. National Maritime Museum, London.

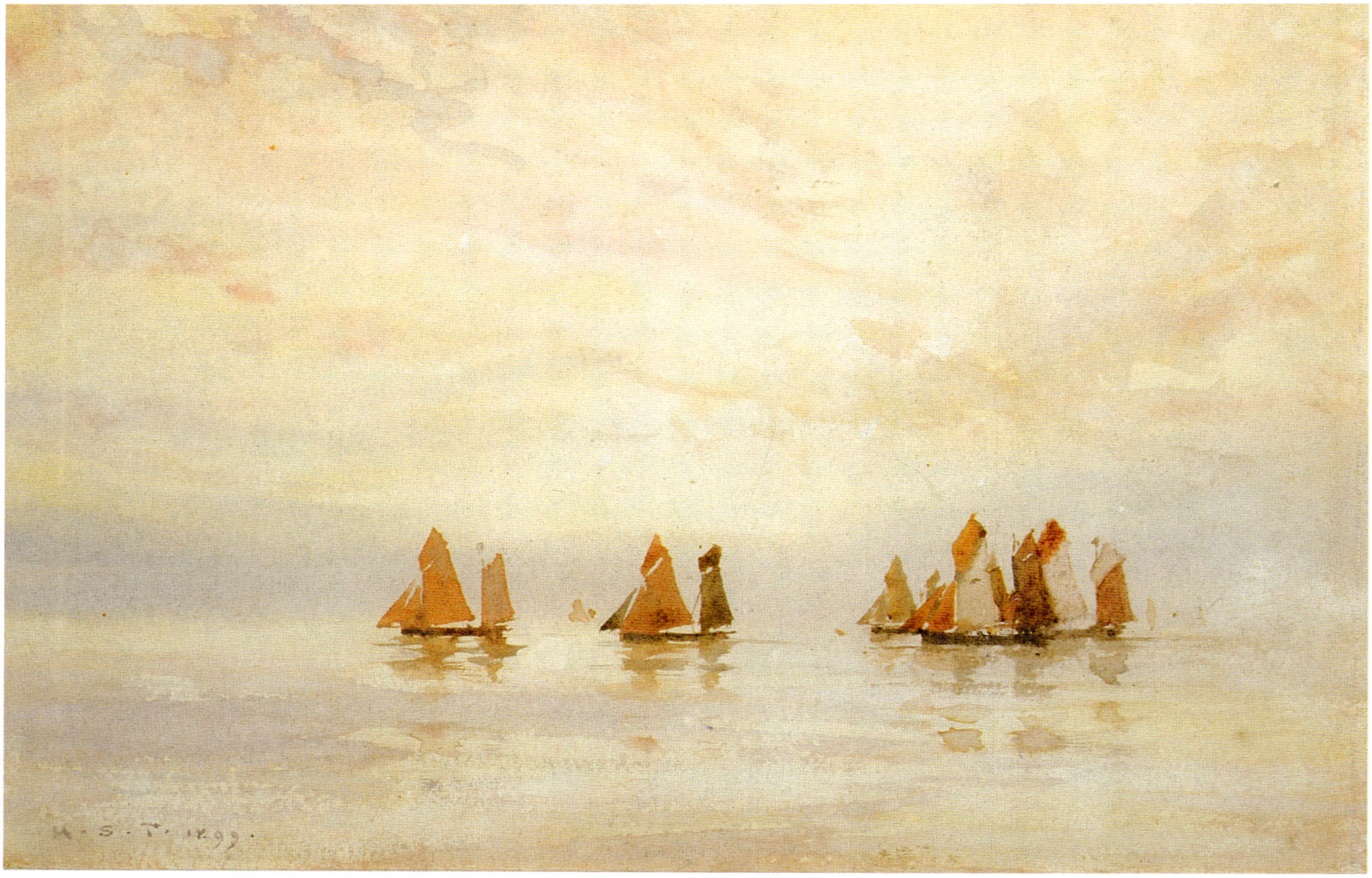

regarded as inferior to oil paintings and not to be taken too seriously. It was this attitude that encouraged a group of watercolour artists to found the Society of Painters in Water-Colour in 1804. This provided a public venue near Bond Street, in central London, for the work of those artists who specialized in the medium. Other venues followed during the next few years. Although watercolours no longer had to compete alongside the more robust oil paintings, there was a tendency from this period onward for them to become larger and more highly finished and to be displayed in elaborate gilded frames.

Nowadays we are so used to seeing watercolours and drawings on public display that it is easy to forget that the majority of drawings were made by artists for their personal use, rather than for public exhibition. For hundreds of years artists have covered loose pages and filled sketchbooks with charcoal, pen or pencil studies of faces and figures, plants and animals, buildings and landscapes. These were learning exercises, experiments, life drawings, copies of other artists' pictures, studies in perspective, and preparatory drawings for finished paintings. Many of these studies

HENRY SCOTT TUKE
Fishing fleet becalmed

In this deceptively simple picture the artist has made maximum use of the transparent qualities of watercolour. The much-diluted washes of colour allow the white of the paper to shine through and create a beautiful pearly light. Tuke was a member of the Newlyn School of artists based in Cornwall and here he shows the local fishing trawlers on an unusually calm day.

Watercolour. Signed with initials and dated 1899. Royal Exchange Art Gallery, London.

were retrieved from artists' studios and have found their way into private collections or into the collections of art galleries and museums. They frequently appear in the sale rooms among the more finished exhibition pieces. Apart from their beauty as works of art, these sketches and studies often provide a fascinating insight into the working methods of the artist.

METHODS AND MATERIALS

Watercolours were traditionally prepared by mixing coloured pigments with gum arabic and diluting this with water. It was the gum arabic, not the water, that enabled the colour to stick to the surface of the paper when the water evaporated. Sometimes the dried watercolour on the page has a transparent appearance, allowing the white of the paper to show through. Sometimes the watercolour is dense and opaque, as was usually the case with illuminated manuscripts and portrait miniatures. Opaque colours (called bodycolour or gouache) were produced by adding an opaque white, which was originally made from white lead and, from the 1830s onward, from zinc oxide. Sometimes a combination of transparent and opaque colours was used. Turner

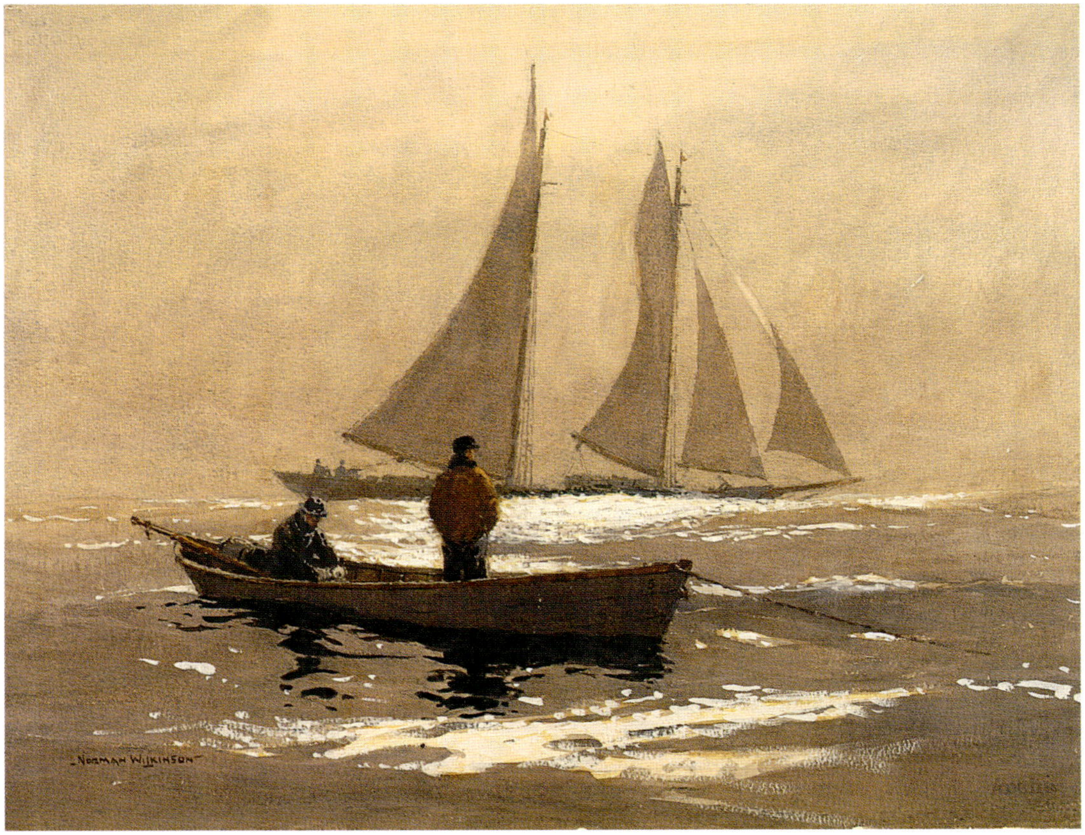

NORMAN WILKINSON
Fishermen on the Newfoundland Banks

Instead of using the white of the paper to create highlights, the artist has made use of opaque white bodycolour. The picture shows two men in a dory on the fishing grounds of the Grand Banks. When they have finished, they will be picked up by the schooner in the background.

Watercolour and bodycolour. Signed. The Tryon and Swann Gallery, London.

and many of the artists who followed him employed a variety of technical means to achieve the effects they wanted. Areas of sky were wiped out with a sponge to create clouds. Blotting paper or bread crumbs were used to absorb and lighten areas of damp colour. And a sharp knife was employed to scratch through the colour already laid down to reveal the white of the paper underneath; in 19th-century marine paintings it is common to find the white crests of waves, the distant masts of ships and the wings of seagulls produced in this way.

Until the introduction of artificial colours produced by chemical means, colours were derived from molluscs, insects, plants, precious stones and earths. Ultramarine blue, for instance, was made by crushing the semi-precious stone lapis lazuli into a fine powder. Indigo blue came from an Indian plant. Raw Sienna was a yellow-brown pigment which was obtained from an Italian clay rich in iron. Sepia came from the dark brown dye produced by cuttlefish. The colours were reduced to powder form, usually by grinding them with a pestle and mortar, and then mixed with gum arabic, which was derived from the sap of the acacia tree. The resulting pigments were diluted with water and then applied with pen or brush to the drawing surface.

Until metal nibs were introduced around 1800, the most common type of pen was made from a reed or a quill, which was carefully cut with a penknife to form the nib. The preferred quills came from the wing feathers of a large bird such as a swan, goose, duck, turkey, or crow. Ink was made from various forms of carbon mixed with gum and water. Ivory black came from burnt bones; lamp black from the soot of oil lamps; and vine black from charcoal. Brushes were made from the hair of squirrels (so-called camel hair) or from ox hair; the best brushes were red sable, which came from the tail hairs of the Siberian mink.

Paper came into general use only in the 14th century; until then, the traditional drawing and writing surface for illuminated manuscripts and sea charts was animal skin. Parchment was usually made from sheepskin; and vellum, which had a smoother surface, was made from calfskin which had been rubbed with pumice or chalk. The skins of cows and goats were also used.

The familiar lead pencil of today was not in general use until the early 18th century; and before that time artists made use of a variety of materials for sketching and drawing. The earliest of these were charcoal and chalk. In ancient times, the charcoal was made from bundles of twigs which were heated in clay pots with sealed lids; later it became the usual practice to make charcoal from vine or willow twigs baked in kilns. For more detailed work, artists discovered that a stylus of silver would draw a fine line on a suitably prepared surface. Graphite was first discovered in Bavaria in 1400, but it was not until a source of pure graphite was found in

Cumberland in 1504 that its potential as a drawing material was realized. For many years it was thought that the deposit was lead, which explains why graphite pencils were called lead pencils, a misleading term that has been used ever since. The first pencil that we would recognize today was made in 1662 and consisted of a mixture of graphite and various gums and resins. Mass production did not begin until 1761 when Faber opened his factory.

The great advantage of pen and wash drawings and watercolours over oil painting was the portable nature of the materials used. Inks and watercolour washes dried rapidly and finished sketches could be carried home without fear of damage, whereas oil paint remained tacky for several days, which posed obvious problems when travelling. Until the introduction of ready-made paint in tubes, the artist working in oils required a fairly complicated inventory of materials, as well as canvases or wood panels to paint on and some form of easel. The artist working in watercolours could stow all his materials in a leather or canvas bag and take them with him to the waterfront or carry them aboard a ship. All he had to do was find a suitable place to sit, rest a board on his knee to hold the paper, and set to work with pen and ink. Washes could be added with a brush, using water to dilute the ink. Since ready-made cakes of watercolour were not generally available until the 1770s, most artists restricted colour to the minimum when travelling and sketching out of doors. The great majority of 17th- and early 18th-century landscapes and coastal views that were made on the spot are little more than tinted drawings. The drawings of Hollar and Francis Place are typical, and it is notable that the sketches of naval battles made at sea by Willem van de Velde the Elder were carried out in pencil, with the addition of a monochrome wash in grey or brown.

The forerunners of the great age of British watercolour painting were a group of artists known as the topographical draughtsmen. They included Thomas and Paul Sandby, Michael Angelo Rooker and Edward Dayes, and they specialized in painting views of landscapes, country houses, churches, castles and market towns. They preferred transparent colours to bodycolour and usually restricted themselves to the use of India ink and no more than three or four colours. Edward Dayes gave the following instructions for painting a picture of Fountains Abbey:

'The whole effect of the light and shade may be acquired by the aid of Indian Ink, indigo (or Prussian blue), and Indian red: after which the tints may be obtained from burnt terra di Sienna, or Roman ochre (according to their brilliancy), combined with more or less of the Indigo for the vegetation.' He concluded 'These materials are enough in the hand of a master to do anything with, from the slightest sketch to the most finished drawing.'

This advice was echoed in a fascinating letter written by Nicholas Pocock in 1804 to a friend in Bristol. By this date, Pocock had established a considerable reputation as a marine artist. His letter gave meticulous instructions on how to paint a seascape in watercolours, and was accompanied by a demonstration sketch, which showed how it was possible to obtain a variety of effects simply by using Indigo blue, light red, and yellow ochre:

'I have inclos'd a Sketch of Scales of tones produced with 3 Colours only and which are sufficient to produce any colour or Effect whatever – the sketch of boats is done as follows. The cloud first with light red and blue only. The Water the same with a little blue added to it the same pencil just touch'd on the yellow oker for the nearest wave. The near vessel blue and red, with rather more red than in the sky, it is the most Aerial tint and any colouring may be wrought upon it with great Clearness and force.'

By the end of the 18th century, a number of manufacturers in London, including John Middleton and Thomas Reeves, were supplying watercolours in ready-made, rectangular cakes. These could be fitted into wooden sketching boxes complete with a tray for mixing paints and a water container. It was now possible for watercolour artists to take a much larger selection of colours with them on their sketching expeditions. This was to have a marked effect on the style of pictures produced and it contributed to the rapidly growing popularity of watercolour painting in Britain. A further development took place in 1846, when Windsor and Newton introduced moist watercolours in tubes. However, the tubes were made from lead, which made them heavy to carry around in any number, and many artists continued to rely on the hard-cake colours when out sketching.

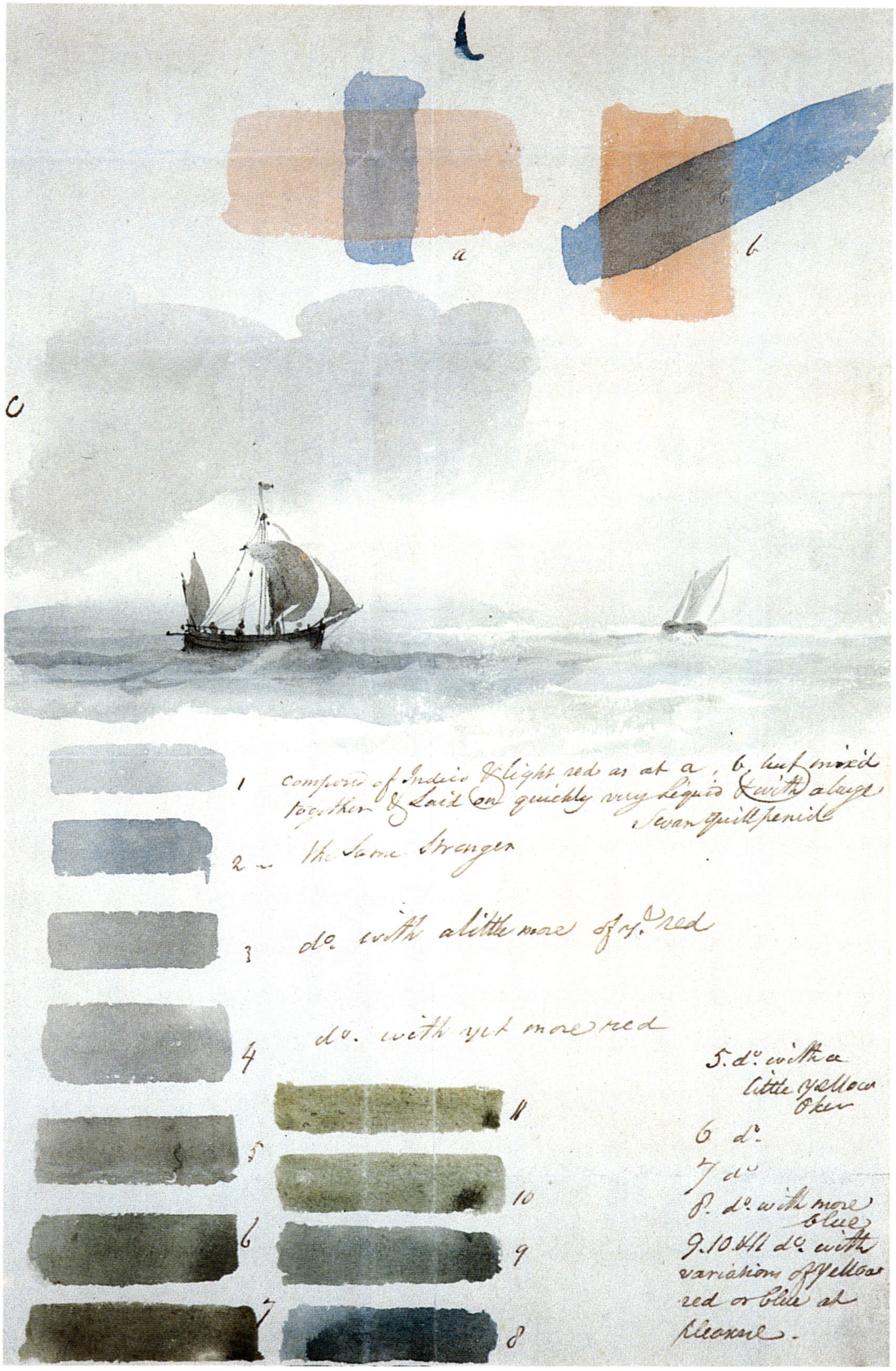

NICHOLAS POCOCK

A sketch of scales of tones produced with three colours only

This sketch accompanied a letter in which Pocock gave advice on watercolour painting to the daughter of a friend. Although a seaman by training and a self-taught artist, Pocock followed the tradition of other watercolour artists of his day and recommended using a limited number of colours, in this instance light red, yellow ochre and indigo blue.

Watercolour. 1804. National Maritime Museum, London.

Chapter three

Prints and processes

Woodcuts, engravings, etchings and other printed images are usually referred to as 'prints'. This is a useful general term, but it gives rise to a number of problems. A photograph produced from a negative is a print, so is a cotton fabric, and so is printed lettering. More confusingly, the word is also used to describe the reproductions of paintings that are sold in huge numbers in shops, art galleries and museums. The discussion here is confined to those printed images made by artists and craftsmen which did not include the photographic process in their reproduction. Lithographs are included, but not photolithographs. Mezzotints and aquatints are discussed, but not collotypes, photogravures or photo aquatints.

Marine subjects have been conspicuously well represented by prints over the years. The delicacy of line and the fine detail which could be reproduced by the process of engraving and etching meant that prints were ideal for depicting the complexitites of ships, gear, sails and rigging. Prints of sea battles were always popular in times of war, and marine artists were able to make a useful additional income by arranging for their pictures of warships and naval actions to be engraved and printed. During the wars between France and England from 1794 to 1815, for instance, hundreds of prints were produced and sold on both sides of the English Channel. But even more popular than sea battles during that period were the humorous and often wickedly satirical caricatures of admirals, sailors and the bawdy life of the waterfront.

The print also made possible the publication and distribution of a series of pictures on a related theme. Favourite maritime topics for such series were views of seaports or pictures devoted to coastal scenery. William Daniell's aquatint illustrations to A *Voyage Round Great Britain* were a particularly ambitious undertaking of this kind, but there were many similar series which concentrated on the picturesque view of a country or region. Another popular subject for a published series of prints was ship types. Outstanding examples of these include the etchings of Dutch shipping by Gerrit Groenewegen published in 1789, the *Liber Nauticus* of 1805 by Dominic and J. T. Serres, and *Fifty Plates of Shipping and Craft* by E.W. Cooke, published between 1828 and 1829.

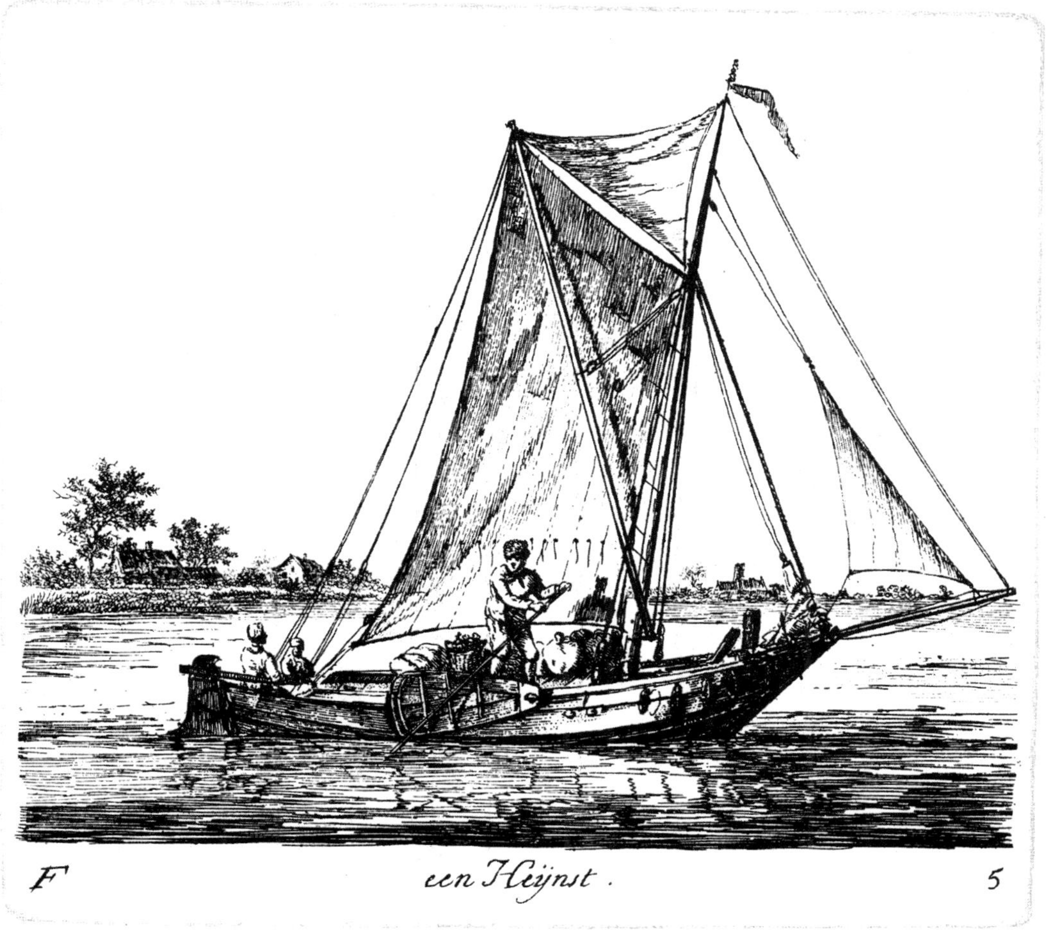

Gerrit Groenewegen
Een Hengst

Engravings and etchings could reproduce very fine detail and were ideal for depicting the complex rigging and hull details of ships and small craft. This picture of an inland vessel called a *hengst* is from a series of 84 prints drawn and etched by the Dutch artist Gerrit Groenewegen. It is reproduced actual size.

Etching from *Hollandsche Schepen* (Dutch shipping) published in Rotterdam in 1789.

Most maritime prints sell for a fraction of the cost of oil paintings and fine watercolours and they are not difficult to find. They are usually included in the marine sales that are held regularly at the major auction houses, and a few specialist galleries, such as the Parker Gallery in London and the Mystic Seaport Gallery in Connecticut, have extensive collections of maritime prints for sale. They can also be found in antique shops, junk shops and street markets.

Apart from being works of art in their own right, many prints include a surprising amount of detail about ships, flags, small craft, harbours and coasts. They provide a useful way of building up a knowledge of ships, and the newcomer to the subject is often assisted by the fact that most prints will include, under the picture, the name of the artist, the name of the engraver, the title of the picture and the date when the print was published. This is in marked contrast to marine paintings, which may bear the artist's signature and a date on a floating log or barrel, but often have neither, and rarely give any indication of the original title and subject matter.

The usual convention in a print is for the name of the artist to be placed under the picture on the left-hand side and the name of the engraver on the right-hand side. The publisher's name and the date are often included as well. Sometimes the words 'painted by', 'drawn by' or 'engraved by' are used, and sometimes the printmakers use Latin or French words to indicate who did what. A list of the words and abbreviations most commonly used will be found on page 160.

Origins and early uses of prints

Prints have been around for a long time. The earliest prints were woodcuts made by the Chinese in the 9th century AD, but it was not until the 15th century that woodcuts were widely used to illustrate printed books in Europe. Around the same time, the technique of printing from engraved metal plates was developed in Germany; Albrecht Dürer used woodcuts and engravings to produce pictorial images of astonishing power and technical virtuosity in the years around 1500. Over the next four centuries, artists and printers developed and refined the various print-making processes. The woodcut and the engraving were joined by the etching, a method of printing that involves the etching of a copper plate with acid. Some of the greatest masters of print-making combined several methods to achieve the results they wanted. Rembrandt frequently combined etching with dry point engraving, which exploited his extraordinary skill as a draughtsman and enabled him to produce the most subtle effects of light and shade.

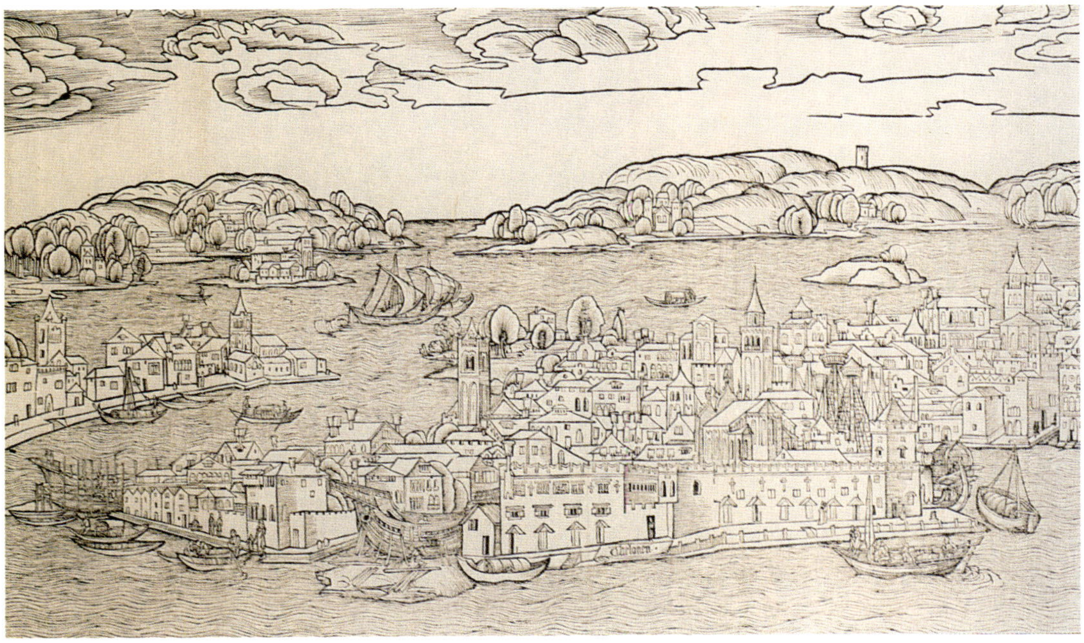

Erhard Reuwich
Detail of a woodcut view of Venice

This is a fine example of an early woodcut with pictures of shipping. It was made by Reuwich to illustrate a book by Bernhard van Breydenbach which was published in Mainz . Among the seven prints in the book are views of the harbours and waterfronts of Corfu, Rhodes and Venice.

Woodcut. 1486. From *Peregrinatio in Terram Sanctam* (Journey to the Holy Land). National Maritime Museum, London.

Some of the earliest prints in which ships and small craft appear are the panoramic views of those European cities that were also major ports. Among the most celebrated of these views are the woodcuts illustrating a book by Bernhard von Breydenbach entitled *Peregrinatio in Terram Sanctam* (Journey to the Holy Land), published in Mainz in 1486, which had seven folding plates, including views of Corfu, Rhodes and Venice. The artist and printer was Erhard Reuwich of Utrecht. His picture of Venice is spectacular and shows an aerial view of the city centre and the surrounding islands, with clusters of ships moored along the waterfront. Amsterdam was another great seaport that attracted the attention of artists and engravers. One of the earliest prints was the bird's-eye view by Cornelis Anthonisz of 1544. This is, perhaps, more of a map than a picture, but it is a powerful image and can be seen as a forerunner of the many views that followed during the next century.

Woodcuts and engravings were also used for reproducing the maps, charts, globes and atlases that followed the voyages of exploration by Columbus, Magellan, Drake and a succession of seafarers from the maritime nations of Europe. The pioneering work was carried out by Abraham Ortelius of Antwerp, who published his great atlas *Theatrum Orbis Terrarum* in 1570. This was the first major work in which the maps were printed from copper engravings rather than woodcuts. The use of watercolour applied by hand, and the addition of ships and sea monsters gave the maps a wonderfully decorative quality.

Another Flemish mapmaker who was working around the same time was Gerard Mercator, who studied under Gemma Frisius and was appointed cosmographer to the Duke of Cleves in 1552. He produced a woodcut world map in 1538, but it was his world map of 1569 and his great atlas of 1585 that brought him lasting fame. He devised a method for projecting the spherical world on to a flat page which was adopted as one of the standard projections by geographers and mapmakers and will be familiar to all cruising yachtsmen today because it is the usual projection used for charts.

The other key figure in the world of map-making and navigation was Lucas Jansz Waghenaer of Enkhuizen in Holland. He gathered together the observations and soundings made by seamen and pilots who sailed the seas around Europe and in 1584 issued his sea atlas, *De Spieghel der Zeevaerdt.* This was a volume of sailing directions [see page 34], and the decorative title page provides a visual summary of the navigational methods and instruments used at the time. The atlas was so valuable for seamen that four years later, in 1588, an English edition was prepared by Anthony Ashley with the title *The Mariner's Mirror.* Its all-embracing contents included 'the courses, heights, distances, depths, soundings, floods and ebbs, risings of lands, rocks, sands and shoals, with the marks for enterings of the harbours havens, and ports of

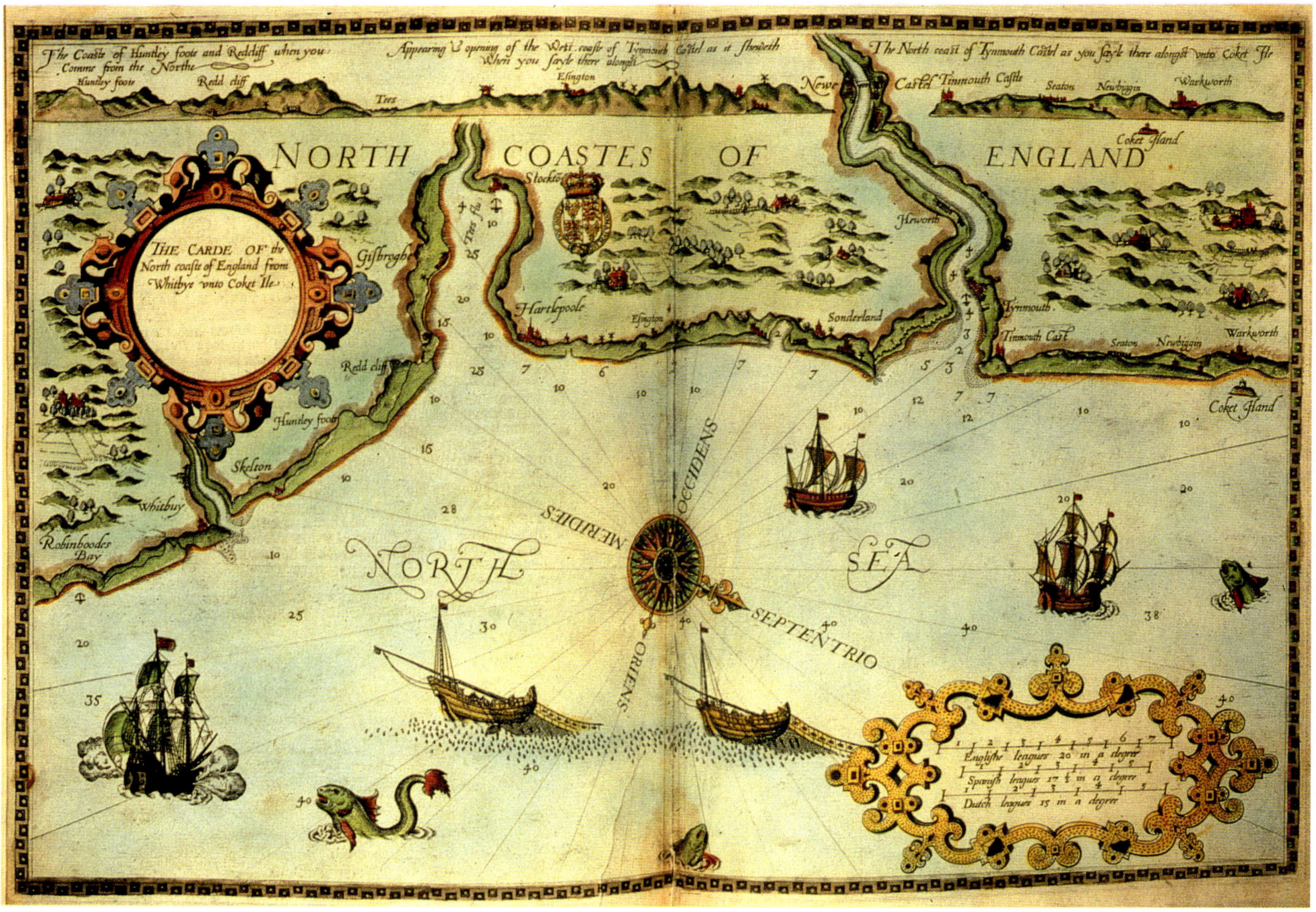

the greatest part of Europe.' It says a great deal for Waghenaer that for many years it was the custom for British seamen to refer to all pilot books and volumes of sailing directions as 'waggoners'.

While the origins of the maritime print may be found in the early views of seaports, and among the decorations of charts, globes and pilot books, the true forerunner of the long tradition of maritime prints was a series of engravings made by Frans Huys after drawings by Pieter Breugel the Elder. Printed in 1561, these vigorous and powerful images of sailing ships set the scene for a century of print-making in the Netherlands, which is properly regarded as the golden age of the print. That century, and the work of the artists and printmakers who followed in the succeeding centuries, are discussed in chapter five and the subsequent chapters.

FACING PAGE
LUCAS JANSZ WAGHENAER
Chart of the North Coast of England, 1583

Most early printed charts were extremely decorative, and in addition to the practical information about depths of water and prominent landmarks they included numerous pictures. On this chart, the ports of Whitby, Hartlepool, Sunderland and Tynemouth are marked by tiny buildings. A coastal profile at the top shows the mariner the appearance of the land from the sea.

Engraving with hand colouring. From *The Mariner's Mirror* (De Spieghel der Zeevaerdt). National Maritime Museum, London.

PRINTING PROCESSES

Print-making is a vast and complex subject. What follows is intended to be an introduction to those processes most likely to be encountered by the collector of maritime prints. The aim is not to show the reader how to make a print but to enable him or her to work out whether a particular print is an engraving, an etching, a lithograph or some other type of print.

A brief description is given of each process, but the accompanying illustrations are the key to identifying the difference between the processes. In each instance, a print or part of a print is reproduced actual size, and this is accompanied by a greatly magnified detail. With practice, it is possible to tell the difference between the major processes without the need for a magnifying glass, but some form of magnifying instrument is essential for the more tricky processes. Photographic suppliers sell a plastic magnifying glass known as a lupe for examining photographs and colour transparencies. It gives a magnification of 8 times. An alternative is a small folding magnifying glass (sometimes called a linen-prover), which is useful because it can be slipped into a pocket. It gives a magnification of 4 times and is often stocked by stamp dealers.

The different types of print are usually grouped under three headings: relief, intaglio and planographic. With relief printing, the ink is carried on the raised parts of the printing surface, as it is with woodcuts and engravings. With intaglio printing, the ink is held in grooves below the printing surface, as with copper engraving, all forms of etching, dry point, aquatint and mezzotint. And with planographic printing the ink lies on the printing surface itself, as it does in lithography.

WOODCUTS

The woodcut was made from a plank of soft wood, such as beech or sycamore. The artist drew his design on the surface of a wooden block, which was usually about 2.5 centimeters (1 inch) in thickness. The wood was then cut away from the lines of the design using a pointed knife for the detail and a gouge for the open spaces. When the cutting was completed, the lines of the artist's design remained in relief ready for printing. Ink was applied to the upstanding surface of the wood block by means of a dabber or roller, and the design was transferred to a piece of paper by applying pressure in a printing press or by burnishing the back of the paper with a spoon or similar instrument.

In order to achieve gradations of tone in a wood block, it was necessary to create a series of parallel lines or cross-hatching, which required considerable skill on the

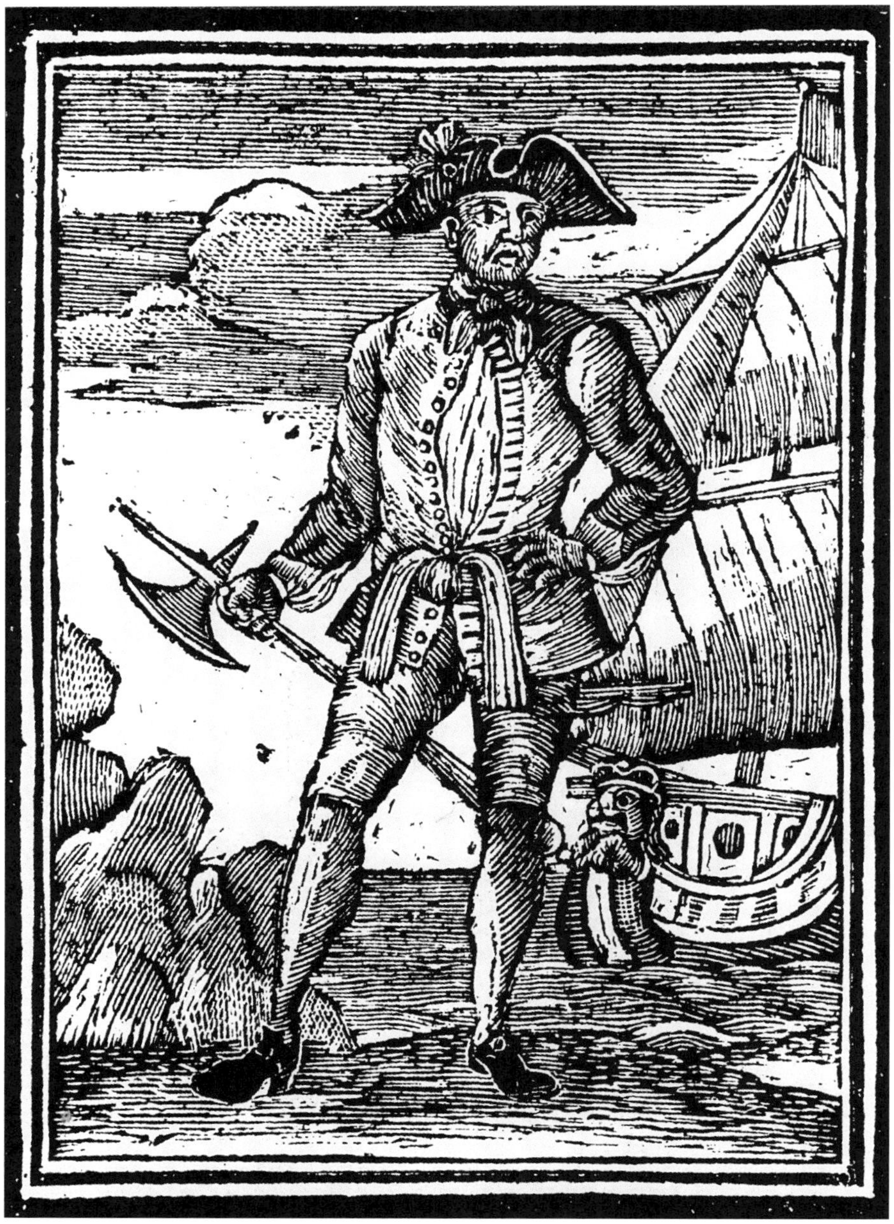

ACTUAL SIZE

Portrait of Edward England, the Pirate

This rather crude picture, reproduced actual size, is typical of many of the woodcuts used to illustrate books in the early 18th century. Woodcuts demanded considerable skill on the part of the craftsman because the wood had to be cut away on either side of a line which was to print in black. Because of the difficulty, relatively simple shading techniques have been used here.

Woodcut. From Captain Charles Johnson's, *A General History of the Robberies and Murders of the most notorious Pyrates,* 1725 edition.

part of the artist. It was, therefore, common practice for an artist to draw his design on the block and to engage a professional woodcutter to do the carving.

WOOD ENGRAVING

Wood engravings were carved out of the end grain of hard woods, such as box. This allowed much finer detail to be produced. Instead of a knife and a gouge, the wood engraver used a pointed graving tool which he pushed into the hard polished wood surface. Once the design had been engraved and the surplus wood cut away, the surface was inked and printed in the same manner as a woodcut.

When wood engravings were pioneered in England by Thomas Bewick in the late 18th century, they tended to be small and were used for vignettes and pictures in finely printed books. With the rapid increase in the production of books, magazines and newspapers from the 1830s onward, the size of wood engravings increased and they were widely used for every type of illustration imaginable. Hundreds of craftsmen were employed to carry out the work required to meet the demands of printers and publishers.

BELOW
THOMAS BEWICK
Vignette showing the ferry at Cherryburn, 1827

By using a hard wood, such as box, pear or holly, and by cutting across the end grain with a graver, it was possible for a skilled artist and craftsman to achieve much greater detail in a wood engraving than in a woodcut. This wood engraving is reproduced actual size.

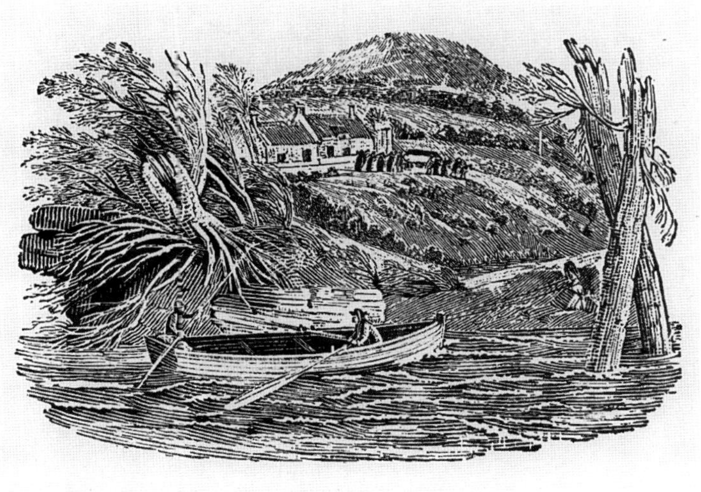

ACTUAL SIZE

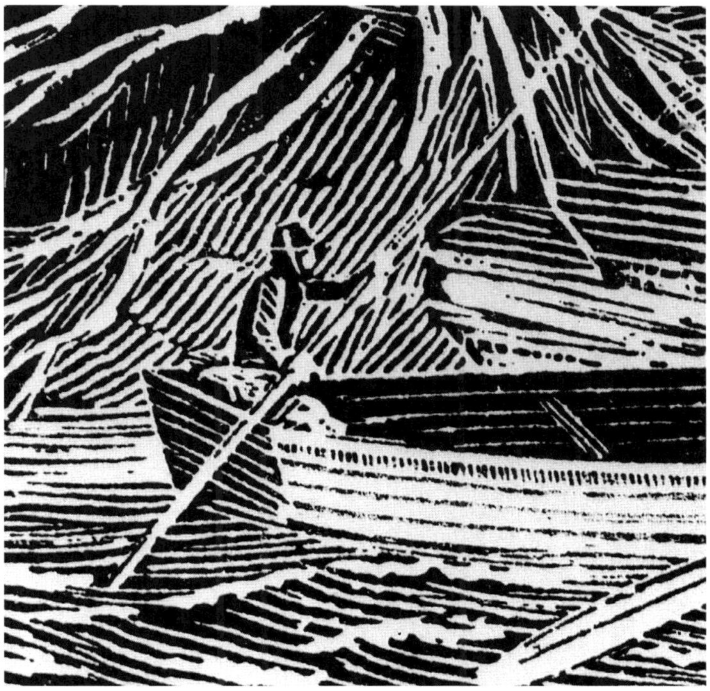

RIGHT
Greatly enlarged detail of Bewick's wood engraving

This shows clearly the various shading techniques a skilled engraver could use. All the white lines have been gouged out of the wood with the graver and the black lines have been left standing by cutting away the wood on either side of them. This produces a crisp, cut-out effect, which distinguishes it from a print made from a copper engraving or etching.

COPPER ENGRAVING

Copper engravings were made by cutting into the surface of a copper plate with a pointed tool called a burin. The V-shaped point of the burin made a groove in the surface of the plate and, when the design was completed, the surface would be covered with a network of incised lines. The burr thrown up by the burin ploughing through the surface was scraped off and then ink was applied to the copper plate with a dabber and carefully worked into all the grooves. The ink lying on the surface was wiped off with muslin, leaving a residue of ink in the grooves. A sheet of dampened paper was laid on the copper sheet and specially resilient felt blankets were laid on the paper. Great pressure was then applied with a printing press, which forced the ink out of the grooves on to the paper.

Printing by this method results in two characteristics which distinguish the copper engraving (and the etching) from the woodcut, the wood engraving and the much later lithograph. The first is that the printed lines of the copper engraving lie proud on the surface of the paper and can actually be felt with the finger tips. The second is that edge of the design is marked by a rectangular indentation or plate-mark which is caused by the pressure of the copper plate being pressed into the paper.

BELOW LEFT
FRANS HUYS after PIETER BRUEGEL
Armed three-master with Daedalus and Icarus in the sky

Because every line must be made by gouging into the plate with a pointed tool, copper engravings invariably lack the freedom of drawing to be found in etchings. Although made by a master from a drawing by a great artist, there is a stiffness and regularity about the shading techniques in this engraving that is characteristic of the process.
Engraving. *c.*1562,

BELOW
Enlarged detail of Huys's engraving

Although the width (and therefore the darkness) of an engraved line can be increased by digging the burin deeper into the copper plate, the lines still have a regular sweep about them. The edges of an engraved line are straighter and cleaner than an etched line and usually end in a sharp point.

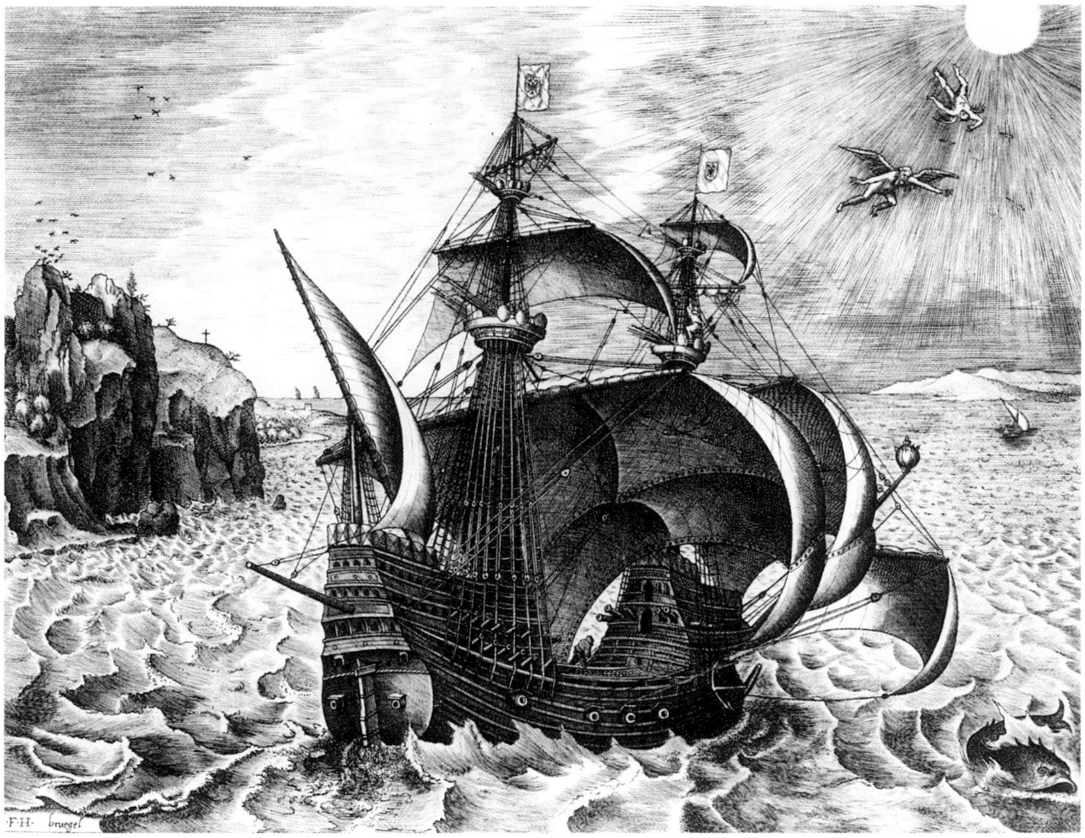

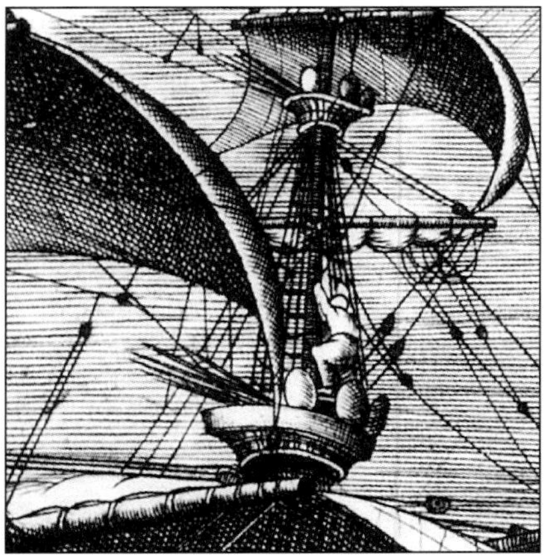

Wood engraving tools and a boxwood block

Several engraving tools are shown here, together with a boxwood block with the surface polished ready for engraving and the leather pad used by the craftsman so that he can swivel the block around as he gouges into the wood.

Also shown are two printed wood engravings from Thomas Bewick's *A General History of Quadrapeds*, published in Newcastle in 1790.

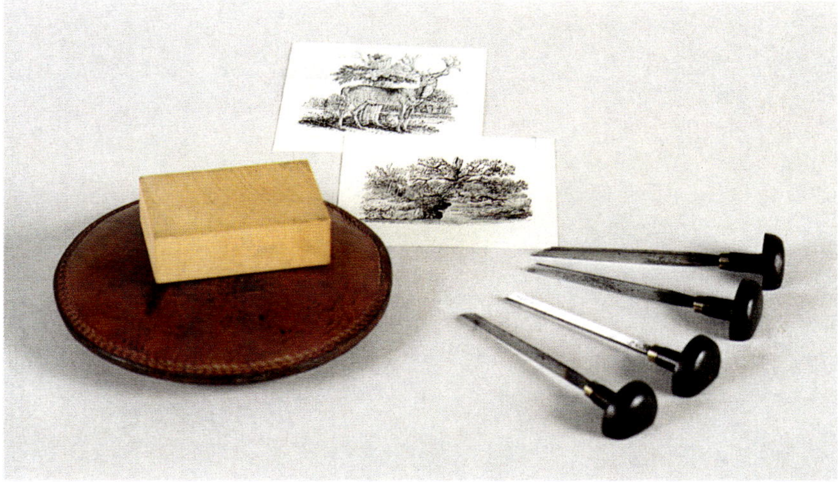

Etched copper plate and tools used for etching and engraving

This is a selection of tools for copper engraving from the studio of an engraver. From left to right, the tools are a pointer for engraving and etching; a pointer and burnisher; an etching needle; and two burins with wooden handles. Included in the picture is a linen-prover for examining prints.This gives a 4 times enlargement.

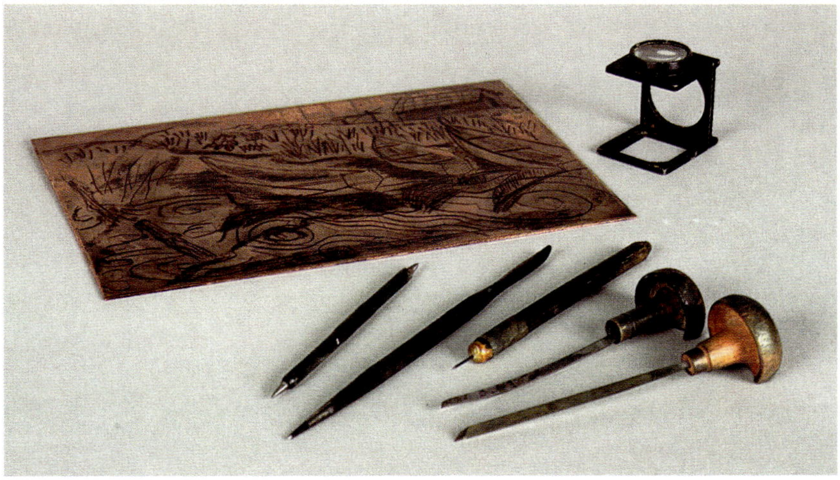

Etched copper plate and print taken from the plate

When the etching process is complete, ink is rubbed into the etched lines and grooves of the copper plate. The surface ink is wiped off leaving the ink in the grooves. A sheet of dampened paper is laid on the plate and pressure applied in a printing press. This forces the ink out of the grooves on to the paper, which is then peeled away. The plate-mark caused by the plate pressing into the paper can be clearly seen around the edges of the image. The tool shown is a general-purpose pointer and burnisher.

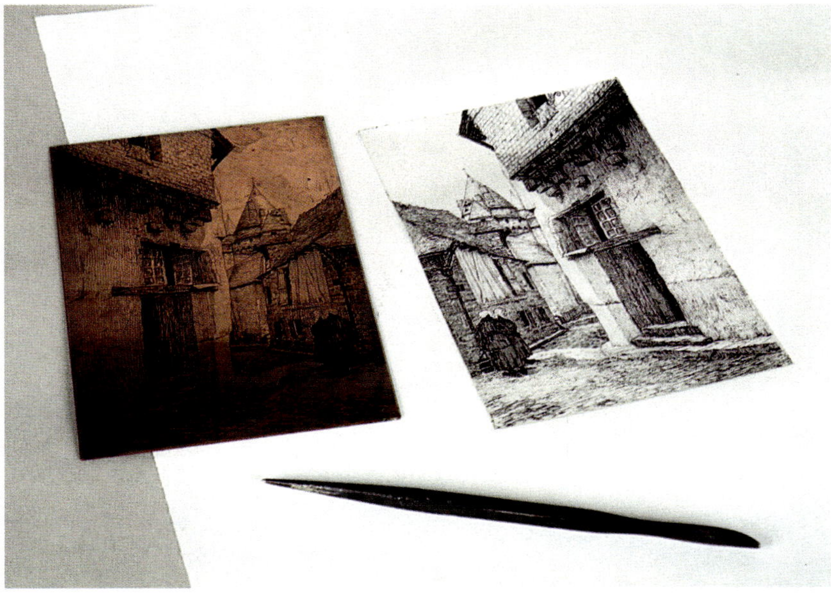

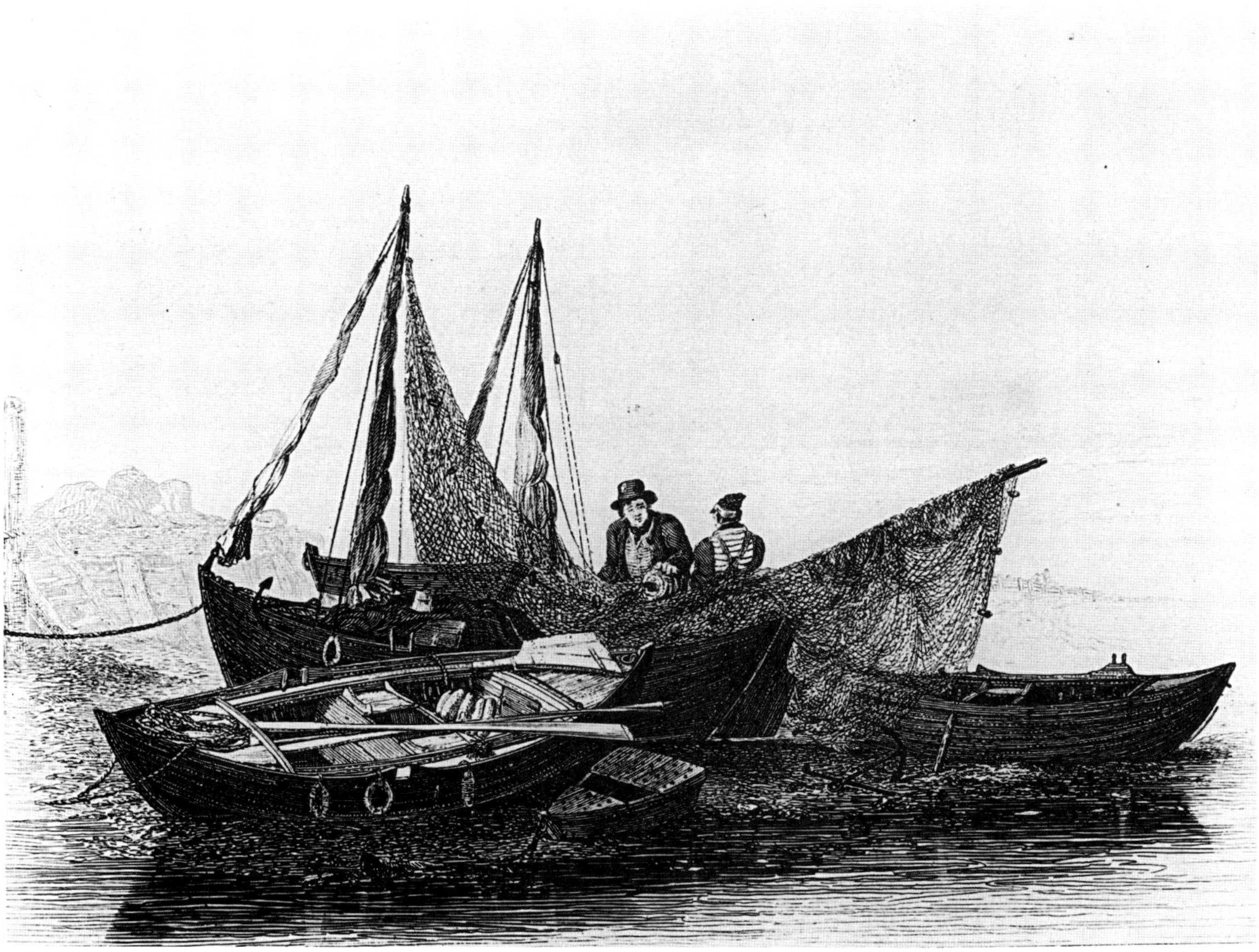

ACTUAL SIZE

E.W. Cooke
Peter boats at Greenwich

An etching requires less skill than an engraving because the artist simply draws on the prepared surface of the copper plate with the etching needle and does not have to dig into the surface. This helps to explain how Cooke was able to achieve such a remarkable effect at the age of only 17.

Etching. From *Fifty Plates of Shipping and Craft,* 1828. Reproduced actual size.

ETCHING

Instead of using the burin to make the grooves in the copper plate, the etching process uses acid to bite into the surface of the metal. A copper plate is heated and wax or gum is spread thinly and evenly over the surface. The artist then draws on the waxed surface with an etching needle to expose the metal beneath. With the back of the copper plate protected by a coat of varnish, the plate is immersed in a bath of nitric acid, which etches away the exposed lines. The width and depth of the lines depends on the strength of the acid and the length of time the plate is immersed.

The plate can be removed from the acid bath at any stage, a proof printed off to check progress, and the whole process repeated. By carefully painting or 'stopping out' some areas with varnish, the depth and thickness of the lines can be varied. Once the etcher is satisfied with the design, the etching is printed in a similar manner to the copper engraving. Ink is spread on the surface and worked into the lines and the surface is wiped clean, leaving ink in the grooves. A sheet of dampened paper is laid on the copper plate, pressure is applied with the printing press, and the ink is transferred to the paper.

Drawing on the waxed ground of a copper plate is much easier than engraving a copper plate with a burin. As a result, the printed lines of an etching have much greater freedom and sensitivity than the lines of a copper engraving, which tend to be rather stiff and mechanical. The quality of the line is different, too: when examined under a magnifying glass the engraved line tends to be fairly even and has a hard edge, while an etched line is somewhat irregular with soft, slightly blurred edges.

Greatly enlarged detail of the etching by E.W. Cooke.

The freedom of the etching process allows the artist to make irregular and wavy lines which are much more like those of a pen and ink drawing than the lines of an engraving. An etched line tends to have a slightly blurred edge and has a blunt, rounded end.

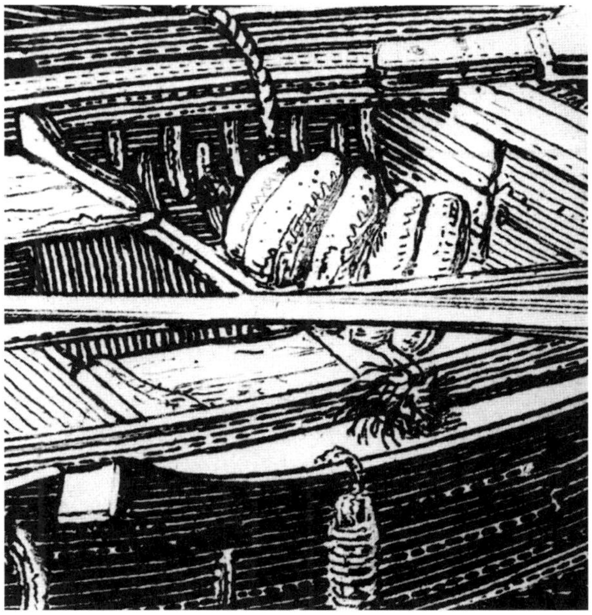

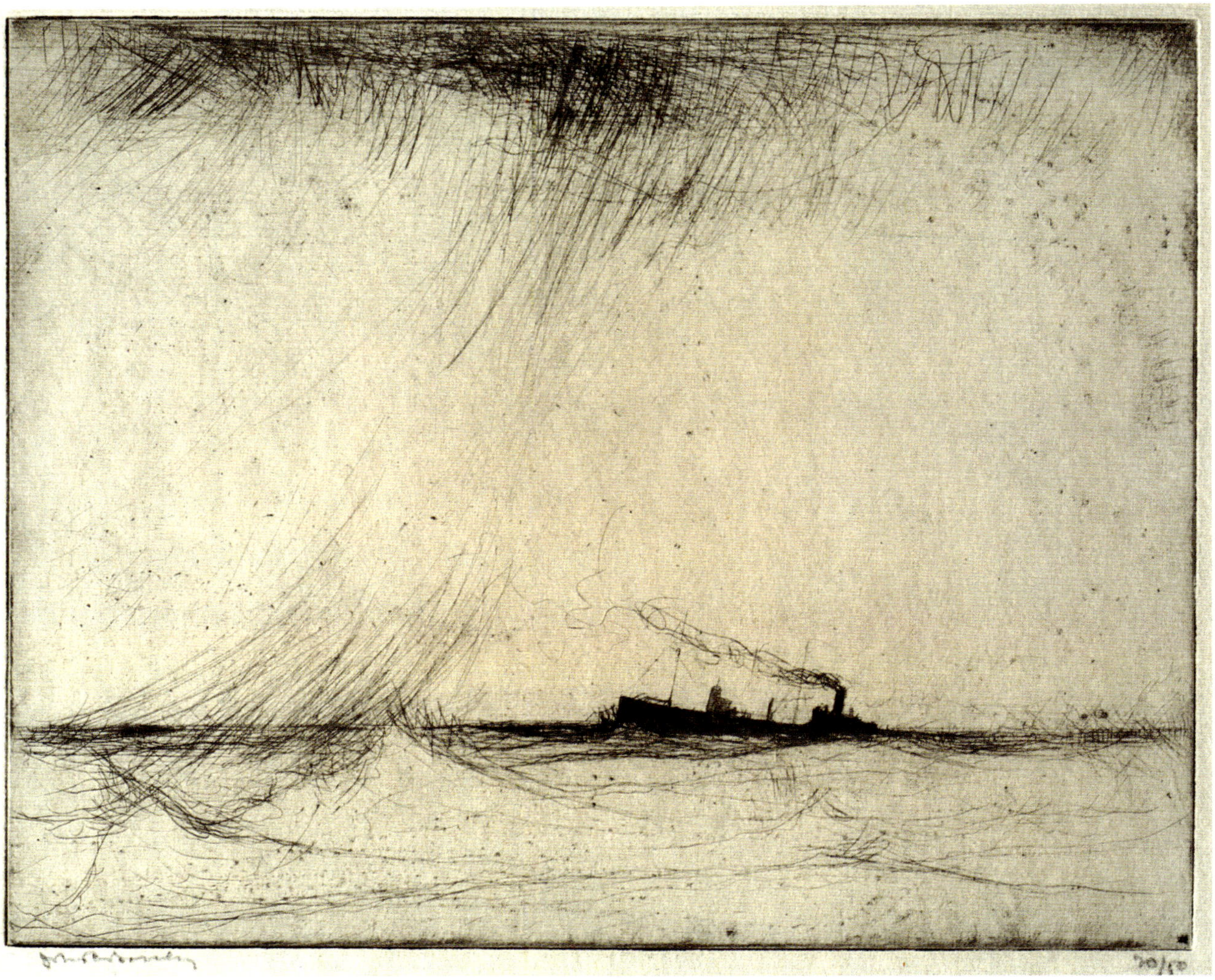

JOHN WORSLEY
A steamship pitching in a squall

Dry point is usually employed in combination with etching. The artist gouges into the surface of the copper plate with a pointed dry point needle. Instead of scraping away the burr left on either side of the line (the usual practice with copper engraving), the burr is allowed to remain. It holds the ink and produces a rich black blotchy line with soft edges.

Dry point. National Maritime Museum

RIGHT
Greatly enlarged detail of the dry point by John Worsley.

The dry point is not very easy to identify. Look for slashed lines with a fuzz of ink on either side. Sometimes there may be a faint white streak resembling a scratch down the centre of the slashed lines.

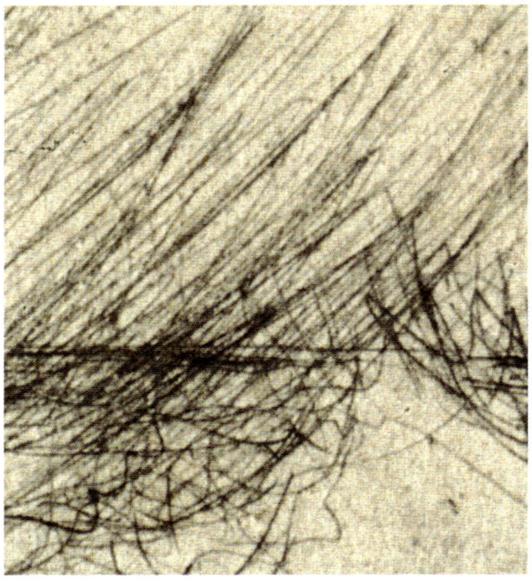

BELOW
HENRY ALKEN
Stag hunting

Marine artists do not appear to have used soft ground etching very often, but it was a favourite medium for many sporting artists. A light brown wash in watercolour has been added over part of the animal's body.

Detail from a print. 1817. Reproduced actual size. The Parker Gallery, London.

BELOW RIGHT
Greatly enlarged detail of the soft-ground etching by Henry Alken.

Soft-ground etching was intended to imitate the effect of a soft pencil or crayon and under the magnifying glass that is what it looks like.

DRY POINT

The dry point process was similar to copper engraving in that the surface of a copper plate was scored with a sharp instrument to create lines which would hold ink. The finished effect was, however, very different because instead of making a deep V-shaped groove with a burin, the surface was scratched with a dry point needle. This threw up a burr, or ridge of metal, on either side of the groove. With engraving, this burr was scraped off, but with dry point, the burr was left because it retained ink and when printed produced an attractive feathery line. If an area was heavily scratched, and the burr retained, the artist could create a rich, dark blotch with hazy edges. One problem with dry point was that the burr would be worn away after 20 or so sheets had been printed from the plate. The other problem was that the dry point needle was nearly as difficult to control as the engraver's burin. Dry point was, therefore, commonly combined with etching, and lines in dry point were added after the etching had been carried out.

SOFT-GROUND ETCHING

This was an easier and less mechanical means of producing a print which had the appearance of being made with a crayon or soft pencil. Although the process was invented in France, it became very popular in England in the period between 1770 and about 1830. Gainsborough and Rowlandson made use of the technique, and it

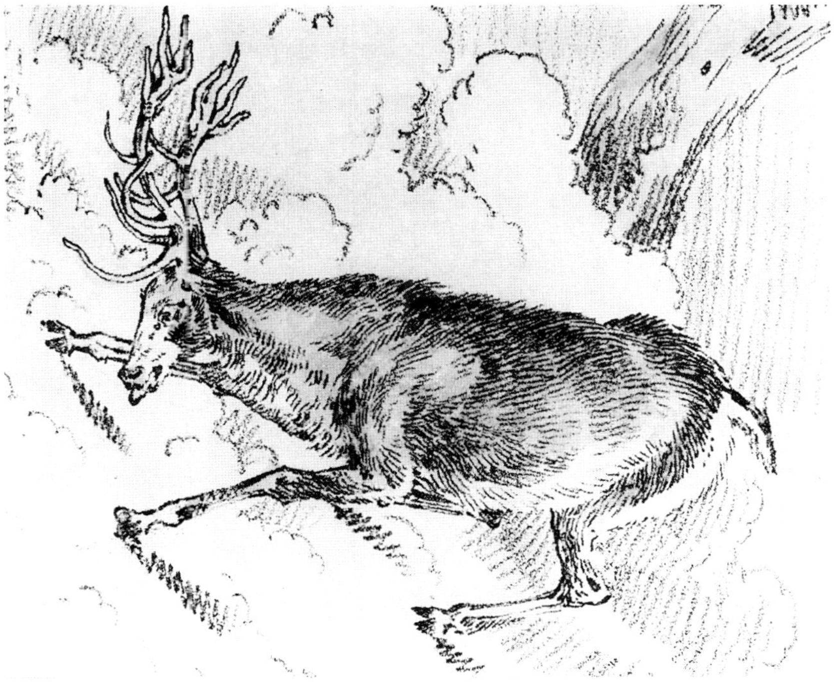

ACTUAL SIZE

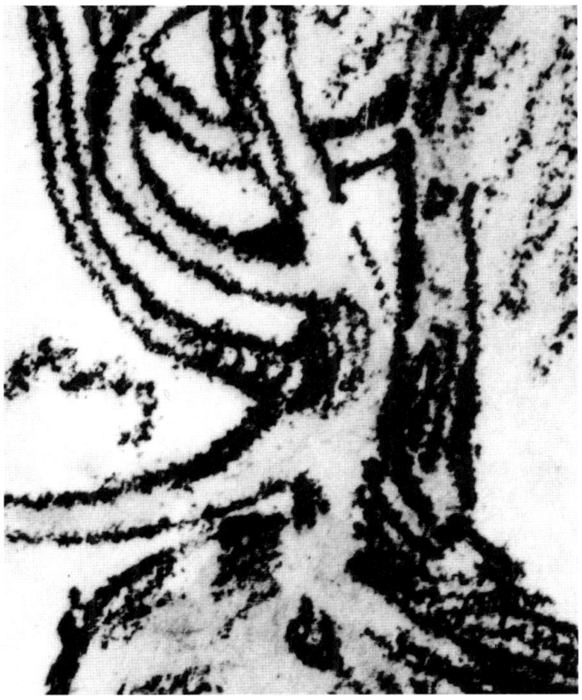

was also used for landscape and seascape subjects by artists such as Samuel Prout, David Cox and John Sell Cotman.

The secret of the process was to add tallow to the wax coating, or ground, on the surface of the copper plate. This kept the ground slightly tacky and soft, hence the name 'soft-ground etching'. A piece of paper was laid on the surface of the prepared copper plate and the artist drew on this with a pencil. When the drawing was completed, the paper was lifted off the plate. The pressure of the pencil caused the softened wax ground to stick to the paper, leaving the lines of the drawing exposed on the copper plate. When the plate was immersed in a bath of acid, these exposed lines were etched into the metal by the acid. What was ingenious was that the quality of the line printed from the plate was almost exactly the same as a pencil line made directly on paper. The width of the pencil point and the amount of pressure applied enabled the artist to produce lines of varying width and density. The technique also allowed the artist to use the same freedom of line as in a normal drawing.

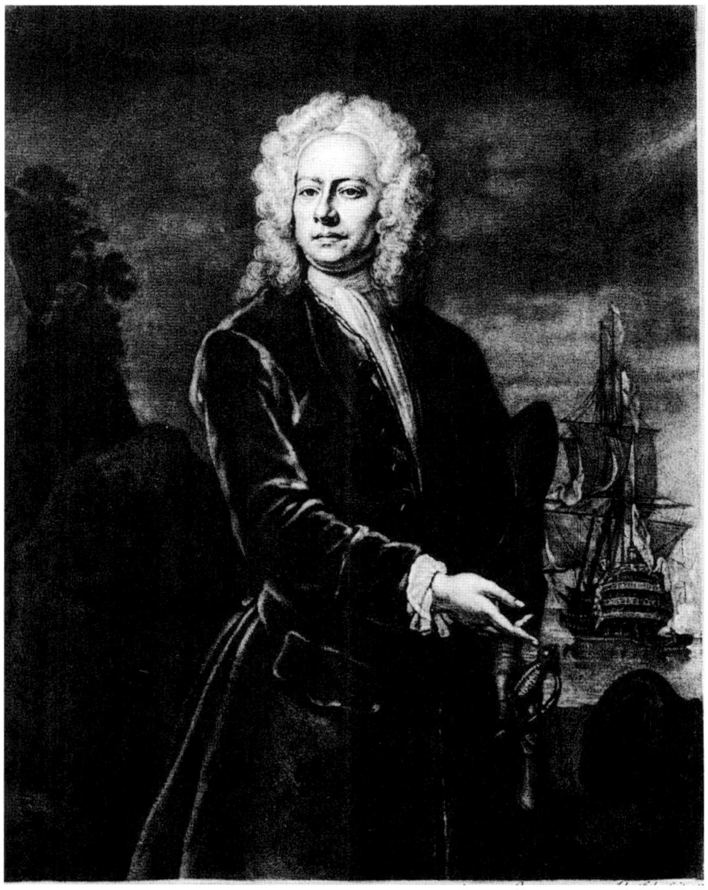

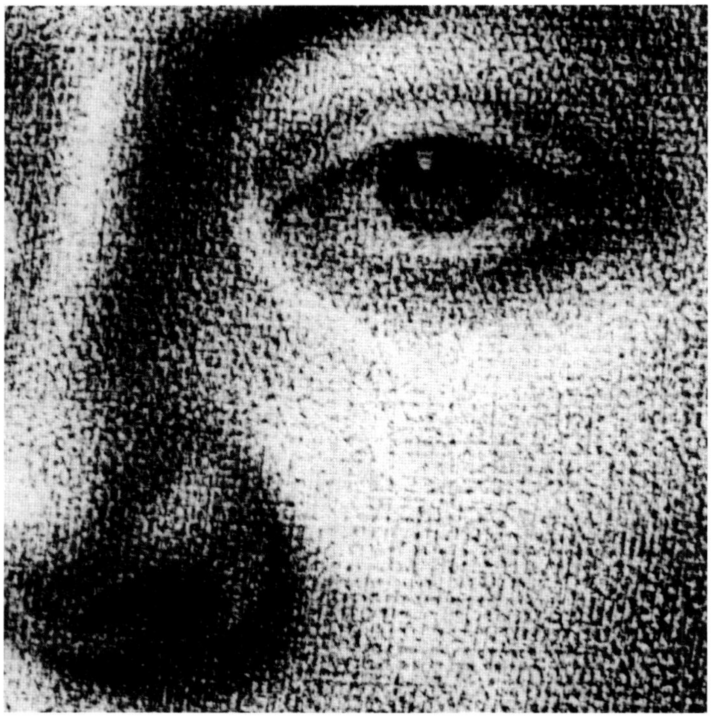

FACING PAGE, LEFT
JOHN FABER after JOHN ELLYS
The Hon. Henry Medley, Rear Admiral of the White.

The mezzotint process was much used for portraits in the period between 1670 and about 1830. Since the engraver worked from black to white by burnishing a surface already scored all over with tiny regular indentations, the overall effect is of a dark velvety surface with lighter areas gleaming out of the blackness.

Mezzotint. 1745. Reduced in size. The Parker Gallery, London.

FACING PAGE, RIGHT
Greatly enlarged detail of the mezzotint of Rear Admiral Henry Medley

The texture of a mezzotint when examined under a magnifying glass is unmistakable. The regular criss-cross pattern made by the rocker and the spiked roulette wheel are clearly visible except in the dark areas that have been left untouched by the burnisher, and in the light areas where the burnisher has polished the copper surface smooth.

MEZZOTINT

Derived from the Italian *mezzotinto*, meaning half-tint, the mezzotint process was able to achieve greys and half-tones. The method was laborious but very effective for producing finely modelled portraits and reproductions of paintings. The copper plate was first prepared by working over the entire surface again and again with a tool called a rocker. This scored the surface and produced a rough texture like sandpaper, which was able to hold an even supply of ink. When printed, this produced a dense black. The engraver then went to work with a burnishing tool and a scraper. Gentle rubbing of an area with the burnisher produced a dark grey, while light greys and white were produced by progressively scraping off the burr and polishing the surface until it was smooth. In the hands of a skilful craftsman, the most subtle effects could be achieved. As with the dry point process, the disadvantage of the mezzotint was that after a number of printings the rough burr holding the ink was worn down and the rich black tones were gradually lost.

AQUATINT

Like the mezzotint, the aquatint process was able to produce a range of half-tones, and in the hands of an accomplished craftsman it could imitate the effect of a watercolour wash, hence its name. It was not able to produce a fine line and therefore tended to be used in combination with etching.

There were two methods of preparing the aquatint plate. The first was to sprinkle the surface of a copper plate with a cloud of resin dust. The plate was then heated and the particles of resin fused to the copper surface. When the copper plate was dipped in acid, the resin particles acted as a partial barrier and only allowed the acid to bite into the network of tiny spaces surrounding each particle. The result was to produce a surface covered with thousands of little depressions. These retained the ink when the surface was wiped over and produced a soft grainy effect when printed.

A similar effect was achieved by dissolving the resin in a spirit such as alcohol. This was poured over the surface of the plate. As with the dust-ground method, the plate was dipped in acid, producing a surface speckled with tiny depressions. With both methods, the artist procured varying affects by using grains of different size and by coating areas with stopping-out varnish before dipping the plate in the acid again.

Although the process is difficult to describe, it is relatively easy to identify an aquatint with the aid of a magnifying glass, when it can be seen that the effect of the resin particles is to produce an area of tone that has a distinctive speckled texture resembling very fine lace.

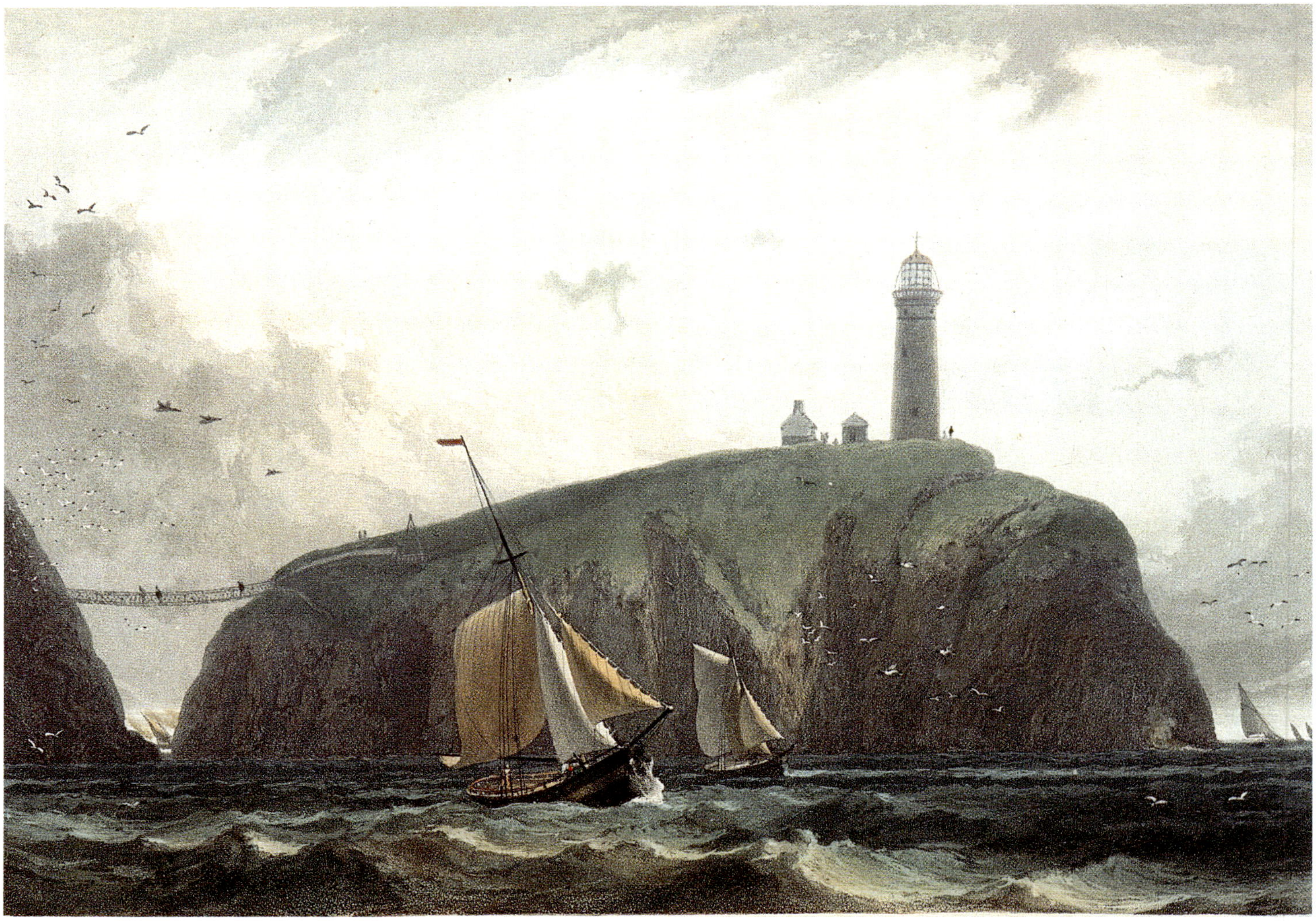

WILLIAM DANIELL *Lighthouse on the South Stack, Holyhead*

The aquatint process produces soft tones and effects similar to those of a watercolour but it is easily identified under a magnifying glass as can be seen in the enlarged detail. This picture is one of the aquatints from Daniell's *A Voyage Round Great Britain.*

Aquatint with additional hand-colouring. 1815. Slightly reduced in size. Private collection.

RIGHT
Greatly enlarged detail of the aquatint by William Daniell

The areas of tone in an aquatint have a distinctive texture, rather like mottled glass or an irregular pattern of fine lace. The seaman's red hat and blue jersey and the blue of the sea have been added later in watercolour.

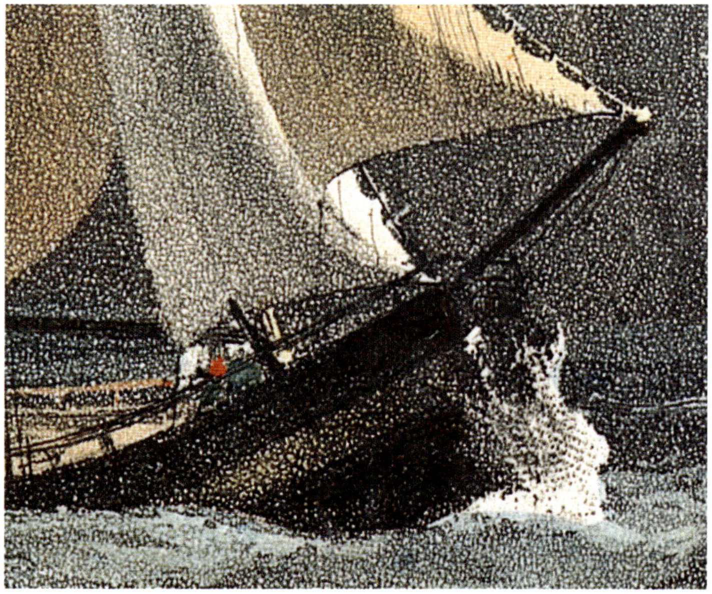

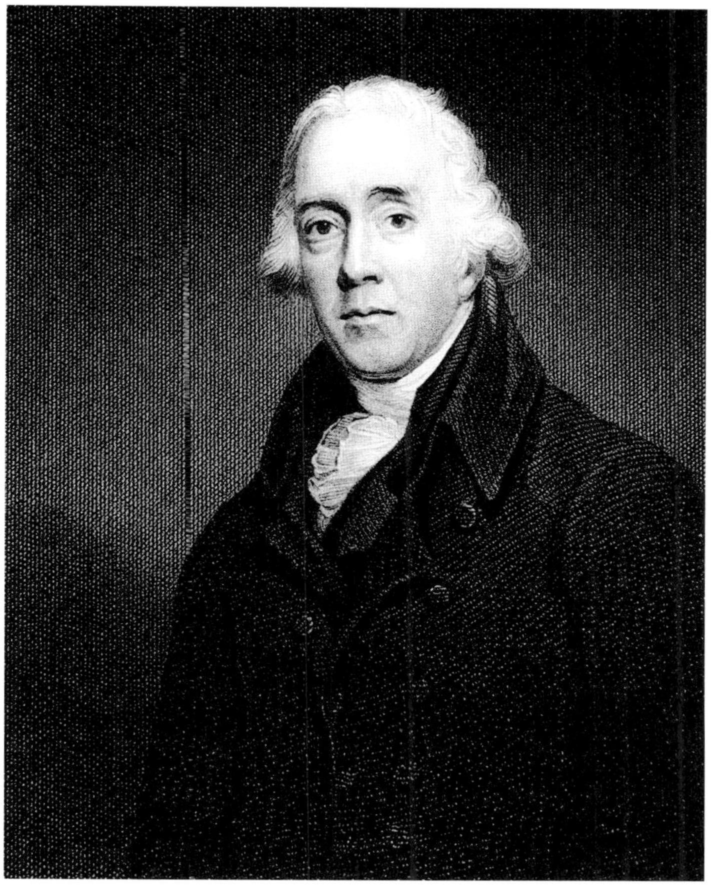

ACTUAL SIZE

BELOW
Greatly enlarged detail of the portrait of Nicholas Pocock.

In a stipple engraving the craftsman punctures or stipples the wax ground on the surface of the copper plate with a hand-held punch, or *mattoir.* This has a metal head covered with a random pattern of spikes and small squiggles. The skilful use of the punch produces a half-tone effect with a distinctive character; when examined under a magnifying glass, it can be seen to consist of numerous small dots and wormlike lines.

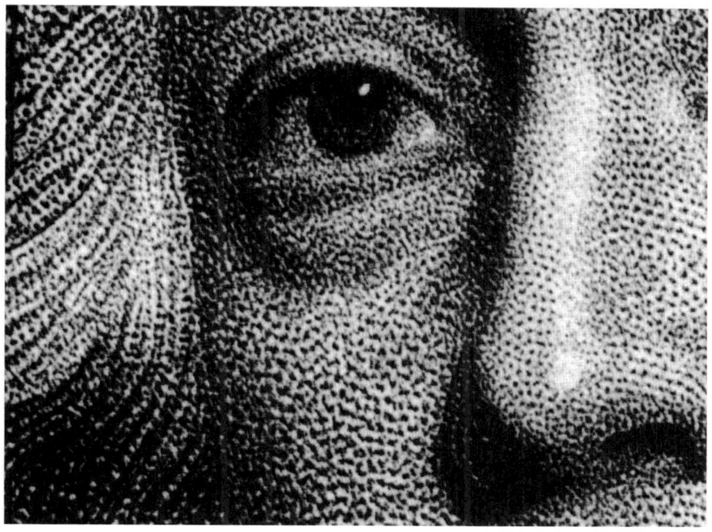

EDWARD SCRIVEN after ISAAC POCOCK
Portrait of the marine artist Nicholas Pocock

Confusingly, a stipple engraving is a form of etching because when the engraver has finished stippling the wax ground on the copper plate, the plate is immersed in acid in order to etch the dots and patterns made by the *mattoir.* This stipple engraving, after a portrait of the artist painted by his eldest son in about 1810, is reproduced actual size.

STIPPLE ENGRAVING AND CRAYON-MANNER ENGRAVING

It was the popularity of the chalk and crayon drawings of Watteau, Boucher and other French artists in the 1750s and 1760s that led to the development of crayon-manner engraving. This technique and stipple engraving made it possible to reproduce lines and areas of coarse, hazy tone that had the appearance of being made with a crayon or soft pencil. The key to the crayon manner was the use of a tool called a roulette, which consisted of a metal wheel, on the end of a handle, the outer edge of which was covered with sharp points. A protective covering of wax was spread on a copper plate and the spiked roulette wheel was run across the surface following the artist's design. When the copper plate was immersed in a bath of acid, the dotted line made by the wheel was etched in the surface of the plate. The ink was retained in the etched line and, when printed, the effect was remarkably similar to a line made with crayon on rough-textured paper.

The stipple engraving was a slightly later development. Instead of relying on the roulette, which produced a coarse-textured line, the stipple technique made use of a tool called a *mattoir,* or mace head, to create areas of tone. The mattoir was like a

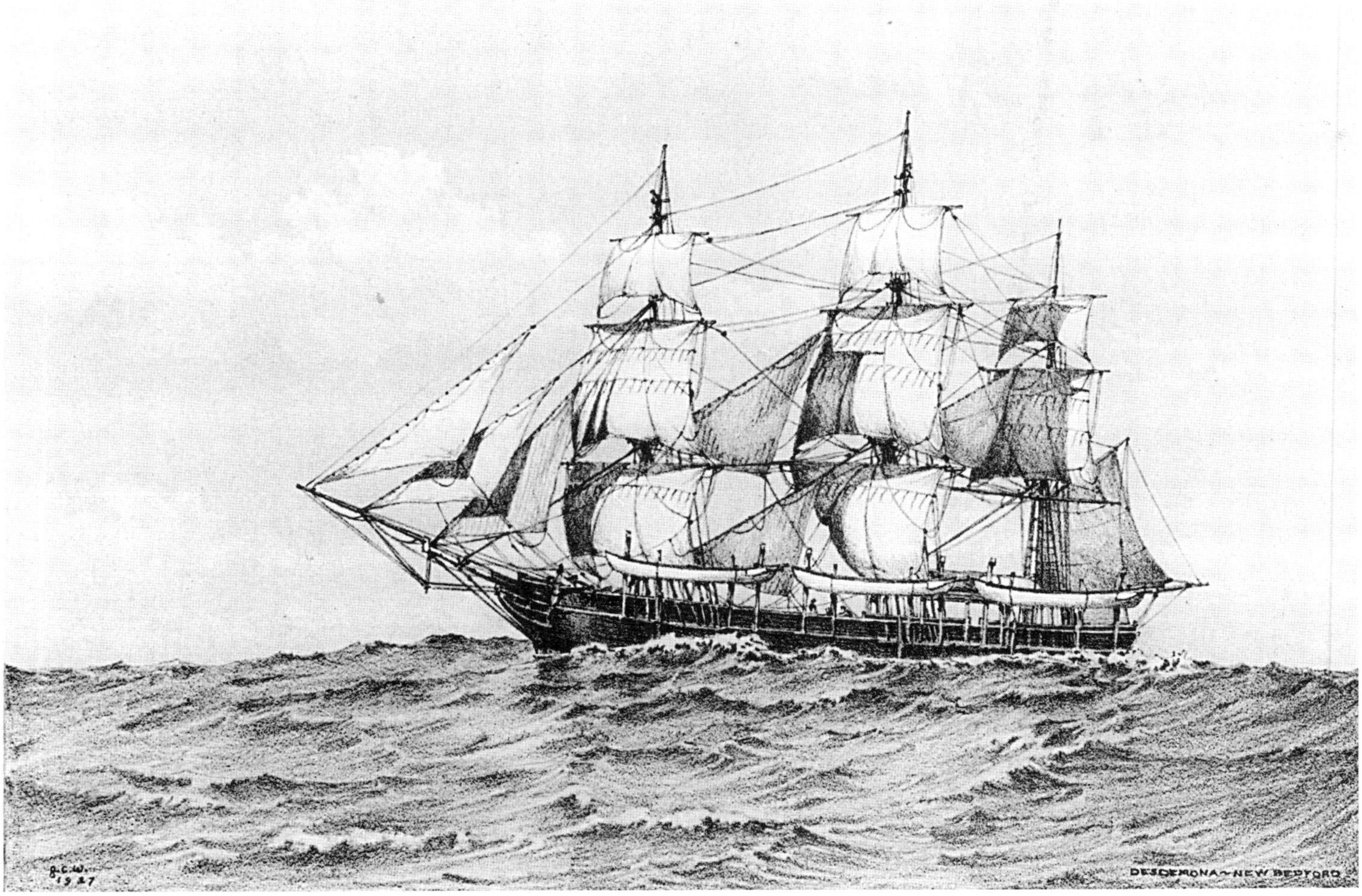

ACTUAL SIZE

George C. Wales
The ship Desdemona *of New Bedford*

The lithographic process can reproduce a variety of tones, depending on whether the artist draws on the stone with a pen and greasy ink, paints a dilute greasy ink on the stone with a brush, or, as here, uses chalk-style lithography, drawing the lines and shading the darker areas with a lithographic crayon.

Lithograph. 1927. Reproduced actual size.

RIGHT
Greatly enlarged detail of the lithograph by George C. Wales.

The quality of the line and shading in this chalk-style lithograph is much like that made by a soft pencil or crayon. There are also similarities with soft-ground etchings, but the two can be told apart because a soft-ground etching has a rectangular plate-mark around the edge of the picture where the copper plate has been pressed into the paper. Lithographs do not have plate-marks.

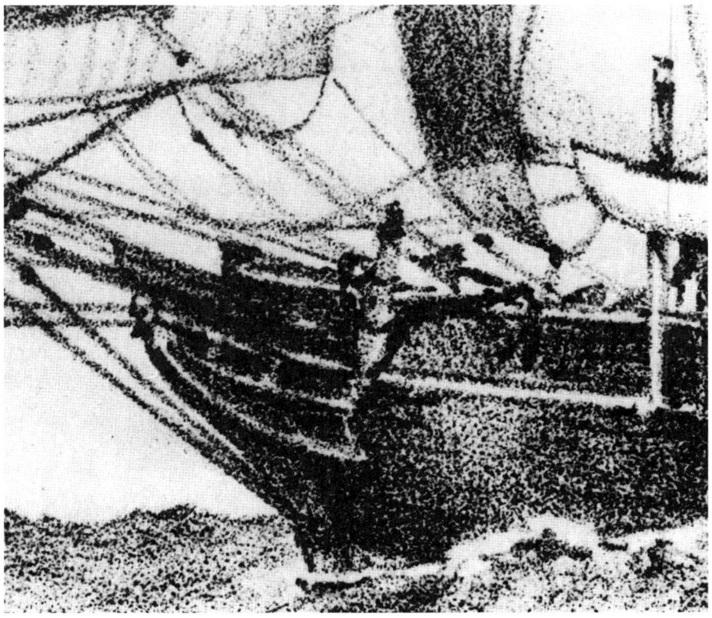

hand-held punch, with the metal head covered with a random pattern of spikes and small squiggles. This was used to puncture the wax ground protecting the surface of the copper plate and, with skilful use, could produce a print which imitated the textured lines and half-tones typical of a crayon or chalk drawing.

LITHOGRAPHY

This process is almost as complicated to describe as the aquatint process, and the following is a much-simplified explanation.

Instead of printing from a wood block or copper plate, the lithograph was printed from the surface of a stone – lithography means stone drawing – and made use of the fact that water and grease repel each other. The artist drew on the flat, polished lithographic stone with a lithographic crayon, which left a greasy mark, or with a pen or brush and a special greasy ink. The stone surface was dampened with water which soaked into those areas not covered with greasy marks. When a roller covered with greasy ink was rolled over the surface, the ink was repelled by the damp areas but stuck to the marks made by the artist. Paper was laid on the stone and pressure was applied to transfer the image from the stone to the paper.

Lithography, which was invented in 1798, proved to have so many advantages over other methods that by the 1820s it was being widely used by publishers and commercial illustrators for a variety of illustrations. The first advantage was that it was almost as easy to draw on the surface of the polished stone as it was to draw on a piece of paper. The second advantage was that hundreds of impressions could be taken off the stone without any loss of image. But perhaps most importantly, the process could create a variety of tones, textures and effects. It could produce a fascimile of a pen and ink drawing, a chalk drawing, a mezzotint, or a watercolour.

HAND-COLOURED PRINTS [see page 50]

The great majority of maritime prints which appear in the sale rooms and are stored in the print rooms of museums and galleries are printed in black ink on white paper. However, there are several types of prints which had colour added after the initial printing. Printed maps and charts were often hand coloured, so were the late 18th-century caricatures of maritime scenes by Rowlandson, Gilray, Cruickshank and others. Topographical views were sometimes hand coloured and it was not uncommon for aquatints of landscapes and seascapes to be printed in two colours from two aquatint plates and then to have additional colour painted on by hand.

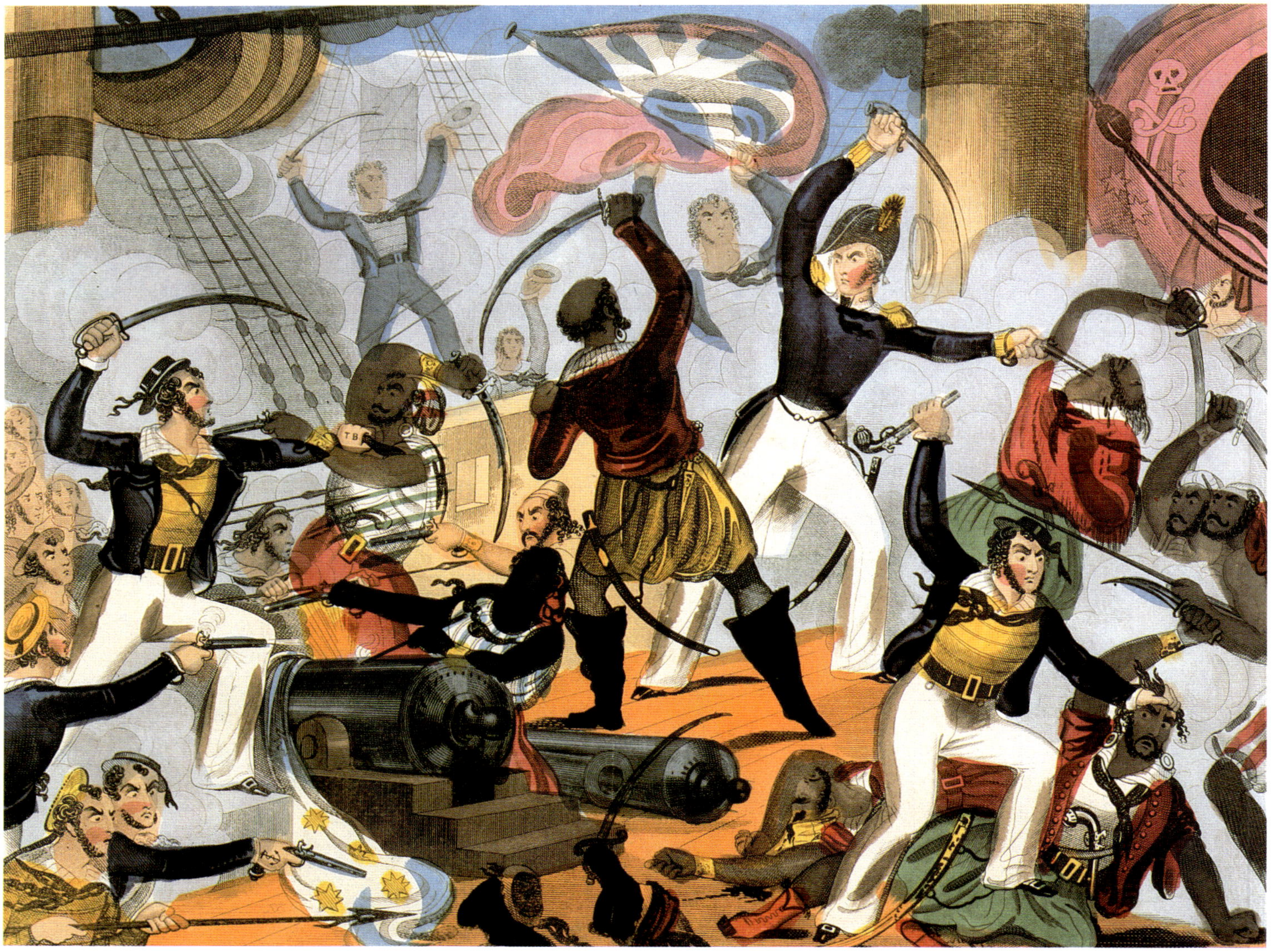

British sailors boarding an Algerine pirate

This is a typical early 19th-century hand-coloured print of the 'Penny plain, tuppence coloured' variety. The bold and rather slapdash application of the colour, and the opaque nature of several of the colours, indicate that the engraving was coloured when it was printed and not much more recently.

National Maritime Museum, London

The problem with hand-colouring is to distinguish between prints which were coloured at the time they were printed and modern hand-colouring. For many years it has been common practice to break up books of topographical views, to cut out and hand colour each print and to sell them individually, either unmounted or mounted and framed. Anthony Griffiths in his admirable book *Prints and Printmaking* suggests a few guidelines to distinguish between the two: 'Eighteenth century original colouring is usually bold and gaudy and applied in a slapdash manner. It is often opaque and completely obscures the lines of the design; modern colouring on such prints, being invariably in watercolour, never does this, and tends to be more carefully applied, with the result that it usually looks timid and anaemic.'

COLOUR PRINTING

This is a complex area which embraces a great number of processes ranging from the colour wood cuts printed from several blocks, which have been around since the 16th century, to the photomechanical processes developed in the 19th century, which form the basis of most of our printing today. Since very few of the maritime prints likely to be of interest to the collector will fall into this category, they will not be discussed here. Many books are available which cover every aspect of early and modern colour printing, and some of these are listed in the Bibliography on page 157.

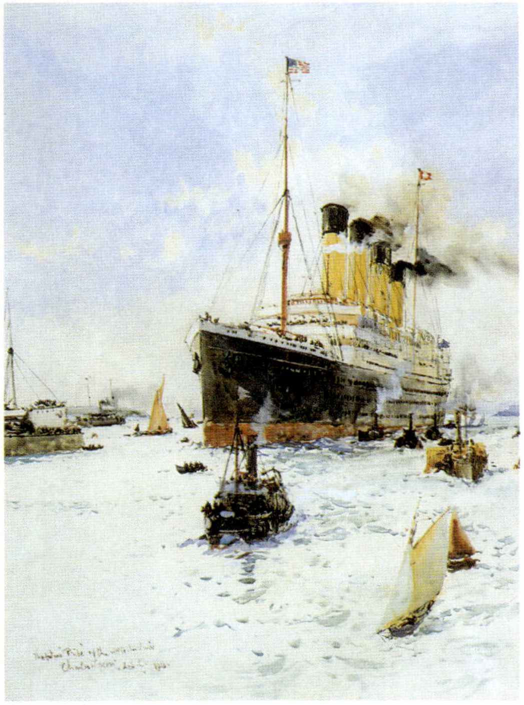

CHARLES DIXON
The White Star liner Olympic *leaving Southampton on her maiden voyage to New York*

This is a four colour half-tone illustration which has been reproduced from an exhibition catalogue published by a London gallery specialising in marine paintings and drawings. The enlarged detail (far right) shows the distinctive pattern of the half-tone process.

Watercolour. Signed and dated 1910. N.R. Omell Gallery, London.

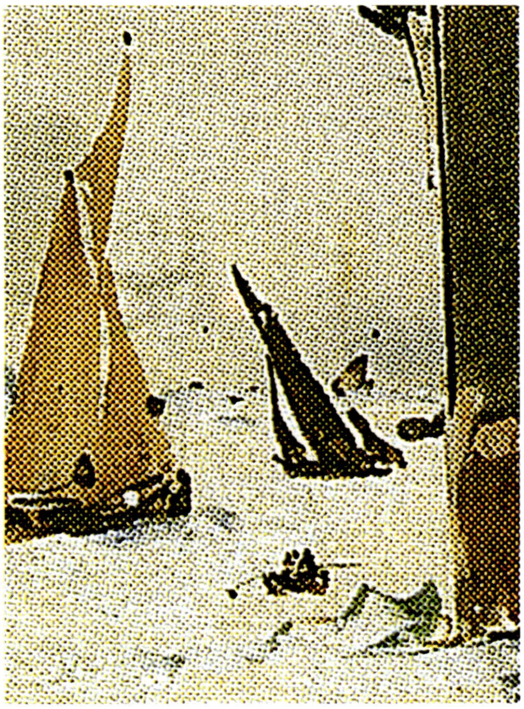

FAR RIGHT Greatly enlarged detail of the four colour reproduction of the picture by Charles Dixon. The photo-mechanical method of reproducing a picture involves photographing the image through a cross-lined screen. When examined under a magnifying glass it will be seen that the various colours and tones are composed of an intricate pattern of dots.

Chapter four

SHIP TYPES

If you had stood on London Bridge 200 years ago and looked downstream towards the Tower of London, you would have seen rows of sailing ships moored alongside the wharves on the north bank, their masts and rigging like a forest lining the waterfront. Larger ships and barges would have been anchored out in the tideway and several vessels would have been on the move. Among these there would be a number of trading smacks and brigs heading downstream with their cargoes, en route to ports in Europe or farther afield. Moving across the river would be a constant stream of small skiffs and wherries ferrying passengers to and fro. Similar activity could have been observed in Amsterdam and Hamburg, and across the Atlantic in the harbours of Boston, Charleston and New York. Nowadays, the only vessels to be seen on the Thames near London Bridge are the river buses, police launches, the occasional tugboat towing a string of barges and, at rare intervals, a coaster headed upstream to Brentford. During the winter months, the river is often deserted for hours at a time.

Apart from professional seamen and yachtsmen, comparatively few people travel by sea any longer. Large square-rigged ships are a rarity, and most of the traditional fishing boats have vanished. The last Brighton hogboat was burned on a Guy Fawkes night bonfire in the 1880s, and yet this distinctive local craft had been a familiar sight on the Sussex coast for centuries and appears in many of the pictures by Constable and Turner. With the disappearance of so many ships and small craft, it is not surprising that people can no longer tell the difference between a schooner and a ketch, or a fishing trawler and a passenger ferry.

The aim of this chapter is to provide an introduction to the various types of ship that will be found in marine pictures. Since it would require a book in several volumes to describe and illustrate the thousands of different sailing, rowing and powered craft that have been built throughout the world over the centuries, the coverage is extremely selective. Most of the vessels illustrated are either British, Dutch or French because it is the ships of these maritime nations that appear in most of the pictures covered by this book. This still leaves a vast field to choose from because the Dutch alone have developed several hundred different types of craft over the years. A selection has, therefore, been made of those vessels that most often appear in pictures and which are representative of particular types. Other types of vessel appear in the illustrations throughout this book and attention is drawn to particular examples.

Given these limitations, the illustrations and the accompanying descriptions should at least enable the reader to work out the difference between a warship, a merchant ship, a fishing boat and a yacht. Even this basic information can often help to unlock the subject matter of a painting and if some of the local small craft in the work of art can be identified, it is often possible to get a very good idea of the picture's geographical location.

The appearance in a picture of a Thames sailing barge, with its great spritsail, [see page 133] is usually a sign that the scene portrayed is somewhere on the Thames estuary or one of England's East Coast rivers such as the Orwell or the Crouch. A vessel rigged with triangular lateen sails [see pages 20, 61, 119] immediately suggests the location is Mediterranean or perhaps on the shores of the Indian Ocean, while junk-rigged craft were mostly to be seen in the ports of China and Indonesia and in the China Seas [see page 95].

Having identified the likely area from the appearance of the local craft, work can begin on identifying any conspicuous towers, spires, forts, lighthouses, piers or distinctively shaped mountains or rock formations. Table Mountain, the Rock of Gibraltar and the white cliffs of Dover surmounted by Dover Castle are among the most easily recognizable places, but there are many others which can be identified with reasonable ease.

WARSHIPS

Before the days of ocean liners, the largest vessels found in marine paintings and drawings were warships. The term 'warship' or 'man-of-war' was the general name given to a ship which was built and armed for war at sea. It was usually restricted to ships belonging to the navy of a sovereign state, and it did not include armed merchantmen or Indiamen, nor did it include privateers or pirate ships. Within the broad category of warships there were several types of vessel, ranging from the flagship of 100 or more guns down to the sloop-of-war.

The most important warships were the ships of the line because they formed the basis of a country's navy and were employed by kings and governments to defend the realm and to make war on foreign powers. The ship of the line [see page 54] was so called because she was powerful enough to take her place in the line of battle when opposing ships went into action. The practice of engaging the enemy in a line to give

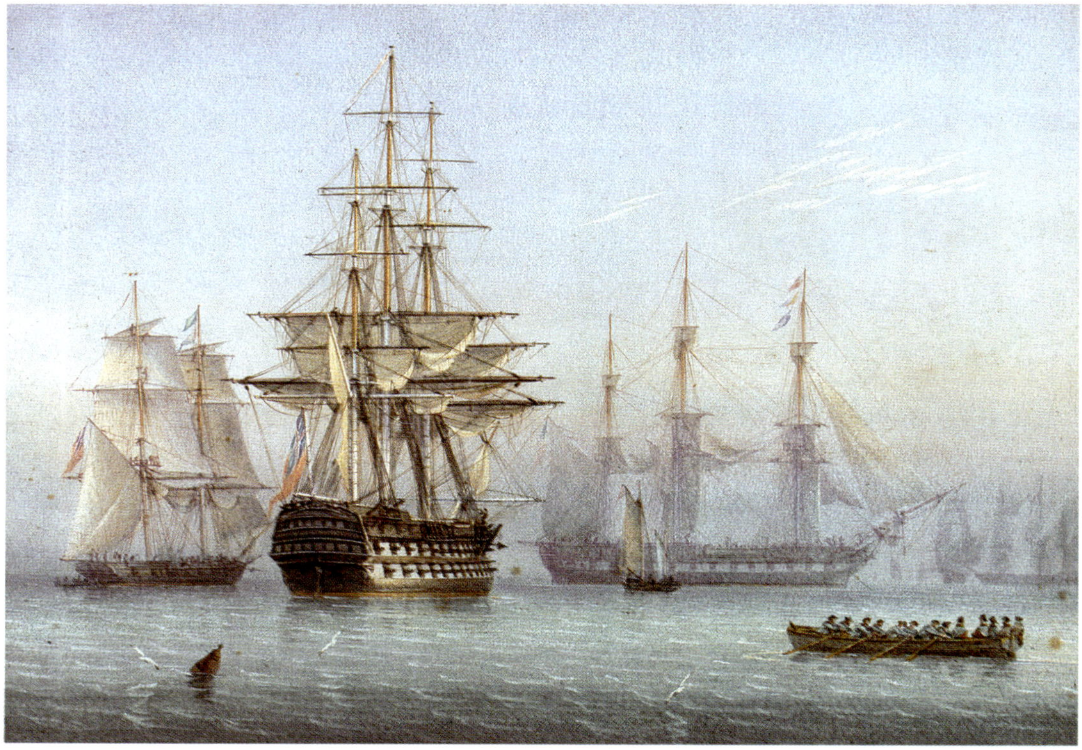

William Joy
British warships preparing to sail

On the left of the picture is a naval brig under sail. The large warship left of centre is a ship of the line whose officers are being rowed out to her in the longboat which can be seen on the right. In the distance, in broadside view, is a frigate.

Pencil and watercolour.
Private collection.

maximum effect to the firing of broadsides was introduced during the first Anglo–Dutch War of 1652–54, and with notable exceptions it remained the standard tactic for European navies until the 1850s. In the 17th century, the ship of the line carried between 50 and 100 guns, but by 1800 the 74-gun ship was the smallest of the line.

For administrative purposes the ships of the line were divided into categories, known as 'rates' in Britain. Originally the categories were based on the number of men required to man the vessel rather than the size of the ship, but it later became the practice to determine the category of the ship by the number of guns she carried. In Britain in 1745 a first-rate ship had 100 guns; a second-rate ship had 90 guns; a third-rate ship had 80 guns if she was a three-decker and 70 if she was a two-decker; and a fourth-rate ship had 50 guns. Fifth- and sixth-rate ships carried between 50 and 20 guns and were generally referred to as frigates [see pages 56-57 fig.1]. They were used for reconnaissance and patrol duties, for escorting convoys of merchant ships and for carrying out raids on enemy coasts and shipping. In a fleet action, they remained outside the line of battle and stood by to give assistance and to repeat the flag signals of the commander in chief.

The largest and most powerfully armed vessel in a fleet was the flagship, so called because she carried an admiral and flew his flag of command at the masthead [see pages 76, 83]. A vice-admiral flew his flag at the foremast, a rear-admiral at the mizzen mast, and an admiral of the fleet at the mainmast; in a major fleet action there might be three or more admirals present. A large warship under sail was a formidable sight, and it is little wonder that warships were favourite subjects for marine artists. Even when they are not the principal subject of the picture, they will often be seen in the middle distance or on the horizon, their masts providing a useful vertical feature in the composition.

Below the sixth-rate ships were a number of smaller vessels. These included bomb vessels, [see page 83] designed to carry one or two mortars which fired explosive shells in a high trajectory against shore defences and other land-based targets. There were fire ships, which were filled with barrels of tar and gunpowder and then let loose among enemy ships. And every navy had on its books a number of small armed vessels such as the sloop-of-war, the brig-of-war and the cutter. In the 18th century, the sloop was armed with 4 to 11 guns on her upper deck and rigged with one, two or three masts. She was the proper command of a master and commander. The brig was a two-masted vessel, fully square-rigged on both masts, with a fore-and-aft sail on the lower part of the mainmast [see pages 56-57 fig.4].

The armed cutter, which frequently appears in maritime drawings and prints, is one of the easiest naval vessels to identify. Single-masted, with a huge gaff sail and two foresails, she is usually shown racing through choppy seas with her lee rail awash [see page 112]. Cutters were fast and seaworthy and were used by navies for reconnaissance and for carrying despatches.

MERCHANT SHIPS

Before the develoment of the tea clippers in the second half of the 19th century, the largest of the sailing merchant ships were the vessels operated by the East India companies [see page 61, fig. 1]. Several European nations set up companies to trade with the East, but the largest by far were those of Britain, France and Holland. The Dutch East India Company was formed in 1602 and the company's ships can be identified by the initials VOC inscribed on the Dutch flag flown at the masthead and the stern. Britain's equivalent was the Honourable East India Company, which was originally set up by a group of merchants in 1600 but did not take over responsibility for the trading operations of the individual members until 1612.

British East Indiamen flew a flag with narrow horizontal red and white stripes. The largest of the East India Company ships were the size of warships and were heavily armed with anything up to 48 guns. They were usually richly decorated with elaborate carving at the stern and finely carved figureheads. The West Indiamen,

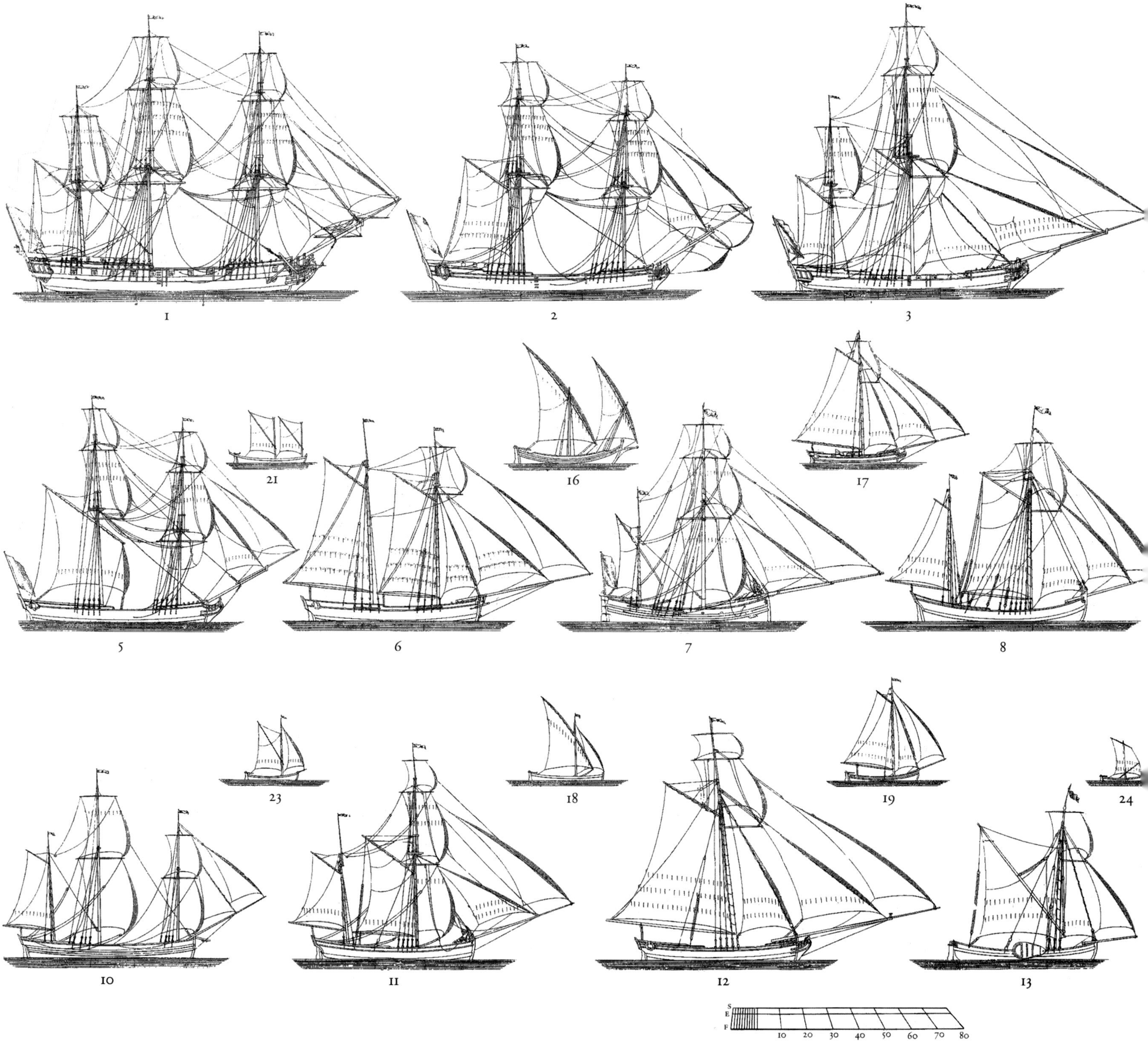
1
2
3
21
16
17
5
6
7
8
23
18
19
24
10
11
12
13
S
E
F
10 20 30 40 50 60 70 80

TWENTY-FOUR TYPES OF 18TH-CENTURY SAILING VESSELS DRAWN TO THE SAME SCALE.

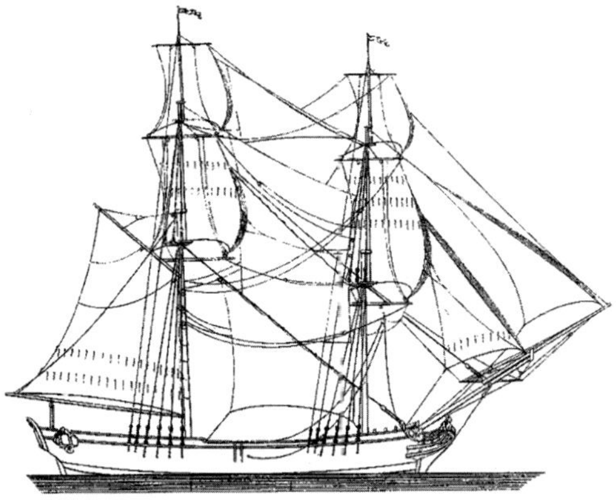

4

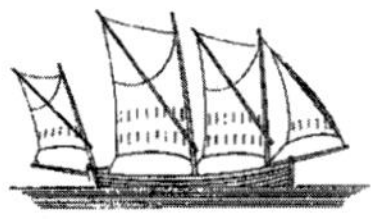

20

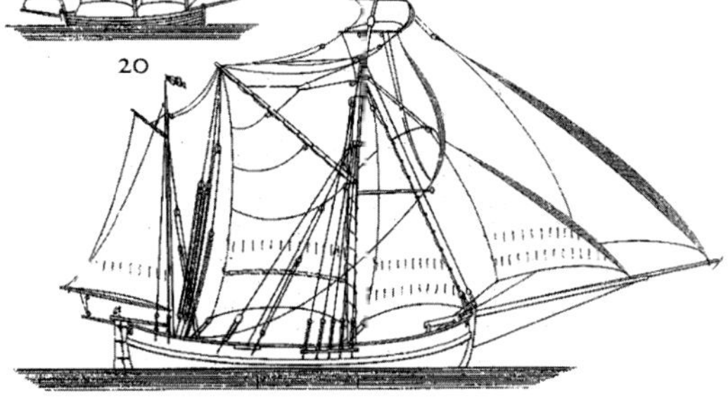

9

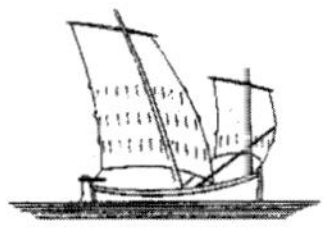

22

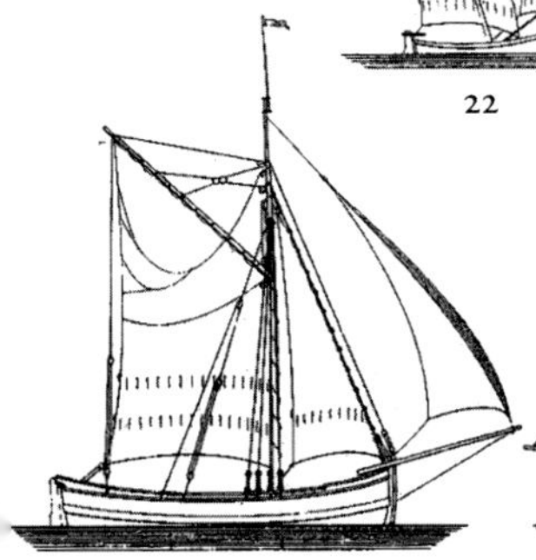

14

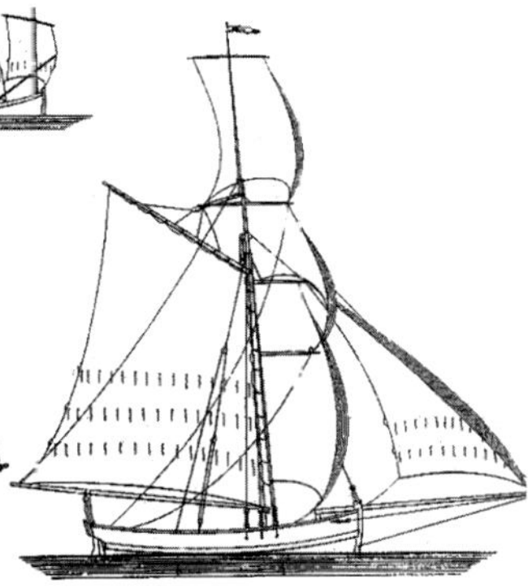

15

These drawings are reproduced from the famous volume of ship plans, *Architectura Navalis Mercatoria*, drawn by the great naval architect Fredrik Henrik Chapman and first published in Stockholm in 1768.

1. *Frigate* An example of a ship-rigged vessel. In the days of sail the term 'ship' was used only for a three-masted vessel with square sails on all three masts.

2. *Snow* A vessel similar to a brig with two masts, fully square-rigged on both masts, but with her spanker (the gaff sail at the stern) set on a separate pole, or trysail mast, just aft of the mainmast.

3. *Ketch* A two-masted vessel with a large fore-and-aft rigged mainmast and a smaller mizen with a fore-and-aft sail. The mizen mast is stepped forward of the tiller or wheel.

4. *Brig* A two-masted vessel, fully square-rigged on both masts, with a fore-and-aft sail on the lower part of the mainmast.

5. *Bilander* A two-masted vessel with square-rigged foremast and square main topsail but a mainsail set from a lateen. This rig was mostly confined to Baltic traders.

6. *Schooner* A two-masted vessel, fore-and-aft rigged on both masts. Some vessels had square topsails on the foremast or on both topmasts.

7. *Dogger* A Dutch fishing boat used for fishing on the Dogger Bank. These vessels had a variety of rigs and could have one, two or three masts.

8. *Dutch hoy* A small coastal craft used for carrying passengers or general cargoes.

9. *Galleass* A Scandinavian vessel used in the Baltic. Very different from the oared galleass that was used in the Mediterranean in the 16th and 17th centuries.

10. *Kray* used in Finland.

11. *Ketch-rigged yacht* used in the Baltic

12. *Sloop* Today the term applies to a vessel having one fore-and-aft rigged mainsail and a single foresail. In the 18th century the term was used to describe a gaff-rigged cutter as shown here, or a small armed vessel with one, two or three masts.

13. *Dutch tjalk* This was a cargo-carrying barge used on the inland waterways of Holland.

14. *English hoy* A small coastal craft used for carrying passengers or cargo and usually rigged as a gaff cutter.

15. *English cutter* A small one-masted vessel rigged with a fore-and-aft mainsail, foresail and jib. In the 18th century a cutter usually had one or two square topsails as well.

16. *Tartane, tartana* or *tartan* Mediterranean coastal vessel with one or two masts and lateen sails.

17. *Pleasure boat,* or *yacht* This is rigged as a gaff cutter with a square topsail.

18. *French longboat* with a lateen sail.

19. *Swedish longboat*

20. *English Deal cutter* with three spritsails.

21. *Pinnace* with two spritsails. This was generally used as a ship's boat.

22. *French fishing boat* used on the coast of Brittany.

23. *Yawl* with spritsail and fore-staysail.

24. *Yawl* used by the pilots at Stockholm.

which were built for trading with the West Indies, were smaller, and a typical ship would be armed with 18 or 20 guns.

In addition to the Indiamen, there was a whole range of merchant ships making trading voyages around the coasts of Europe and across the Atlantic. In the 17th century the most common of these was the flute, [see page 61, fig. 5] which has some claim to being one of the most successful merchant ships of all time. Built cheaply and in large numbers, and able to operate with a small crew, the flute gave the Dutch a competitive advantage over the other maritime nations of Europe and played a major part in the extraordinary growth of the Dutch Republic in the 17th century. The first flute was built at Hoorn in 1595 and the design proved so successful that flutes were soon being built in shipyards throughout Holland. They were also built in Britain, France and Scandinavia.

Another three-masted merchant ship that was a common sight in North European waters in the 18th century was the cat; several designs for cats are shown in F.H. Chapman's volume of ship plans, *Architectura Navalis Mercatoria.* They were beamy, flat-bottomed ships, with heavy whales, or rubbing strakes, running the length of the vessel, a stout stempost and well-rounded bows; their principal cargo was timber from the Baltic [see page 61, fig. 3].

The workhorses of trading operations across the Atlantic in the 18th century were three-masted ships of between 100 and 300 tons and the two-masted brigs and snows [see pages 56-57]. In addition to these, there was a variety of sailing barges operating around the coasts and up and down the rivers of Europe. Among those in use in the Netherlands were the *tjalk*, the *aak*, the *poon* and the *praam*, but there were dozens of local variations of these with different names. Of the English barges, it is the Thames barges that are most often illustrated, but there were also Norfolk wherries, which frequently appear in pictures by East Anglian artists, and Humber keels, which operated on the coast of Yorkshire.

Steam-powered vessels, with their distinctive, tall thin funnels, began appearing in pictures surprisingly early in the 19th century. The pioneers were the *Charlotte Dundas*, which made her maiden voyage on the Forth and Clyde Canal in 1802, and Robert Fulton's famous paddle steamer the *Clermont*, which began service as a passenger ferry on the East Hudson River in 1807. The advantage of steam over sail for regular ferry services was quickly grasped by shipowners and operators. In 1814 a steam ferry service began operating on the Thames between London and Margate, and two years later the first steamship passenger service across the English Channel was opened between Brighton and Le Havre.

A major breakthrough was the first crossing of the Atlantic made by a steam-powered ship in 1818, when the American steamship *Savannah* made the crossing from Georgia, South Carolina, to Liverpool. The engines were used for only 85 hours during the 27-day crossing, but it was the start of a new era. Samuel Cunard established the British and North American Royal Mail Steam Packet Company in 1839, and the following year his wooden paddle steamer *Britannia* carried the mail from Liverpool to Boston. Charles Dickens sailed on her second voyage and gave a graphic account of the turbulent crossing during which most of the passengers were violently seasick.

FISHING BOATS

Probably a greater variety of fishing boats has been built over the centuries than any other type of vessel. They have developed distinctive hull forms and rigs, as a result of local traditions and in response to local conditions and building materials. Fishing boats have been built of reeds, logs, dugout tree trunks, skins stretched over a frame, overlapping planks of wood and planks of wood laid side by side and caulked. More recently they have been made from iron or steel and glass fibre. Some fishing boats have been designed to operate on lakes and rivers, others among mud banks in estuaries, and yet others in the open seas and oceans. Some were launched into the surf off exposed beaches, and some operated from deep-water harbours. Every country and every region has come up with its own solutions over the years, and a few representative types are shown in the accompanying illustrations [see pages 20, 21, 62, 70, 85, 111, 130]. These are only a handful of the hundreds of different types of hull shape and rig that can be found around the coasts of the Western world.

The most obvious way to identify fishing boats in pictures is by their nets and fishing gear or by the activities of their crews. However, a schooner on her way to the fishing grounds is likely to look very like a merchant schooner, and there are many instances where there was little apparent difference between the vessels used for fishing and those used for transporting cargoes.

YACHTS AND YACHTING

The Dutch word *jacht* was derived from the verb *jagen*, meaning 'to hunt, chase, shoot or pursue', and the first yachts were fast sailing ships used for chasing enemy ships during the Dutch wars of the 16th century. They operated in coastal waters and the estuaries of the great rivers, and were employed during the skirmishes against the Spanish. There were variations in the size and rig of the earliest of these yachts, but by the 1620s their basic form had been established. They were armed with 8 to 10 guns, were richly decorated at the bow and stern with carving and had a raised state cabin aft, which provided comfortable accommodation. The vessels used by government officials on state business were called States yachts (*Statenjachten*) and those used by royalty were called Princes yachts. Originally designed for carrying despatches, providing support to the warships and fighting in shallow waters inaccessible to larger ships, the vessels came to be used as pleasure yachts during times of peace [see pages 64, 73].

The States yachts were, in effect, small warships, but during the course of the 17th century the Dutch developed another form of yacht that was not armed and was used purely for pleasure [see page 64]. These were usually owned by wealthy merchants and were elegant in design, with carved decoration and gilded coats of arms at the stern. They were 10–20m (33–66ft) in length and were rigged with one or two masts and fitted with fore-and-aft sails. They sometimes appear in the paintings of the two Willem van de Veldes and are much in evidence in pictures of the mock battles that were held in Amsterdam harbour for the entertainment of visiting dignitaries. Some indication of the growing popularity of these yachts can be gathered from the records of the yacht havens, the forerunners of the yacht marinas of today. In 1622 a yacht haven was opened in Amsterdam which had berths for 41 pleasure yachts; later in the century there were four yacht havens in the city, each providing private berths for about 40 yachts.

It was the States yacht, and the similar but more richly decorated Princes yacht, which provided the pattern for the yachts introduced into England during the early years of the reign of King Charles II. While Cromwell ruled England under the Commonwealth, the exiled Prince Charles spent much of his time in Holland, since his sister was married to Prince William of Orange. With the ending of the Commonwealth and the Restoration of the Monarchy in 1660, Charles travelled in state to England. The first part of the journey took him from Breda, past Rotterdam, to the Hague and he travelled in a yacht which had been built for the Prince of Orange. According to a contemporary account, 'The King found his yacht so comfortable that he remarked, while discoursing with his deputies, that he might order one of the same style so soon as he should arrive in England, to use in the River Thames.'

In August 1660 King Charles was presented with a similar yacht as a gift from the city of Amsterdam. She was named the *Mary* after Charles's sister, the Princess Royal, and was moored in the Pool of London; she was the first yacht seen in England and attracted considerable attention. She was 15.8m (52ft) in length, with a beam of 5.8m

The prints of ship types opposite are taken from three different sets of etchings: *Navis Mercatoria Hollandis* by Wenceslaus Hollar published in the 1640s; *Hollandsche Schepen* by Gerrit Groenewegen, published in Rotterdam in 1789; and *Collection de toutes les especes de batimens de guerre et de batimens marchands qui naviguent sur l'Ocean et dans la Mediterranee* by Jean-Jerome Baugean, published in Paris in the early 19th century.

Fig. 1 *A Dutch East Indiaman*
Etching by Groenewegen.

Fig. 2 *An English merchant ship*, with a brig in the distance.
Etching by Baugean.

Fig. 3 *A Dutch flute, or fluit*, the most successful type of merchant ship in the 17th century.
Etching by Wenceslaus Hollar.

Fig. 4 *A Dutch kat coming to anchor*
These vessels were used for transporting timber from the Baltic and were known in England as cats.
Etching by Groenewegen.

Fig. 5 *A French chasse marée and a dogger*
Etching by Baugean.

Fig. 6 *A Spanish xebec, or chebec*, with lateen sails.
Etching by Baugean.

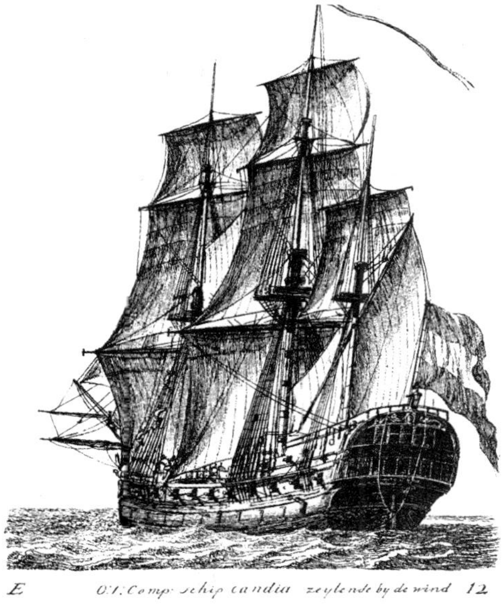

Fig. 1

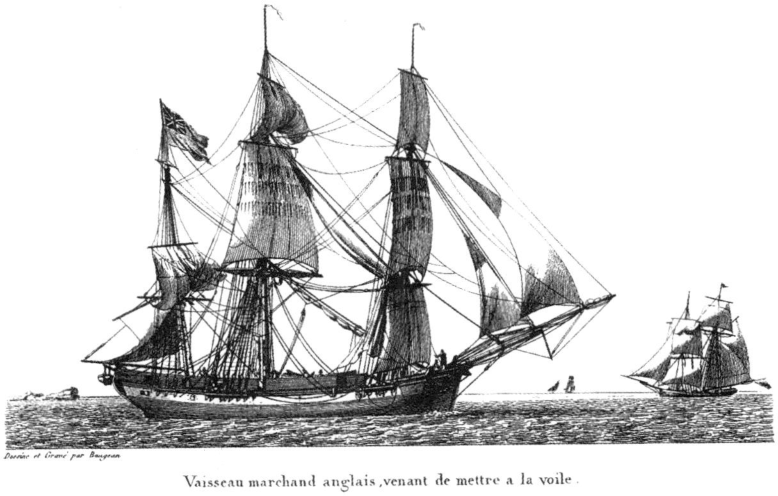

Fig. 2

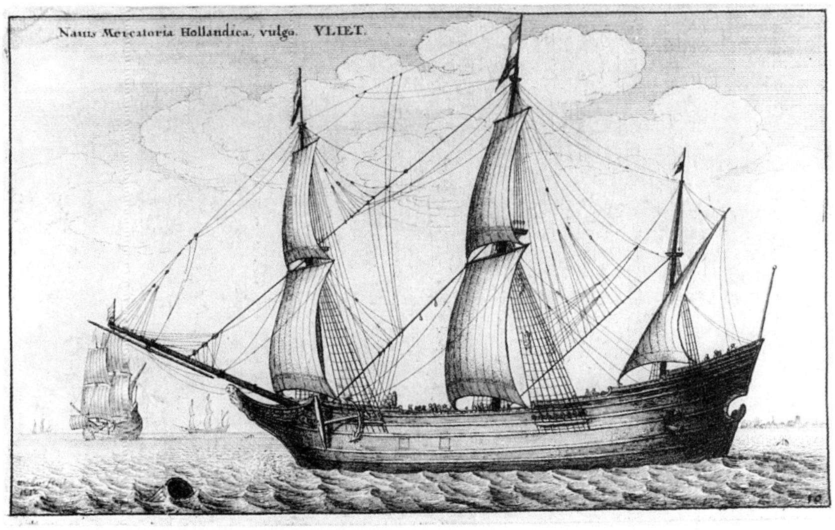

Fig. 3

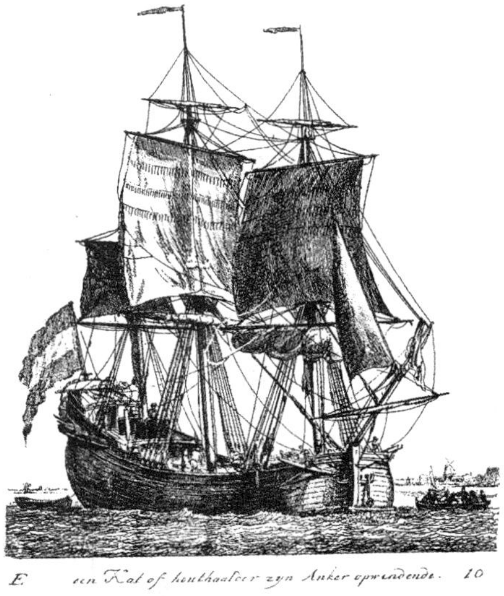

Fig. 4

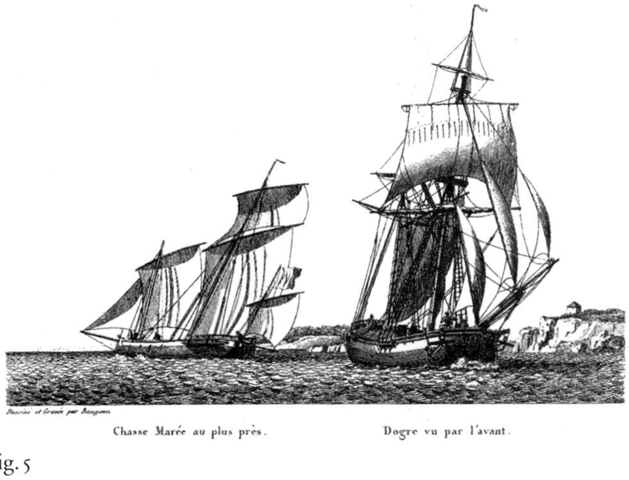

Fig. 5

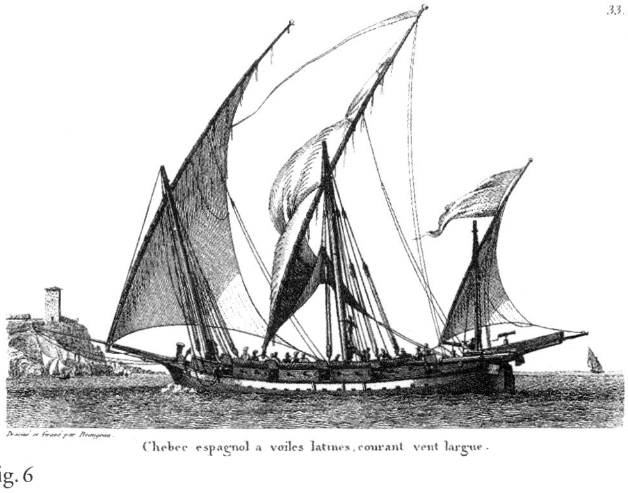

Fig. 6

Charles Napier Hemy
A fishing boat in a fresh breeze

Powered by a heavy brown lugsail, a Cornish fishing boat heads towards the fishing grounds.

Signed with initials and dated 1912. Sotheby's, London.

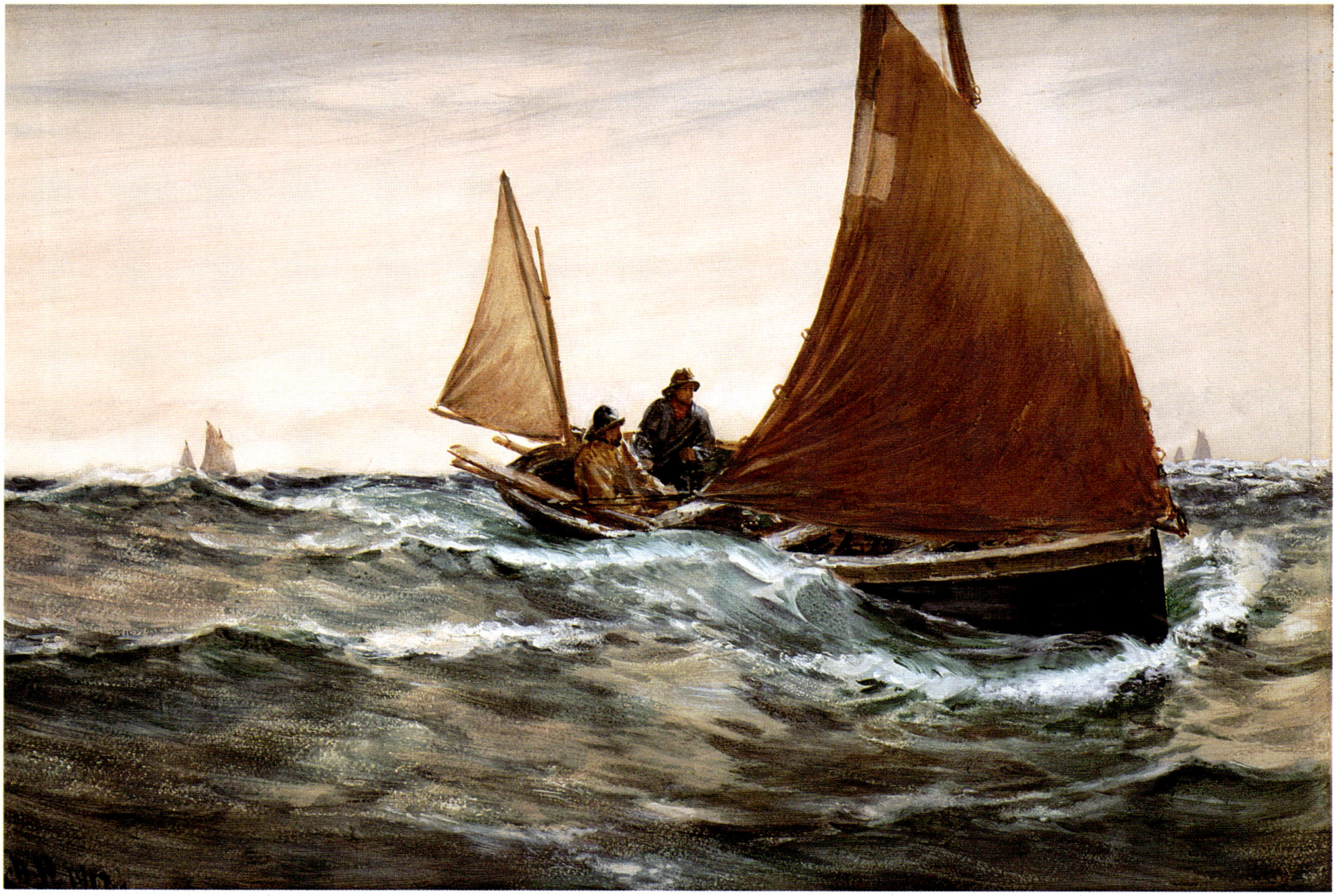

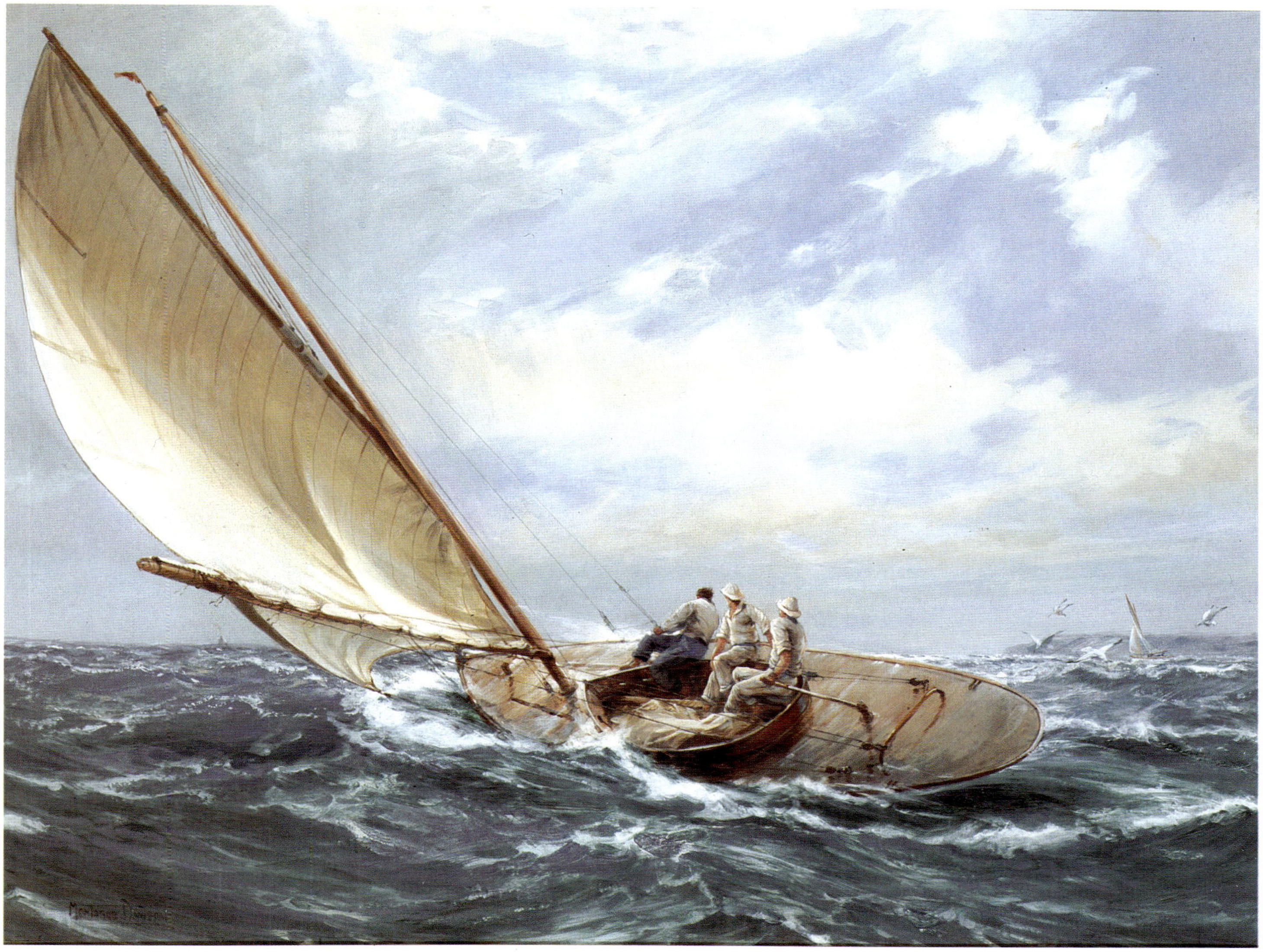

MONTAGUE DAWSON
Going free

A racing yacht with reefed mainsail is shown running before a fresh breeze with her lee rail awash.

Gouache. Signed. Sotheby's, London.

(19ft) and a draft of 2m (7ft). The king was delighted with her and ordered four similar yachts to be built, which became a familiar sight on the Thames and were frequently used for races in which King Charles and his brother James took part. It is these races that mark the beginning of yachting in England.

During the course of the 18th century two clubs were formed which were to be the precursors of yacht clubs all over the world. The earliest was the Water Club of Cork, which was in existence by 1720. Originally it had no more than 25 members and held regular rallies in Cork harbour in southern Ireland. In 1775 the Duke of Cumberland, brother of King George III, presented a cup as a prize for races which for some years had been held on the Thames between Westminster Bridge and

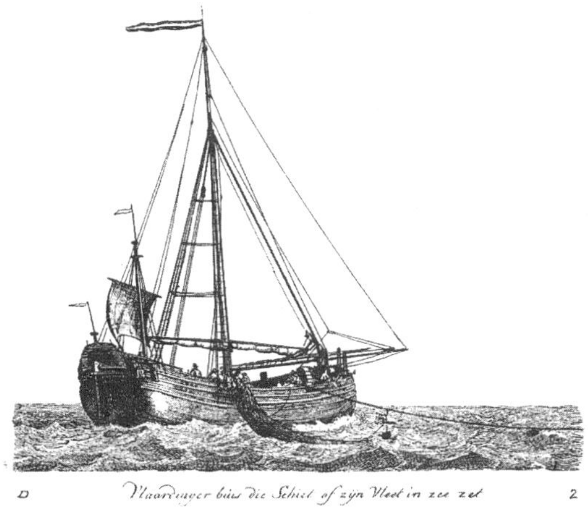

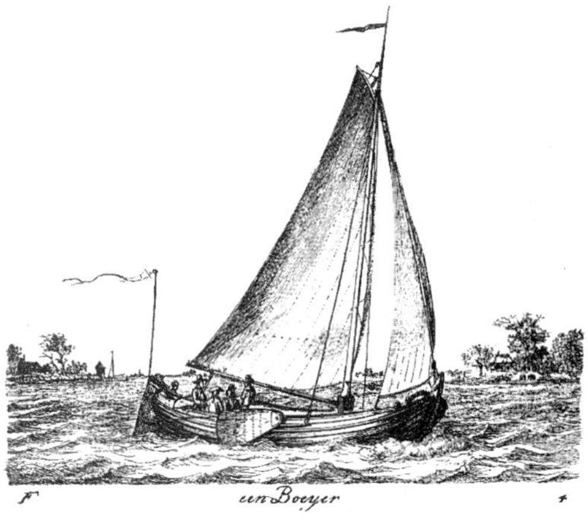

FAR LEFT
Dutch fishing buss shooting her nets
Etching by Groenewegen.

LEFT
Dutch boeier yacht
Etching by Groenewegen.

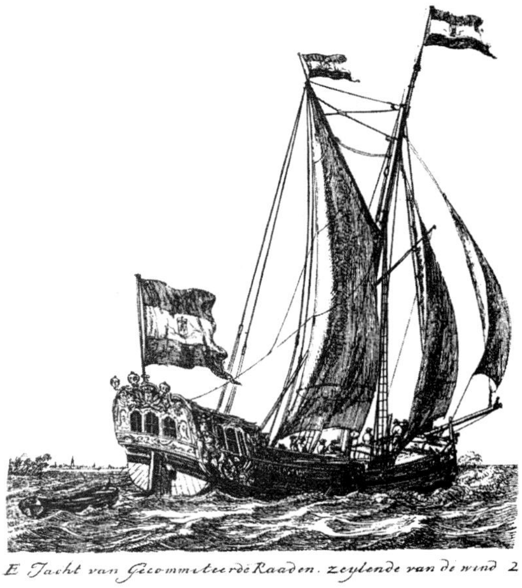

Dutch States yacht
Etching by Groenewegen.

Putney Bridge, and the participants formed themselves into the Cumberland Sailing Society. Following a dispute in 1823, several members departed to form the Thames Yacht Club, which held its first race in September of that year.

The Royal Yacht Squadron at Cowes on the Isle of Wight can trace its origin to a meeting of English aristocrats and gentlemen held in London in 1815. It was originally called The Yacht Club and was for yachtsmen wanting to sail on the sea, rather than the Thames. Meetings were held every August at Cowes, where a building on the seafront was leased in 1824. King George IV had become a member when he was Prince Regent, and in 1833 his successor, King William III, announced that it was his wish 'that it shall be henceforth known and styled "The Royal Yacht Squadron" of which His Majesty is graciously pleased to consider himself the head.'

The prestigious New York Yacht Club was formed a few years later. The first meeting was held on board the schooner *Gimcrack* in New York harbour in July 1844, and in August seven yachts cruised to Newport, Rhode Island. The following summer the club organized a race through the New York Narrows of Staten Island, around a buoy in the Lower Bay and back again. In 1850, one of the founders of the New York Yacht Club received a letter from England suggesting that the Americans send across a boat as part of the international celebrations connected with the Great Exhibition to be held the following year. A schooner based on the lines of the New York pilot boats and measuring 31m (101ft 9in) in length overall was built; she was named *America*. She sailed across the Atlantic in 20 days and dropped anchor at Cowes in August 1851

The Royal Yacht Squadron organized a race around the Isle of Wight, which was open to all comers. The *America* and 14 British yachts took part in the race, which began at 10am on 22 August 1851. Although the *America* was last off the mark, she steadily overtook every other yacht and led the fleet around the island and back to Cowes, where John Cox Stevens, the commodore of the New York Yacht Club, was presented with the solid silver trophy that was later to become known as the America's Cup.

The Dutch, the British and the Americans were among the first to develop yachts and yacht races, but they were soon joined by other maritime nations. Yachts were introduced into France shortly after they had been taken up by the English Court, mainly due to the encouragement of Jean-Baptiste Colbert, Louis XIV's chief minister, who commissioned them into the French navy. The Royal Swedish Yacht Club was founded in 1830; the Societé des Regates du Havre in France in 1838; and the Royal Bermuda Yacht Club in 1844. By the end of the 19th century, yachts and yacht clubs were to be found all over the world.

Chapter five

THE DUTCH SCHOOL

Although it is possible to find pictures of ships in early charts, in medieval manuscripts and tucked away in the background of Renaissance paintings, it was the artists working in the Netherlands during the 17th century who were the first to make ships and seascapes their major preoccupation. Their greatest work was carried out in oil paint on oak panels or canvases, but they also worked in pen and wash and produced a large body of engravings and etchings. The finest examples of their work in all these areas has rarely been surpassed, and it provided an inspiration for the generations of marine artists who followed them.

The development of marine painting in the Netherlands was part of that astonishing era which is often described as the Golden Age of Dutch art. It was a period that produced some of the greatest names in the history of art, including Rembrandt, Vermeer, Frans Hals and Jacob van Ruisdael. It was also a period which saw specialist art forms developed to an unusual degree of perfection. Among these were flower paintings; still life subjects; architectural interiors; genre scenes of peasants in taverns; winter landscapes with people skating on frozen ponds and canals; beach scenes with fishing boats; and pictures of ships and the sea.

The pictures were painted not for aristocrats and royalty but for the merchants, town councils, shopkeepers and shipowners who were turning the newly created Dutch Republic into the most successful trading nation in Europe. After years of struggle against Spanish rule, the Dutch gained their freedom and threw their energies into building up a strong internal economy and developing overseas trade. Shipping played a crucial part in the story. The Netherlands were criss-crossed by a network of waterways. The low, exposed landscape lacked the shelter provided by mountains and hills, but it enabled the maximum use to be made of the wind. The Dutch harnessed wind power to drive windmills, which not only ground corn but pumped water from flooded fields into canals and operated sawmills in the shipyards. The wind also provided the motive power for hundreds of sailing craft on the Zuider Zee and the innumerable inland waterways. Small boats were used to deliver milk and vegetables and to take people and their livestock to market. Fishing boats cast

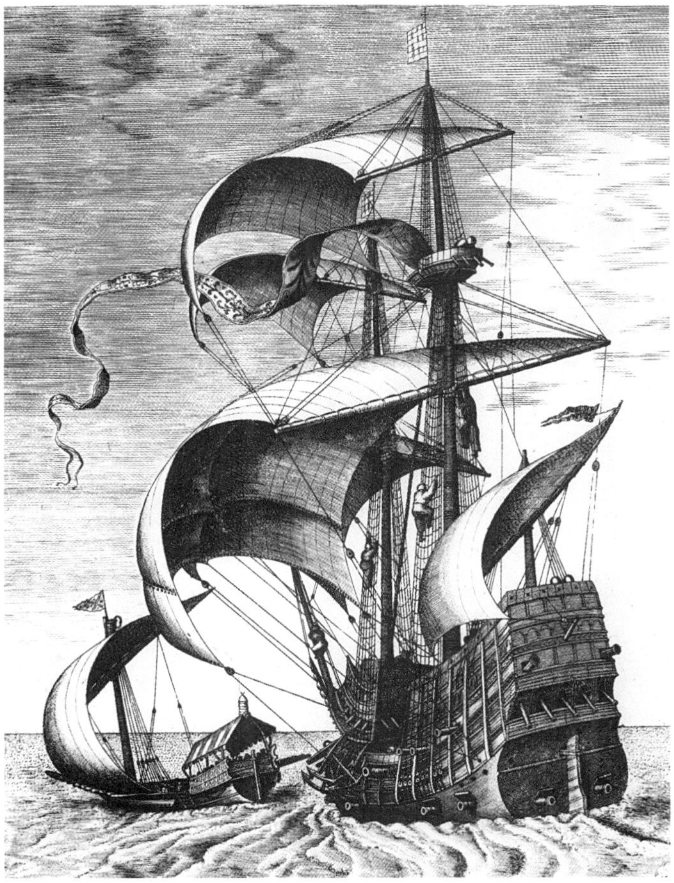

FRANS HUYS after
PIETER BRUEGEL
A galleon and a galley

This is one of a series of ten prints of ship types engraved by Huys from drawings by Bruegel. The work of a great artist is here translated into a lively and decorative print by an accomplished engraver.

Engraving. Inscribed BRUEGEL/F.H. *c*1565. National Maritime Museum, London.

their nets on the rivers and in the North Sea. Coastal vessels and barges traded with neighbouring countries, and the ships of the Dutch East India Company set off on voyages to the Far East. It is not surprising, therefore, to find that seascapes were much in demand.

In 1565 a series of ten prints of ship types, based on drawings commissioned from Pieter Breugel the Elder and engraved by Frans Huys, was published in Antwerp. The engravings are frequently reproduced in books on ships as key examples of early sailing vessels, but they are equally important as examples of print-making. Bold and vigorous in design and alive with movement, they show what can be achieved by a skilful engraver working from designs by a great artist. Breugel had painted several pictures which showed ships viewed from afar, but the prints show his interest in all the intricate details of rigging and reveal an understanding of how sailing vessels reacted to differing weather conditions.

The year following the publication of Breugel's prints, Hendrick Cornelisz Vroom was born in Haarlem. Vroom is usually regarded as the founding father of Dutch marine painting, and he was certainly the first artist to make his name in this specialized area. He spend some time in Italy as a young man and was employed by Cardinal Ferdinand de Medici to paint pictures of ships and harbours. He travelled in France and Spain and made a number of coastal voyages, one of which ended in shipwreck. On his return to Holland he devoted himself to marine paintings and almost single-handedly created a market for seascapes. He received commissions from the Dutch East India Company and the various Admiralties, and in 1594 was exempted from military service by the burgomasters of Haarlem 'because of his unique skill in painting of marine subjects in which he excels all others.' Although there are many examples of Vroom's paintings in the collections at Greenwich and in Amsterdam, very few of his drawings have survived. The National Maritime Museum has a delicate study in pen and brown ink of Dutch herring busses, which gives some indication of his style in this medium.

A follower and probably a pupil of Vroom was Cornelis Claesz van Wieringen, who also came from Haarlem and spent his early years as a seaman before taking up painting. In 1621 he was commissioned by the Admiralty of Amsterdam to paint *The Battle of Gibraltar*, a dramatic work showing a ship exploding; there is a version in the Netherlands Scheepvart Museum and another in the Rijksmuseum. The Frans Hals Museum in Haarlem has an impressive painting, *Arrival of Frederick V, Elector Palatine, at Flushing in May 1613*, and the National Maritime Museum has a fine

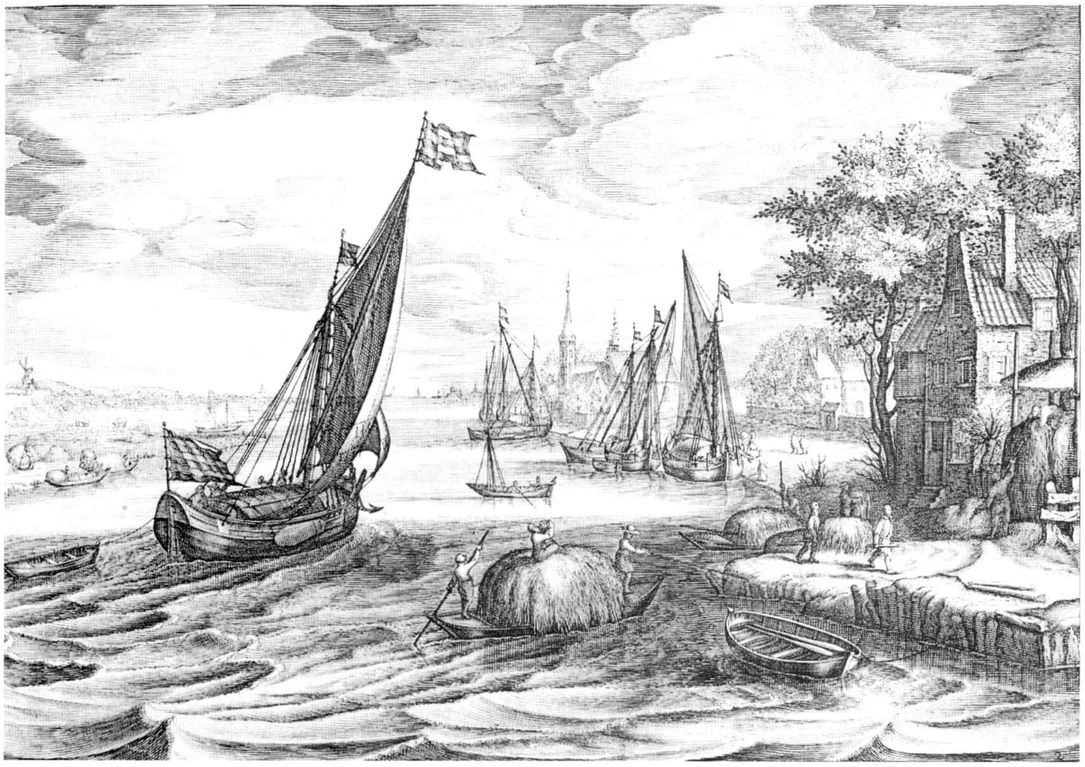

ROBERT DE BAUDOUS after CLAESZ VAN WIERINGEN
Aestas or Summer

In the second of four engravings illustrating the seasons the artist has depicted a peaceful summer scene with haymaking in progress. The Latin inscription under the picture can be translated as 'Summer: while the summer sun still blazes down, safely choose the open sea. Gentle summer breezes blow, with mind at ease, leave land's lee.

Engraving. 1618. Private collection.

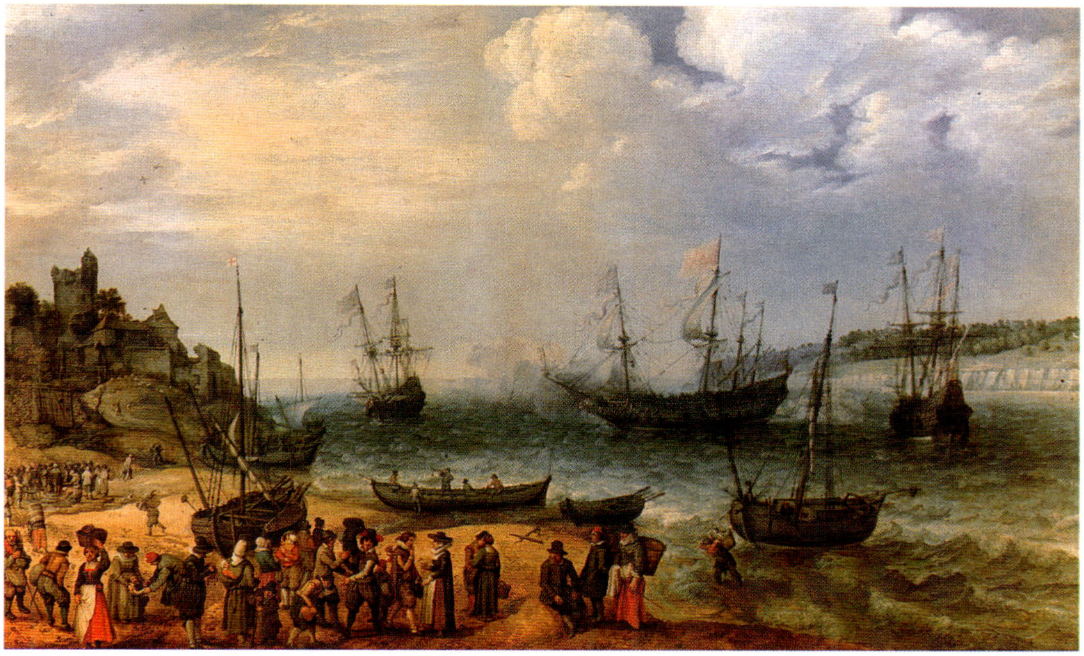

ADAM WILLAERTS
The departure of an East Indiaman, 1640

One of the first Dutch artists to concentrate on painting seascapes, Willaerts' speciality was decorative pictures which celebrated the embarkation of kings and princes or, as shown here, the departure of a ship on a voyage to the East. His drawings are fairly rare and this oil painting has been included as an example of the work of the early Dutch School.

Oil on canvas. Signed and dated 1640. National Maritime Museum, London.

example, *An English privateer off La Rochelle*, which has some wonderful detail and a fascinating and patriotic inscription. But more relevant here than Van Wieringen's paintings are the very fine engravings that were made from his designs by Robert de Baudous, in particular a series depicting the four seasons. These are centred around shipping activities, and perhaps the most charming is the engraving illustrating summer. A small boat ferries a mound of hay from the distant fields across a river to a barn, while a sailing vessel sets off downstream towards the sea, heeling before the summer breeze.

The paintings of the Flemish artist Adam Willaerts are similar in subject matter to those of Vroom but show a lighter touch. The foregrounds of his many embarkation scenes are usually filled with colourful detail. Fishermen are shown loading or unloading baskets of fish; departing travellers take leave of their families; and curious onlookers, accompanied by their dogs, stand around watching the activity on the shore. Willaerts was born in Antwerp but moved to the inland city of Utrecht in 1600, and this was his base for the rest of his life. His eldest son, Abraham, became his pupil and followed in his footsteps as a marine painter. Abraham's decorative and somewhat stylized paintings are similar in style to those of his father, and it is often difficult to tell them apart.

Jan Porcellis pioneered the second phase in the development of Dutch marine painting. Instead of recording the comings and goings of big ships and important historical events, he turned to the activities of local fishermen for his subject matter. In

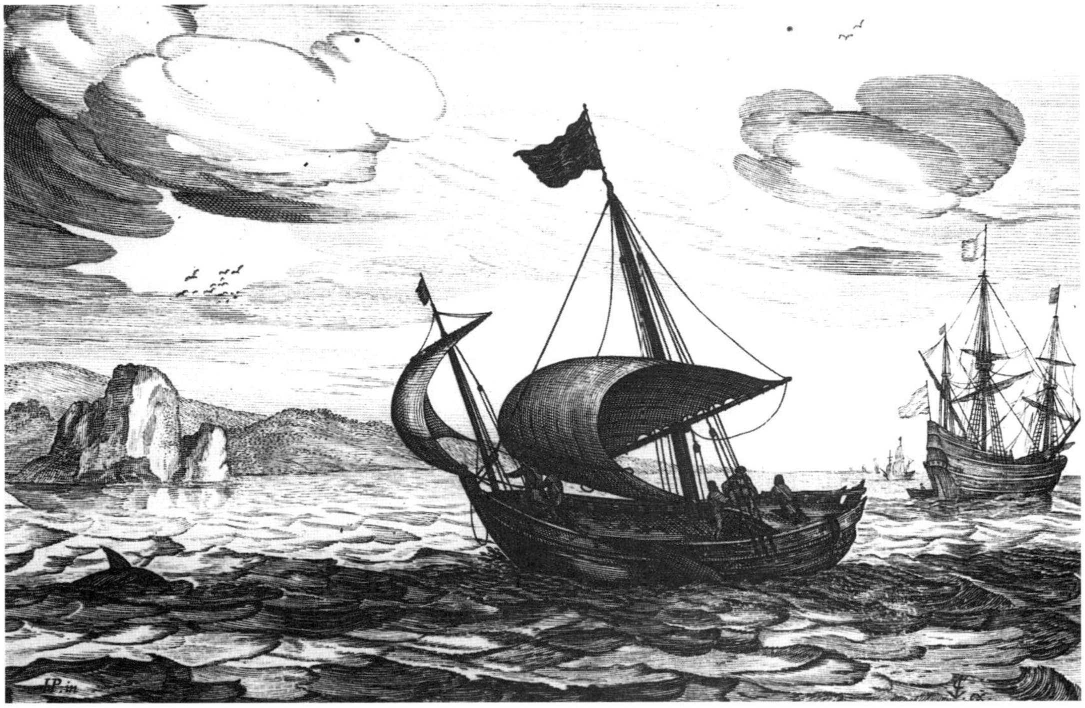

CLAES JANSZ VISSCHER after JAN PORCELLIS
A Dutch dogger in a fresh breeze

Compared with the free and sensitive drawing of the etchings by Nooms and Bakhuizen, this engraving is curiously stiff and stylized. This reflects the difficulties of cutting the lines directly into the copper plate. Visscher was a fine craftsman but had to adopt the rather mechanical form of shading associated with most engravings. The dogger was a type of Dutch fishing boat used for cod fishing on the Dogger Bank in the North Sea.

Engraving. 1627. National Maritime Museum, London.

place of the bright colours of Vroom and Willaerts, he painted in a muted palette of sombre browns and greys. His pictures are dominated by great cloudy skies, with sunlight and shadow sweeping across windswept beaches and the surface of the sea.

Porcellis was born in Ghent around 1584 and moved to Rotterdam, where he was married in 1605. His early years as an artist were plagued by poverty, and at one stage he went bankrupt. In 1622 he moved with his family to Haarlem and, following the death of his first wife, married the daughter of a prosperous painter and print publisher. His life took a turn for the better as the quality and originality of his work were recognized, and by the time of his death in 1632 he was a rich man and his reputation eclipsed that of Vroom. His work was particularly admired by later artists. Rubens owned one of his landscapes, Rembrandt had six, and Jan van de Cappelle had sixteen.

In 1627 a set of 12 prints after designs by Jan Porcellis was published in Amsterdam. The prints were engraved by Claes Jansz Visscher and depicted the various types of fishing boats and ferries to be seen on the Dutch waterways. Compared to later series of ship types by Reinier Nooms and Gerrit Groenewegen, the prints are curiously stiff and stylized. This partly reflects the limitations of copper engraving, which is difficult to work in and lacks the freedom and spontaneity of line possible with etching. This is clearly demonstrated by the many fine prints that Visscher carried out as etchings based on his own designs: these are lively views of everyday life in the ports and shipyards and are packed with incident.

The moody seascapes of Porcellis inspired a number of gifted artists, the greatest of whom was Jan van Goyen, whose river scenes are among the most beautiful of their kind. Van Goyen travelled the waterways of Holland in a boat, filling his sketchbooks with drawings in black chalk. He was an acute observer of clouds and weather and liked to depict grey, overcast days with fishermen huddled in small boats beside their nets, and brown-sailed boats drifting through the flat Dutch fields.

Another painter of river scenes was Salomon van Ruisdael, the uncle of the landscape painter Jacob van Ruisdael. The National Gallery in London has a typical example of his work entitled *A view of Deventer.* Painted in 1657, this depicts the small town of Deventer on the Ijssel, with the tower of the Grote Kerk in the middle distance. It is a tranquil summer day and sailing vessels laden with passengers are heading for market. A cluster of masts near the church tower indicates the position of the town's busy harbour. The seven windmills visible in the picture are not simply picturesque additions to the landscape but were essential for grinding corn, pumping water and working machinery.

Simon de Vlieger followed the lead of Porcellis but applied his talents to a much wider range of subjects. He was equally at ease working on small-scale views of beaches and rocky coasts as on large paintings of warships. An original and talented artist, he experimented with perspective and developed a distinctive silvery grey palette, which is instantly recognizable. He was born and grew up in Rotterdam, but after his marriage there he moved to Delft, where he became a member of the artists' guild. In 1649 he bought a house in Weesp, 16km (10 miles) from Amsterdam, where he spent the last four years of his life. The National Maritime Museum at Greenwich has some spectacular examples of his work and there are also fine paintings in the National Gallery in London.

Jan van de Cappelle painted winter landscapes and a remarkable series of pictures showing groups of vessels becalmed beneath soaring clouds. Barges filled with people move slowly across the mirror-smooth waters. Sails lie limp, creating intricate patterns as they recede into the distant haze [see page 72]. The art historian Walter Stechow regarded Cappelle as the greatest of the marine artists and observed how his subtle tones of brown and grey are 'held together by an atmosphere of an almost palpable moisture such as had never been painted before; all the details are steeped in it.' Cappelle lived all his life in Amsterdam, where his father owned a successful dyeworks. He married a girl from a wealthy family and when her mother died he inherited three properties in the city. His wealth enabled him to build up a fabulously rich art collection of some 200 paintings and 6,000 drawings, which included 10 paintings and 500 drawings by Rembrandt and works by De Vlieger, Van Goyen and Jan Porcellis.

Of the same generation as Van de Capelle, was Aelbert Cuyp, who is famous for his peaceful rural scenes with cows and horses gathered on the riverbanks. He also painted some memorable marine paintings. These include stormy scenes of boats heeling before squalls under lowering skies, and tranquil calms with beautifully drawn sailing vessels illuminated by a golden light. Fine examples of the latter are the *View of Dordrecht* at Kenwood House in Hampstead, London, and *The Passage Boat* in the Royal Collection. Cuyp was born in Dordrecht, an ancient port, where he lived all his life. He went on numerous sketching trips around Holland, but it was the countryside around his home town, and the dominating tower of its church, which appear in so many of his paintings. His work was greatly admired by the later English landscape painters, notably Turner, whose magnificent painting *Dordrecht,* in the Yale Center for British Art, was directly inspired by Cuyp.

The third phase of Dutch art was dominated by Willem van de Velde the Elder and his son, Willem van de Velde the Younger. These two artists worked as a team, the Elder going to sea with the fleet and recording sea battles at first hand, and the Younger making use of his father's drawings for the detail in his paintings of naval actions. Between them they portrayed all the major sea battles of the Anglo–Dutch wars, as well as royal visits to the fleet, ship portraits and many of the merchant ships,

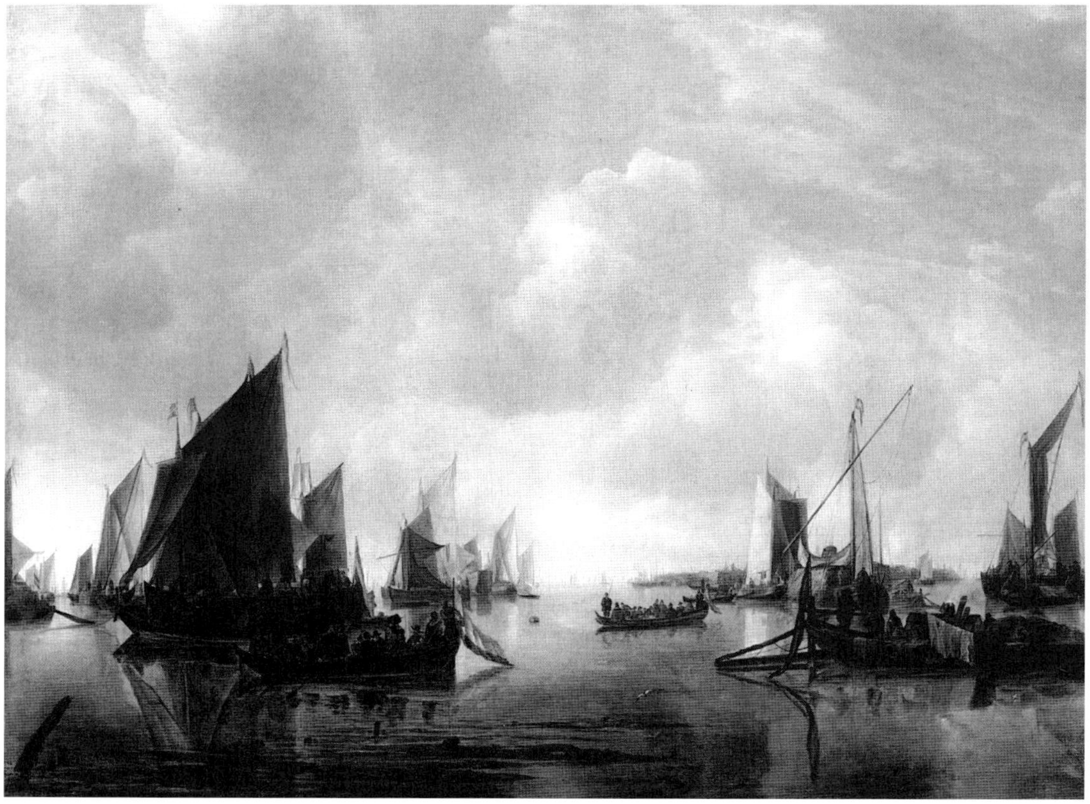

JAN VAN DE CAPPELLE
A river scene with many Dutch vessels becalmed

A miscellaneous collection of vessels, including a hay barge, a ferry, a yacht and several fishing boats, lie becalmed in a vast expanse of shallow water. An extraordinary illusion of depth is created so that the foreground melts imperceptibly into the distance, and the horizon vanishes into the sky. This serene work by one of the greatest of the Dutch marine artists typifies the achievement of the Dutch School.

Oil on canvas. The National Gallery, London.

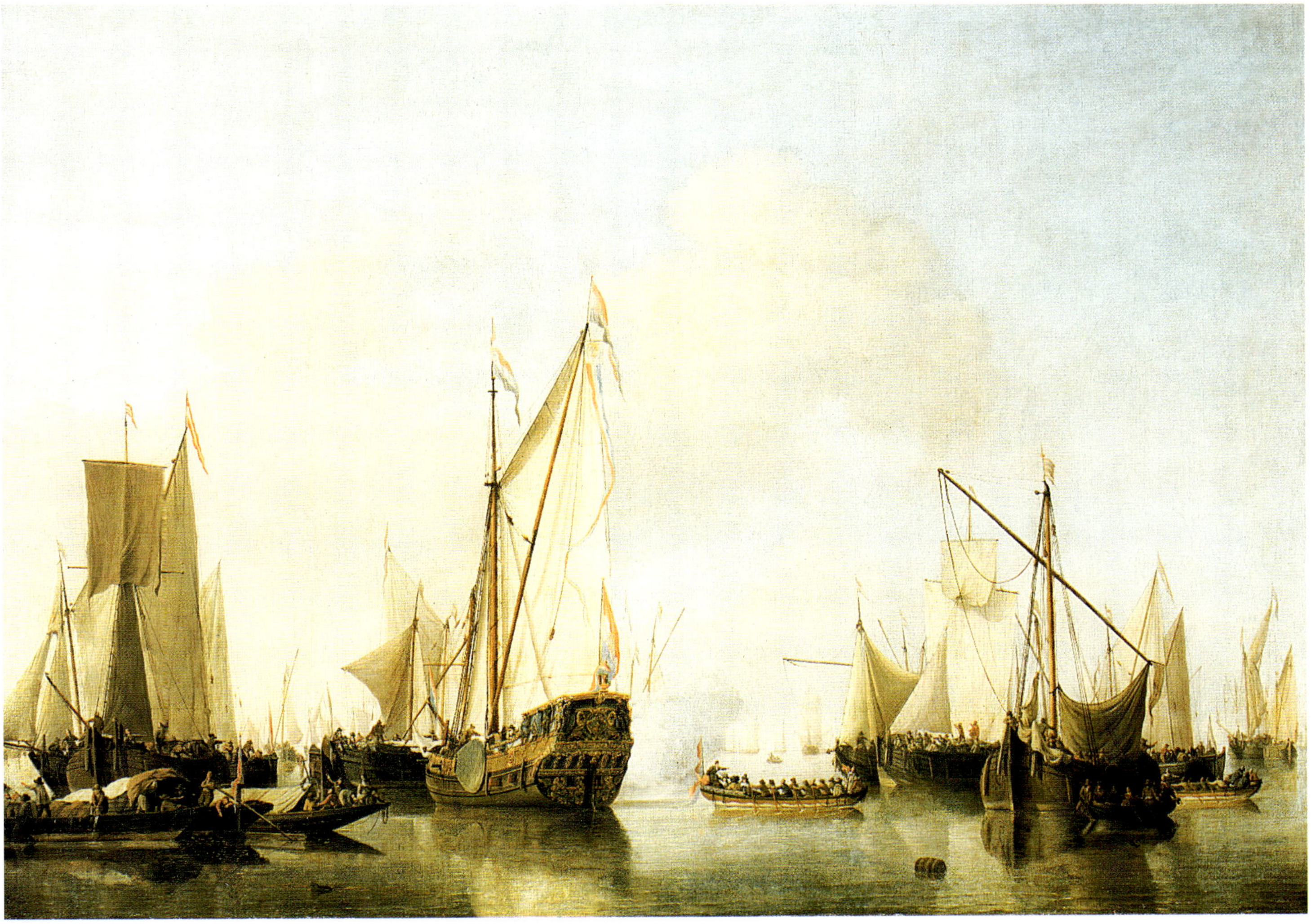

WILLEM VAN DE VELDE THE YOUNGER
Calm: a States yacht and many other vessels in a very light air

The beautiful calm scenes painted by the younger Van de Velde made his reputation and were greatly admired by later generations of artists and collectors. The elaborately decorated vessel in the centre of the picture is a States yacht, which is firing a salute as a ship's barge pulls away from her stern.

Oil on canvas. Signed with initials. 1658. Private collection.

yachts and small craft to be seen around the shores of Holland and southern Britain in their day.

It has to be said that their work seldom achieved the poetic intensity and atmospheric effects of Cuyp, Van Goyen and Van de Cappelle, but they had no rivals in the range of their subject matter and the accuracy with which they depicted ships. In particular, Van de Velde the Younger achieved lasting fame with his pictures of becalmed vessels. Painted between 1653 and 1655, when he was in his twenties, these calms established him as the leading marine artist of his day.

Willem van de Velde the Elder was born in Leiden, the son of a local seaman who was master of a troop transport vessel. By 1636 he was married and living in Amsterdam, which remained his home until he emigrated to England when he was in his sixties. He devoted his entire life to drawing ships, much of it in an official capacity for the Dutch Admiralty and later for the English monarch Charles II. His

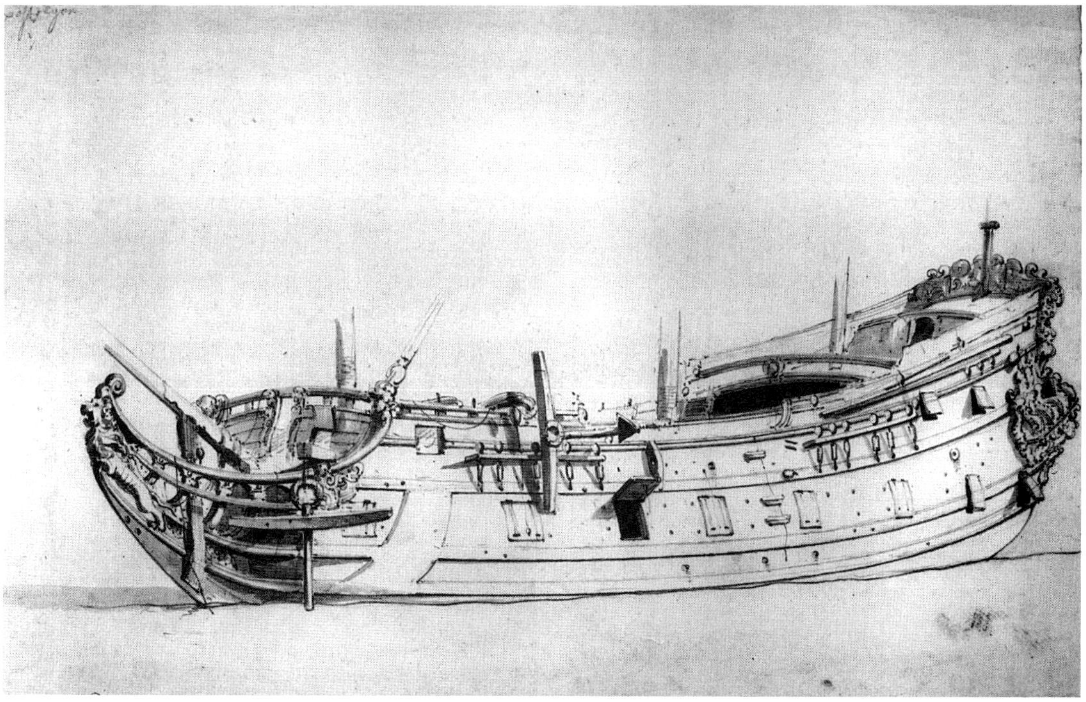

WILLEM VAN DE VELDE THE YOUNGER
Portrait of the Postiljon, *a Dutch ship of 24 guns*

Van de Velde was so adept at drawing ships that he could convey all the essential detail and create an almost three-dimensional effect with an enviable lightness of touch.

Pencil and wash. Signed. 1665. National Maritime Museum, London.

value as a war artist is underlined by a letter written by Admiral de Ruyter to a ship's captain shortly before the Four Days' Battle in June 1666: 'Captain Govert Pietersz is hereby ordered to receive and take on board the galliot under his command Willem van de Velde, ship's draughtsman, and to go with him ahead or astern or with the fleet, or in such manner as he may judge serviceable for the drawings to be made without failing in any way whatsoever under penalty of severe punishment.'

Hundreds of drawings made by Van de Velde the Elder have survived, but he was also famous for his *penschildering* – pen paintings – sometimes called grisailles. These were drawn with a quill pen and a brush on a prepared canvas or wood panel. The resulting work has the appearance of a very large engraving, except for the use of pale grey paint for clouds and smoke. Van de Velde seems to have pioneered this particular art form and was the greatest exponent of it in his day, although pen paintings were also made by Ludolf Bakhuizen, Heerman Witmont and Adriaan Van Salm.

The younger Van de Velde was trained by his father who no doubt taught him how to draw ships, but he also received some instruction from Simon de Vlieger in Weesp. The son's drawings, usually in pen and grey wash, tend to be looser and freer than those of his father, and he often uses a charming shorthand to suggest the shape of ships at sea. There are some interesting drawings at the National Maritime Museum which show how he worked out the perspective in his seascapes; these seem to have been made to instruct pupils in the Van de Velde studio.

When the Van de Veldes emigrated to England in 1672, the field was left open for Ludolf Bakhuizen. He was two years older than Van de Velde the Younger but made a late start as a painter. He trained as an accountant and worked as a merchant's clerk in Emden before moving to Amsterdam in 1650. There he turned first to calligraphy and then to the production of pen paintings in the manner of Van de Velde the Elder. Not until the early 1660s did he become established as a marine painter. However, he proved to have formidable gifts, and his accomplished and theatrical paintings soon led to a series of important commissions. In 1665 he was commissioned by the Amsterdam city magistrates to paint the large canvas *Shipping before Amsterdam*, which shows the city at the height of its prosperity; other impressive clients included the Duke of Saxony, the Archduke of Tuscany and Tsar Peter the Great.

Bakhuizen became the undisputed leader of marine art in the Netherlands when Van de Veldes moved to London. In 1701, at the age of 70, he made a series of ten

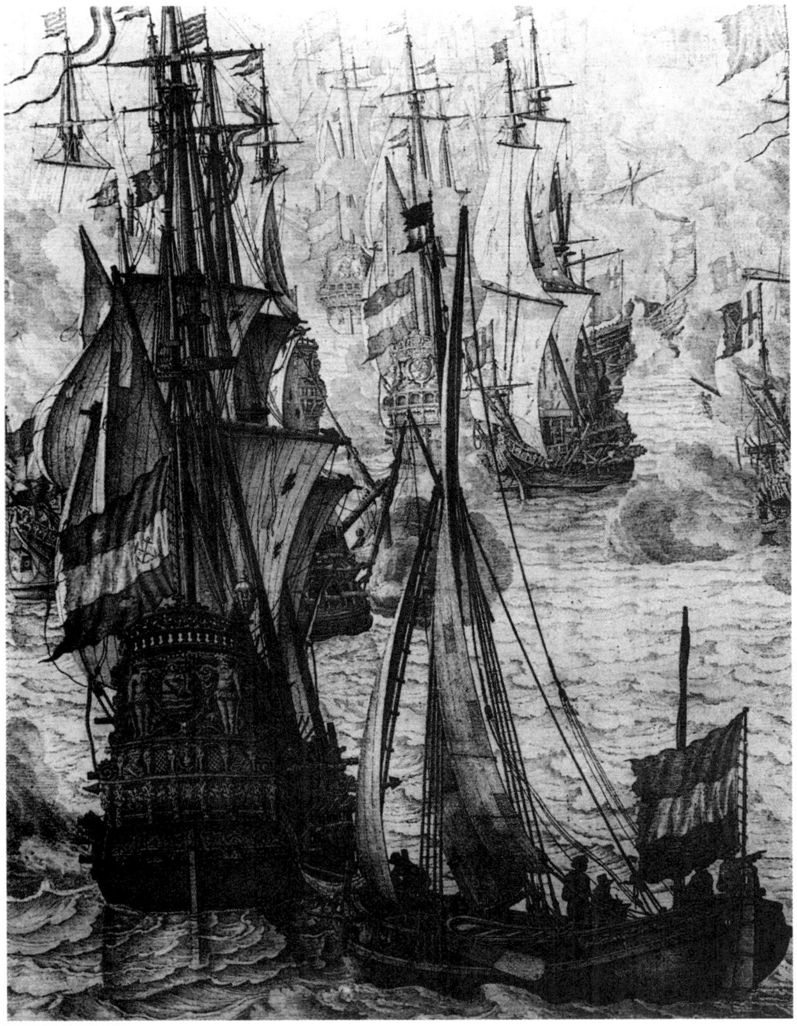

WILLEM VAN DE VELDE THE ELDER
The battle of Scheveningen, 31 July 1653

In this detail from a panoramic view of a sea battle, the artist has shown himself seated on the deck of a galliot with his drawing board on his knee as he sketches the action. This is an example of a pen painting (*penschildering*, or grisaille) which was carried out with a quill pen on a primed wood panel or canvas.

Grisaille on canvas. Signed and dated 1655. National Maritime Museum, London.

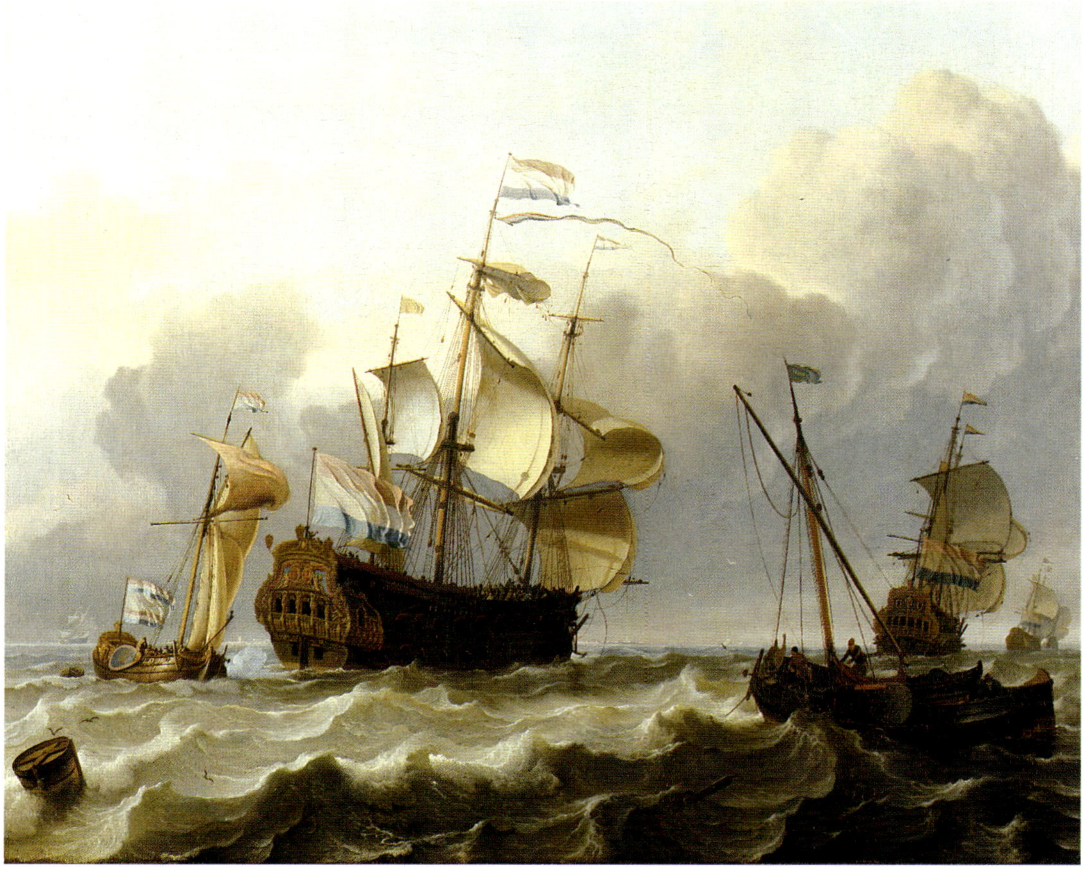

LUDOLF BAKHUIZEN
A flagship with a yacht under her stern

In addition to his skill at drawing ships, Bakhuizen was able to bring a sense of drama to his seascapes. He frequently used a backdrop of dark storm clouds and liked to show his ships splashing through heavy seas and heeling before a strong breeze.

Oil on canvas. Signed. National Maritime Museum, London.

etchings of river views with shipping. They are among the finest of all marine prints, executed with his customary panache and so full of atmosphere that one can almost hear the thunder of canvas as the warships sweep up the river propelled by a rising gale which whips up the waves and sends small craft scudding for shelter [see facing page].

The only maritime prints of this period that can compete in quality with those of Bakhuizen are the etchings of Reinier Nooms. Almost nothing is known of this artist and printmaker apart from the fact that he was married and lived most of his life in Amsterdam. He acquired the nickname 'Zeeman' (seaman), which suggests that he was at one time a professional sailor. He painted pictures of sea battles and harbours, and was a prolific draughtsman. His lively pen and wash drawings compare favourably with those of any of his talented contemporaries, but it is his etchings that are his most important legacy. He made more than 160 of these, and they include topographical views, seaports, innumerable river scenes and depictions of most of the fishing boats, ferries, barges and warships of his day. Although his drawing of people and figures is sometimes clumsy, he had a natural talent for etching. He never resorted to a formula but used a searching, sensitive line to render the sea in all

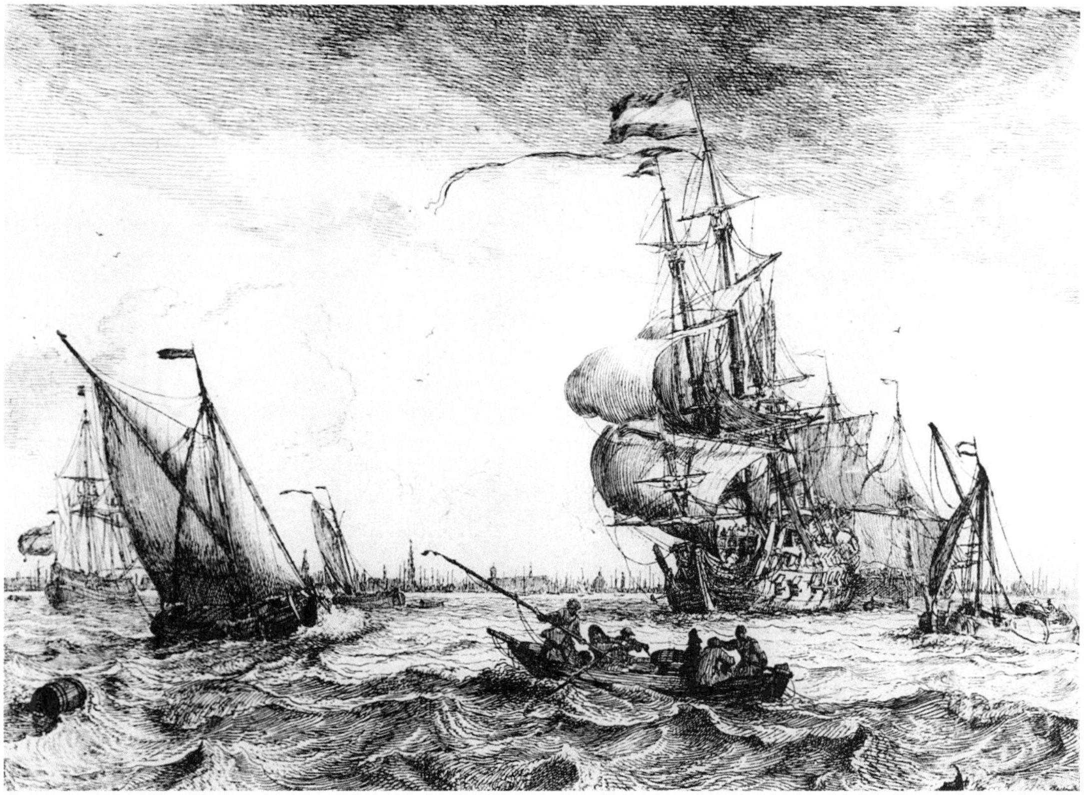

LUDOLF BAKHUIZEN *Shipping on the Ij at Amsterdam*

This is one of a series of ten etchings of river scenes made by Bakhuizen when he was 70 years old. They were the only prints he ever made and reveal his extraordinary powers as a draughtsman. The scene is a windy day in the approaches to Amsterdam, with numerous small craft in the foreground and a ship of the line on the right, heading out to sea.

Engraving. 1701. National Maritime Museum, London.

conditions of wind and tide. A careful study of his prints provides a window on to the busy maritime life of Holland in the 1640s and 1650s.

THE VAN DE VELDES AND THEIR CIRCLE IN LONDON

In June 1672 King Charles issued a proclamation from Whitehall entitled 'His Majesty's gracious Declaration for encouraging the subjects of the United Provinces of the Netherlands to transport themselves with their estates, and to settle in this His Majesty's Kingdom of England.' The Netherlands was in turmoil at this time. King Louis XIV of France had crossed the Rhine with an army of 100,000 men and set up his headquarters in the province of Utrecht. The country around Amsterdam was deliberately flooded to impede the invading army. Mobs roamed the streets and in August a crowd attacked Johan de Witt, who had governed as Grand Pensionary for 20 years, and his brother and murdered them in the streets of the Hague.

Having spent some time in exile in Holland, King Charles was aware of the skills and talents of the Dutch people. His offer was taken up by a number of artists, engravers, mapmakers and craftsmen. The Van de Veldes, who already had contacts

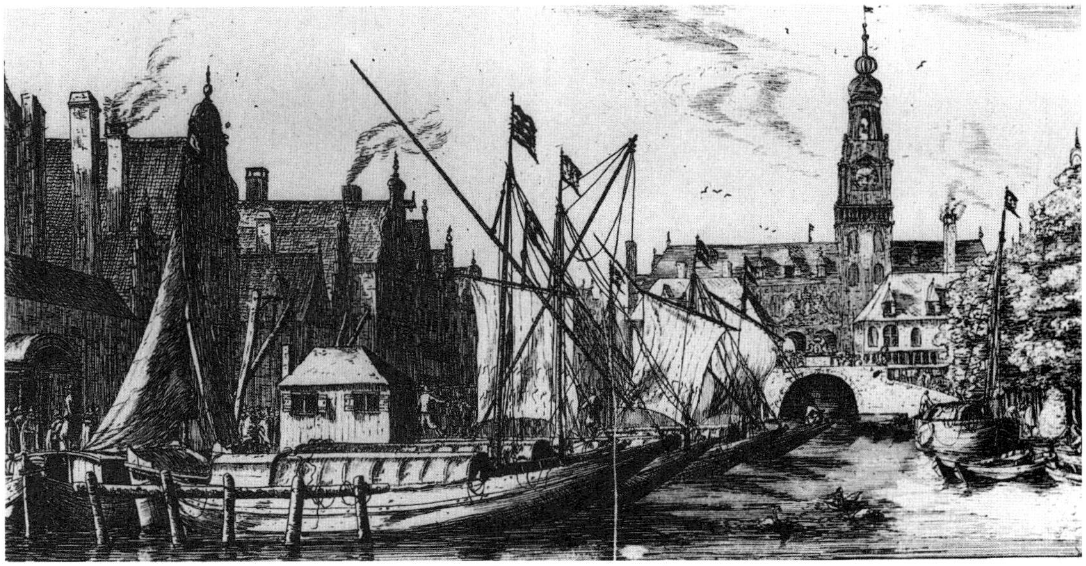

REINIER NOOMS
Rokin, with the Exchange

A line of passenger ferries is shown moored along the waterfront in Amsterdam, with the great tower of the Exchange building rising up behind.

Etching. Private collection.

in England, arrived in London during the winter of 1762–63 and were immediately welcomed by the king and his brother the Duke of York. They set up a studio in Greenwich and had so many commissions that they were able to employ a number of studio assistants, including several members of their family. Two years later Pieter Blaeu, van de Velde the Elder's agent met him in Amsterdam and noted that, 'He had come to collect his wife, since he intended to stay for many years and perhaps for ever in London. The King of England had been so kind as to grant him a salary of 100 pounds sterling...as well as a large house. Furthermore the Duke of York had promised to pay him in addition 50 pounds sterling a year and all this would be apart from the money he would receive for each picture he did.'

The Van de Veldes created a market for marine painting in England and trained a generation of marine artists. Their paintings were widely imitated and their influence was disseminated further afield by the publication around 1725 of a series of 16 mezzotints based on their sea-pieces. These were engraved by Elisha Kirkall and were particularly distinctive because they were printed in an appropriate sea-green ink.

Chapter six

THAMES VIEWS, NAVAL ACTIONS AND VOYAGES OF DISCOVERY

The arrival of the Van de Veldes in London in the 1670s established a tradition of marine painting in Britain that was to flourish for more than two centuries, but in the realm of print-making another foreigner had already made his mark. During his years in London the Bohemian artist Wenceslaus Hollar produced some of the finest views of the city and the surrounding countryside that have ever been made. His celebrated *Long view of London from Bankside*, which was published in 1667, is generally regarded as his masterpiece. This wonderful etching provides a panoramic view of the Thames, the dozens of merchant ships, laden barges and rowing boats making their way up and down the river, and the jumble of buildings on both banks. It is only one of more than 2,700 prints which this industrious artist made during the course of his life. During his travels around Europe he drew and etched a variety of subjects from castles and country villages to portraits and exquisitely observed studies of birds, butterflies and seashells. Conspicuous

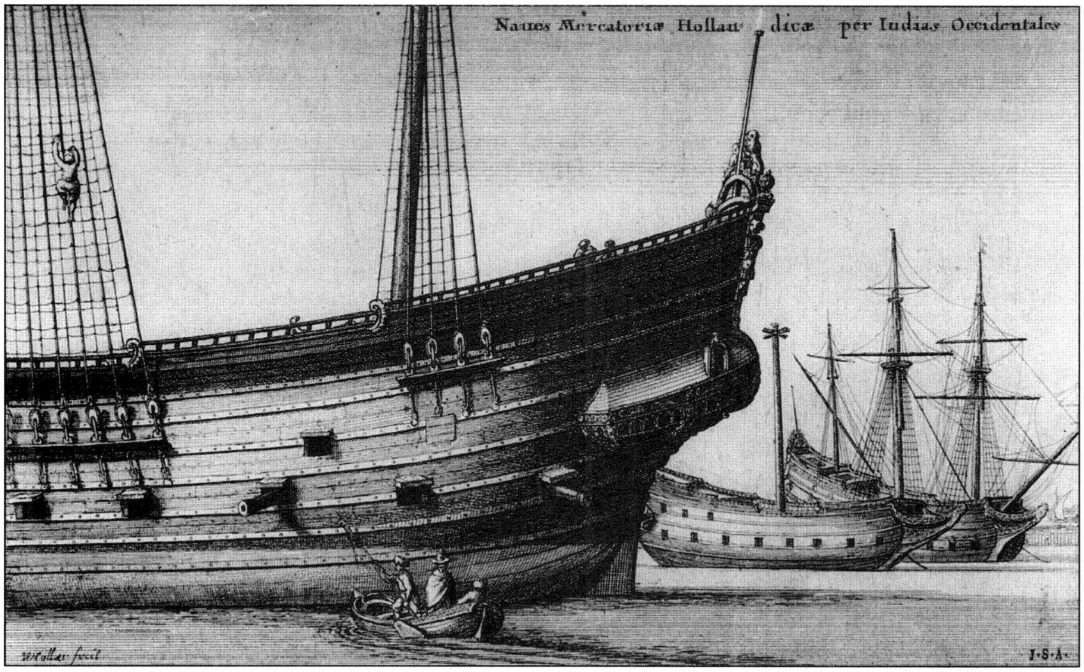

WENCESLAUS HOLLAR
The stern of a Dutch merchant ship fitted out for a voyage to the East Indies

Hollar made several visits to Holland and drew ships undergoing repair in the shipyards. He subsequently made a number of etchings of Dutch East Indiamen at anchor and sailing vessels tossed by gales in mountainous seas.

Etching. Signed. 1640s. National Maritime Museum, London.

among his prints are several views of dockyards showing huge warships undergoing repair and artfully arranged groups of ships at anchor.

Wenceslaus Hollar was born in Prague and spent his early years working and travelling in Germany and the Netherlands, but in 1636 he entered the service of the Earl of Arundel and came to England. He married a lady-in-waiting to the Countess of Arundel and spend six productive years in London before the English Civil Wars of 1642–1645 compelled him to seek refuge in Antwerp. He returned to London in 1652 and recorded many of the key events of the subsequent decades, notably the effect of the Great Fire of London on the city. The biographer John Aubrey wrote of Hollar, 'He was a very friendly, good-natured man, but shiftless as to the world, and died not rich.'

In the years following Hollar's death in 1677, marine art in Britain continued to be enriched by the work of foreign-born artists. The contribution of the Van de Veldes and their studio has already been noted; among their followers were L.D. Man, Jan van Beecq, Jacob Knyff and Isaac Sailmaker. Jacob Knyff was the elder son of the Dutch landscape painter Wouter Knyff of Haarlem, and brother of Leonard Knyff, who painted aerial views of English country houses and their gardens. Jacob emigrated to England in about 1673 and he painted views of Dover, Sheerness and other English ports. One of his most attractive pictures is *The Thames at Chiswick*, a colourful glimpse on a sunny day of the houses fronting the river.

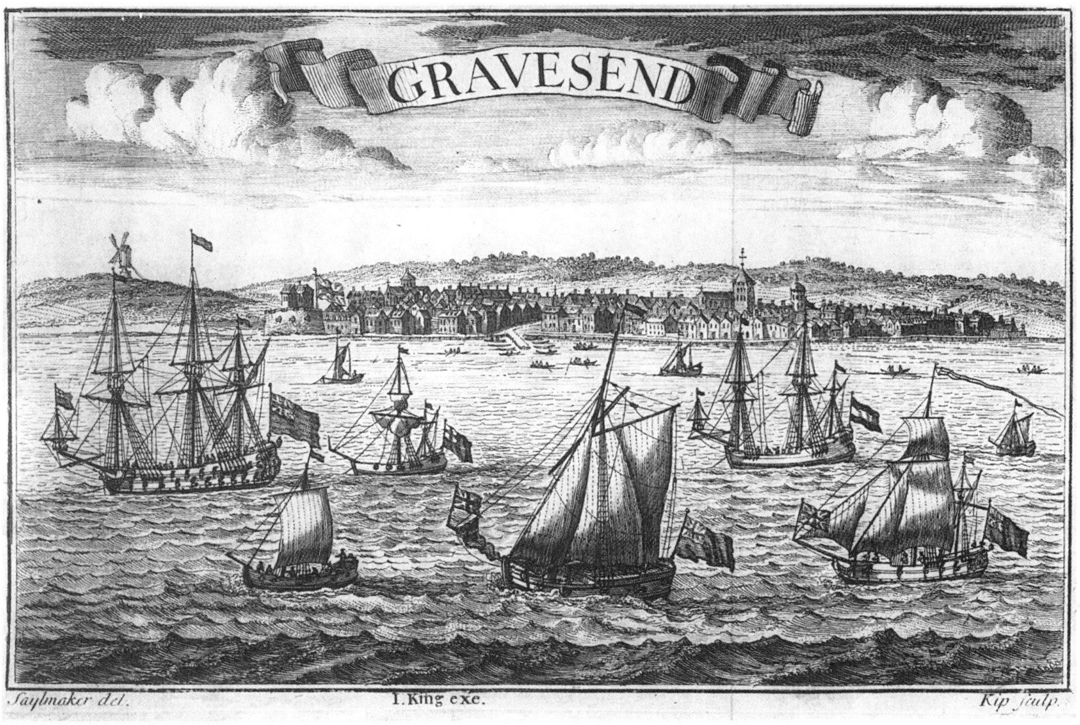

ISAAC SAILMAKER
Gravesend

Sailmaker painted a number of views of English coastal towns and ports which were engraved. Gravesend lies on the south side of the Thames estuary and in the early 18th century it was still surrounded by countryside. Among the numerous vessels depicted in the foreground are a warship, several yachts and a Dutch flute.

Engraving. Private collection.

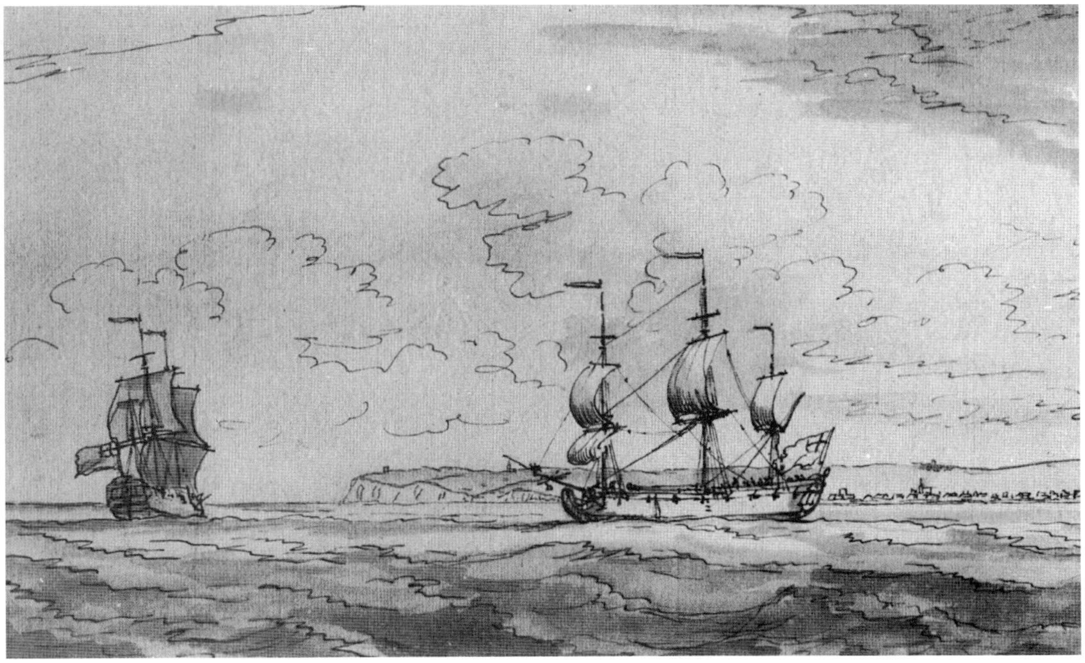

PETER MONAMY
A view of Deal from the Sea, South Foreland in the distance

This pen and wash drawing has a fresh and breezy quality which suggests that it was made on the spot. George Vertue, who was a contemporary of Monamy, noted that the artist 'made many excursions towards the coasts and seaports of England to improve himself from nature.'

Pen and sepia ink and grey wash. Signed and inscribed on the reverse. Private collection.

The paintings of the minor artist Isaac Sailmaker were first identified in the 1970s, when a painting of the Eddystone lighthouse was discovered and was identified by its close resemblance to an engraving of the same subject. Other engravings after Sailmaker paintings include a spirited depiction of *The Battle of Malaga*, 1704, and another of *The Battle of Barfleur*, 1692, inscribed 'Designed by I. Sailmaker according to the special direction of several on board during the action.' Sailmaker, whose original family name was Zeilmaker, was born in Scheveningen, emigrated to London during the period of the Commonwealth and took up residence in Drury Lane. When he died at the age of 88, the engraver and antiquary George Vertue noted that 'His contemporaries the Van de Veldes were too mighty for him...but he outlived them and painted to his last.'

A more considerable artist than Knyff or Sailmaker was Peter Monamy, who was born in Jersey but moved to London while still a young man. He was trained as a housepainter and the start of his seven-year apprenticeship was recorded in the registers of the Company of Painter Stainers in 1696. He turned to marine painting and soon had a respectable reputation. Hogarth painted a portrait of him standing in front of his easel, palette in hand, and showing a picture to Thomas Walker, who was a Commissioner of Customs and a noted collector. The picture on the easel shows shipping becalmed in an estuary, the type of painting at which Monamy excelled.

Samuel Scott was the first English marine painter to break away from the Dutch tradition and establish a style of his own. He owned a large collection of Van de

Velde drawings and many of his early works are clearly inspired by them, but when he began painting views of the Thames waterfront he showed a refreshing individuality. He never achieved the glittering quality of Canaletto's London views, but he gives us a real glimpse of what life would have been like on the river in the middle years of the 18th century. He shows us the building of Westminster Bridge, the massive pile of London Bridge in its heyday, and stretches of the river at Deptford and Chiswick with men loading barges and mending boats. He seems to have lived most of his life in London and around 1758 moved to Twickenham; in his old age he retired to Bath in the hope of curing his gout. He was working up to his death and sent a view of the Tower of London to the Royal Academy in 1771, the year before he died. Many of Scott's drawings have survived [see facing page, above]. A few of these are in pen and watercolour, but most are carried out in pen and wash or in black chalk on blue paper, heightened with white.

Scott was well served by the engravers. In 1734 John Bowles published mezzotints by Elisha Kirkall after the paintings by Scott and George Lambert of six of the principal forts and trading stations of the East India Company. Scott's views of London Bridge and Westminster Bridge were engraved by Peter Canot and several of his naval actions were engraved and published.

Drawings by Charles Brooking are fairly rare, which is a pity because those that have survived have some of the delicacy and masterly drawing of ships that are so characteristic of his oil paintings. They are usually carried out in pen and grey wash, the ships defined with precision, the waves somewhat stylized, and the clouds more loosely handled. Brooking had great natural gifts as a marine painter. He seems to have taught himself by making copies and versions of paintings by Van de Velde the Younger, but he soon went his own way. No artist more accurately observed ships at sea, the set of sails and the effect of wind and tide on the surface of the water. Edward Dayes, the painter and engraver, wrote of Brooking's work, 'his colouring is light and clear, his water pellucid and transparent, with a firm, broad, spirited touch.'

Brooking was brought up in Deptford, where his father was employed as a painted and decorator at Greenwich Hospital. He evidently began painting marine subjects from an early age because there is a sea-piece inscribed 'C. Brooking pinxit, aged 17'. He fell into the hands of an unscrupulous picture dealer for several years but was discovered by Taylor White, the Treasurer of the Foundling Hospital, who became his patron and encouraged him to exhibit at the Hospital, which had a fine collection of pictures by Scott, Hogarth and Monamy.

Unlike Brooking, whose life was a constant struggle against illness and poverty, Dominic Serres led a charmed existence and although by no means the most talented

SAMUEL SCOTT
A ship near the shore with yachts alongside

Scott spent most of his life in London, and apart from various outings on the Thames and one coastal voyage in a yacht he had no experience of seafaring. This drawing probably depicts a scene on the Thames and has every appearance of having been drawn on the spot.

Pen and sepia ink. National Maritime Museum, London.

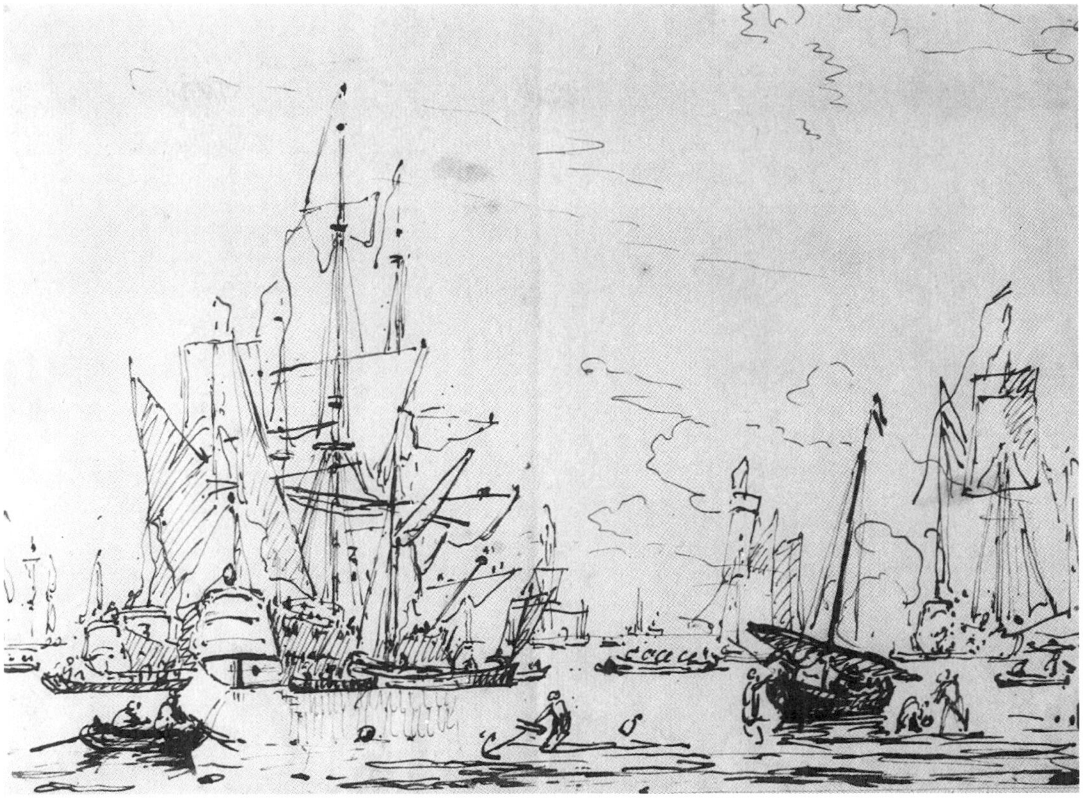

CHARLES BROOKING
A Vice-admiral of the Red and a squadron at sea

The strongly patterned clouds, beautifully drawn ships, and breezy atmosphere of this small oil painting are typical of Brooking's work. The flag flying from the foremast of the warship on the left indicates that she is the flagship of a vice-admiral. On the far right is a ketch-rigged bomb vessel.

Oil on canvas. Signed. National Maritime Museum, London.

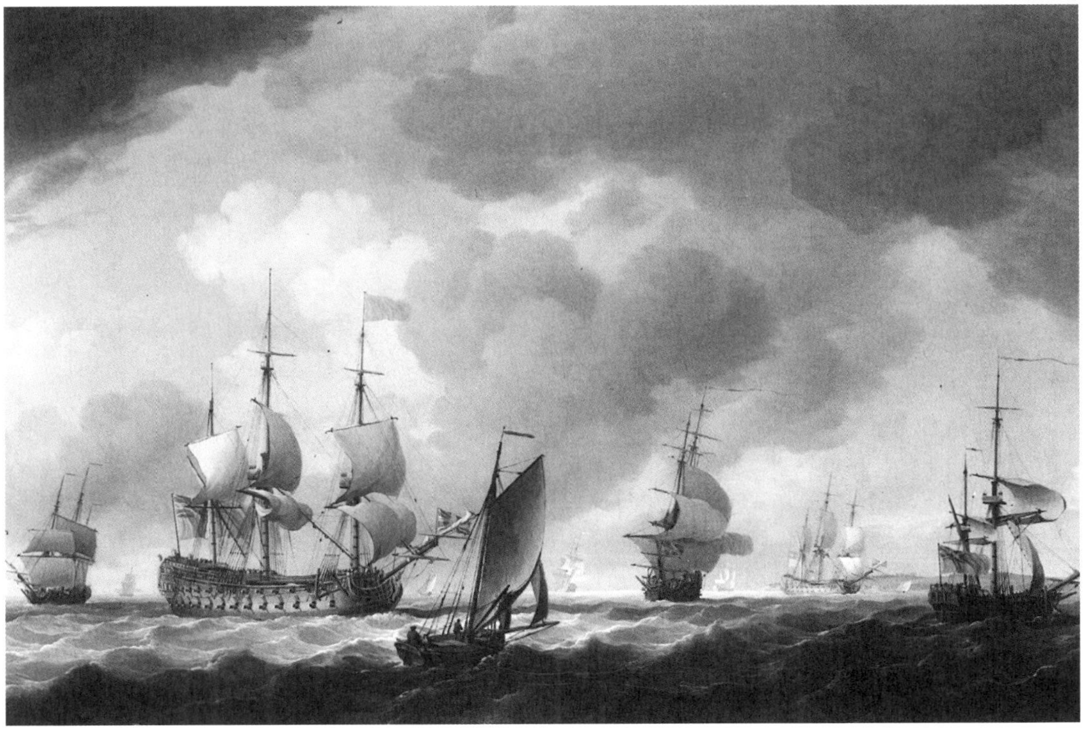

marine artist of his day, he was by far the most successful. He was a founding member of the Royal Academy, where he showed 108 paintings and later became the librarian. He also exhibited at the Incorporated Society of Artists and the Free Society and was made marine painter to King George III. 'But Dom is grown a very great man,' wrote his friend Paul Sandby in 1784, 'has been to Paris, seen the grand exhibition, dined with the King's architect, and is going to paint for the Grand Monarque.'

The secret of Serres' success lay in his aristocratic background, his charm and intelligence (he spoke five languages) and his practical experience as a seaman. He was born at Auch, near Toulouse in southern France, and was brought up to be a priest, but he ran away to sea and eventually became captain of a trading vessel. Following the capture of his ship by a British frigate, he was brought to England, where he decided to settle and become a marine painter. He met Charles Brooking and was much influenced by his style, and although Serres never achieved the subtle atmospheric effects of Brooking, he was expert at drawing ships and naval actions.

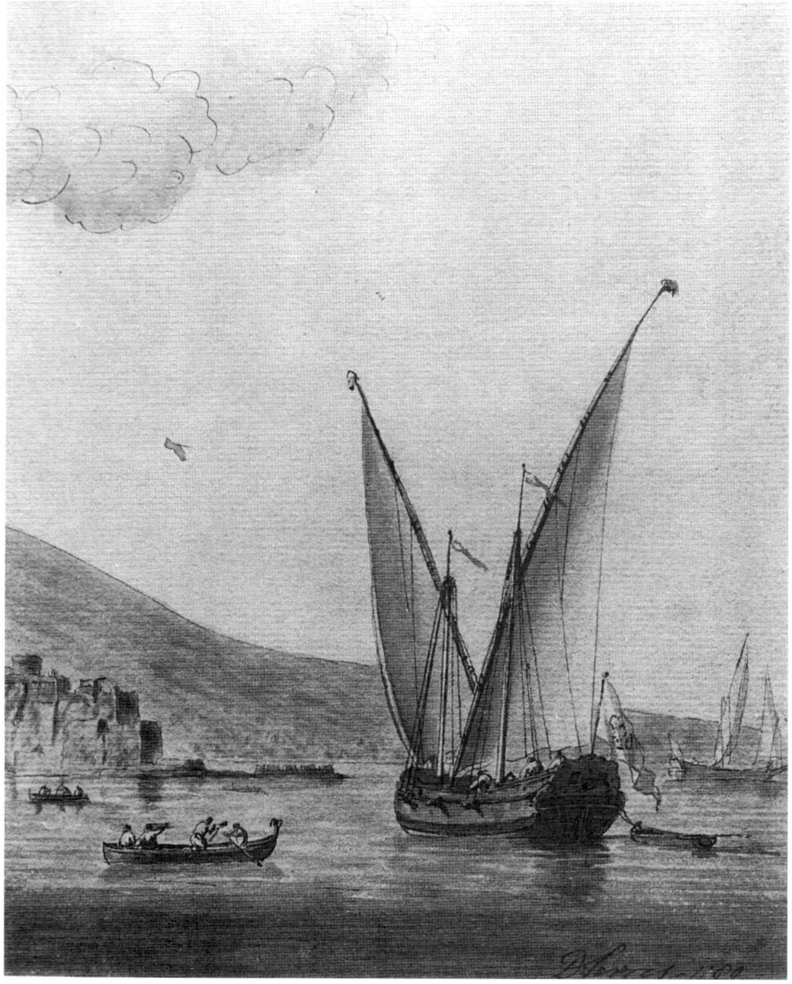

DOMINIC SERRES
Shipping in the Mediterranean

This picture, showing a two-masted vessel with lateen sails, known as a settee, sailing in light airs off a fort, is a typical of numerous studies of shipping made by Serres.

Watercolour. Signed and dated 1780. Thomas Agnew and Sons, London.

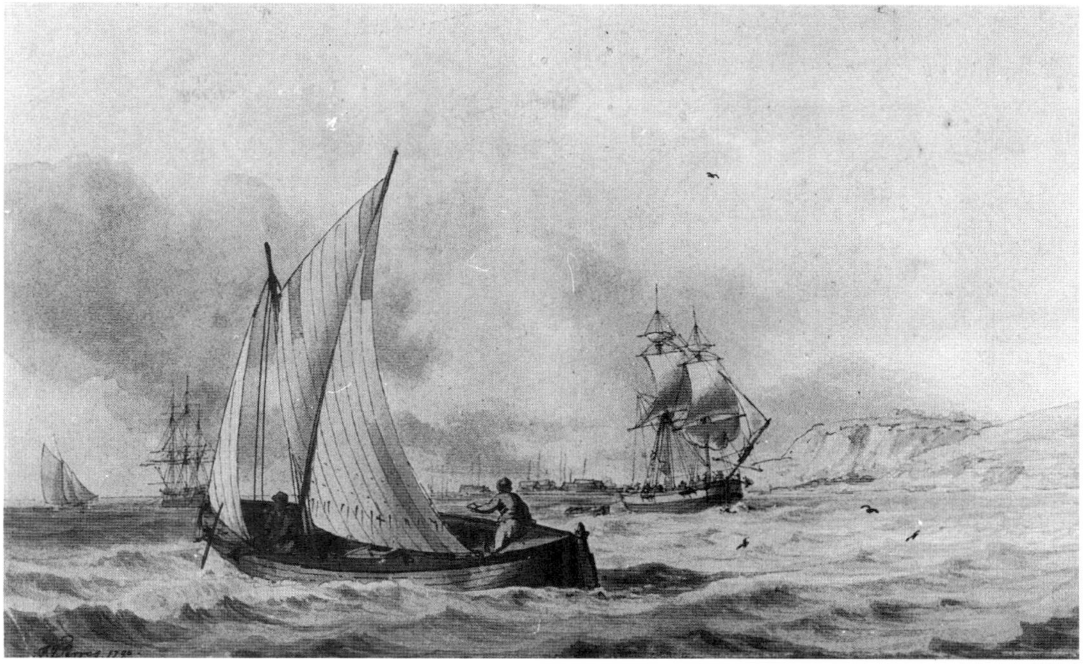

JOHN THOMAS SERRES
A Peter-boat and other vessels in the Thames estuary

Peter boats, named after St Peter the fisherman, were the most common type of small fishing boat used in the Thames. They had a wet-well amidships for storing live fish and, like the much larger Thames barges, were fitted with spritsails.

Watercolour. Signed and dated 1790. National Maritime Museum, London.

His impressive output included pictures of most of the battles of the Seven Years' War, many ship portraits and a series of 11 paintings picturing the capture of Havana. His watercolours and pen and wash drawings are workmanlike studies with careful attention paid to sails and rigging.

Serres' two sons both became artists. His younger son, Dominic, had no great talent but his elder son, John Thomas Serres, became a drawing master and an accomplished marine painter. He succeeded his father as marine painter to the king and was appointed Marine Draughtsman to the Admiralty in 1800. He travelled widely in Europe and spent some time at sea with the navy, making drawings of French harbours.

In 1805 he published an instruction manual entitled *Liber Nauticus and Instructor in the Art of Marine Drawing*, which consisted of 41 aquatint plates accompanied by useful instructions on the parts of a ship, the ranks of admirals, the principles of sailing and practical hints on the drawing of water. The first 17 plates of explanatory drawings were taken from his own watercolours and the remainder were based on pictures by his father. These depicted a variety of yachts, fishing boats and coastal craft. It was an impressive production and comparable with some of the great series of maritime engravings produced by Dutch artists such as Nooms and Groenewegen. Unfortunately, the career of J. T. Serres was blighted by a disastrous marriage. His wife was constantly unfaithful and wildly extravagant, which led to Serres being charged with bankruptcy and dying in a debtor's prison.

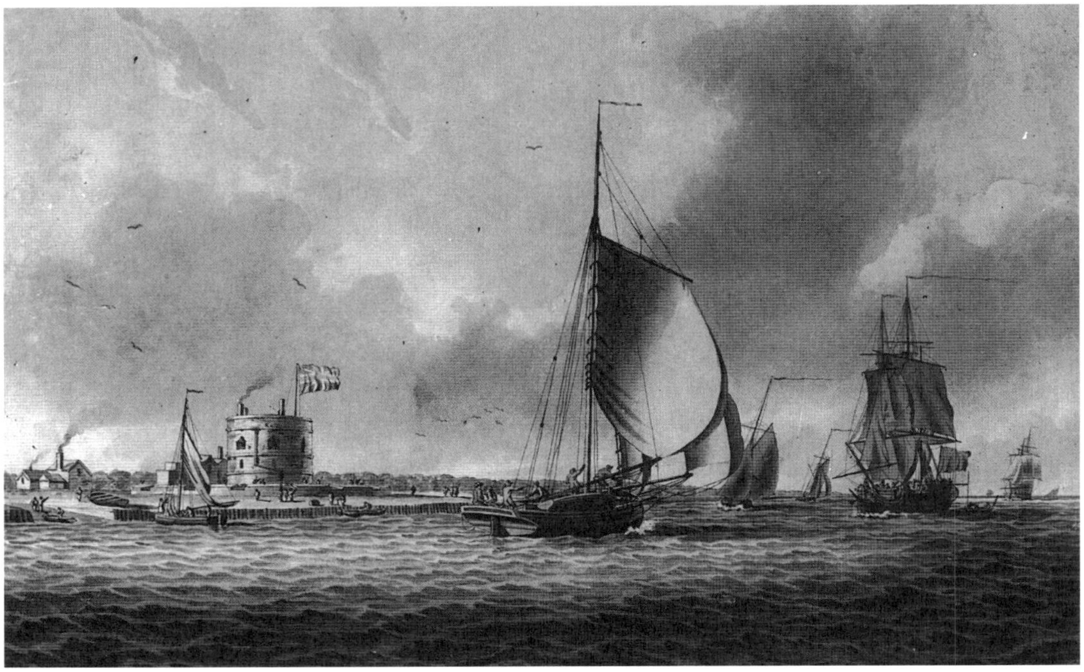

JOHN CLEVELEY THE YOUNGER
Calshot Castle from the Solent

The younger John Cleveley was an accomplished watercolourist and travelled on several expeditions as a draughtsman. Calshot Castle was built to guard the entrance to Southampton Water which has always been one of the busiest waterways in Britain.

Watercolour. Signed. Private collection.

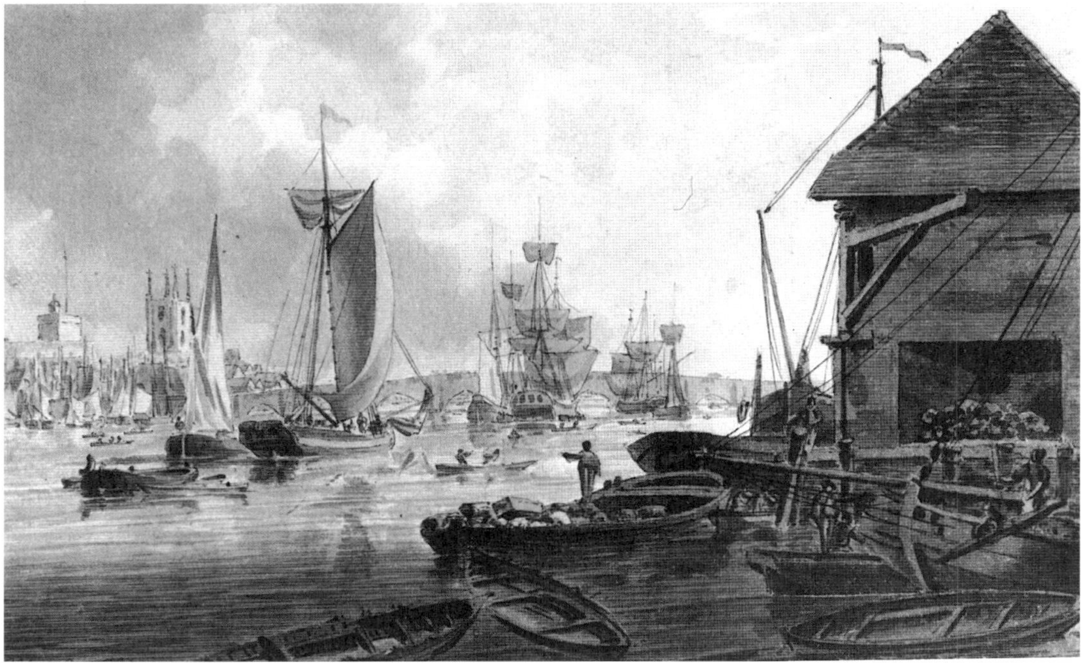

ROBERT CLEVELEY
The Pool of London looking towards London Bridge and Southwark Cathedral

This view is taken from the north bank of the Thames among the warehouses and wharves lining the waterfront near the Custom House and the Tower of London. In the foreground are barges and skiffs, while out on the river numerous merchant ships are on the move.

Pencil and watercolour. Signed and dated 1791. Christie's Images, London.

The Cleveleys were another family of marine painters working in London around this time. Like so many other British marine artists in the 18th century, they all had a professional connection with the sea. John Cleveley the Elder was the son of a Southwark joiner and became a shipwright at Deptford. When he died in 1777, he was recorded as being 'Carpenter belonging to His Majesty's Ship the Victory in the

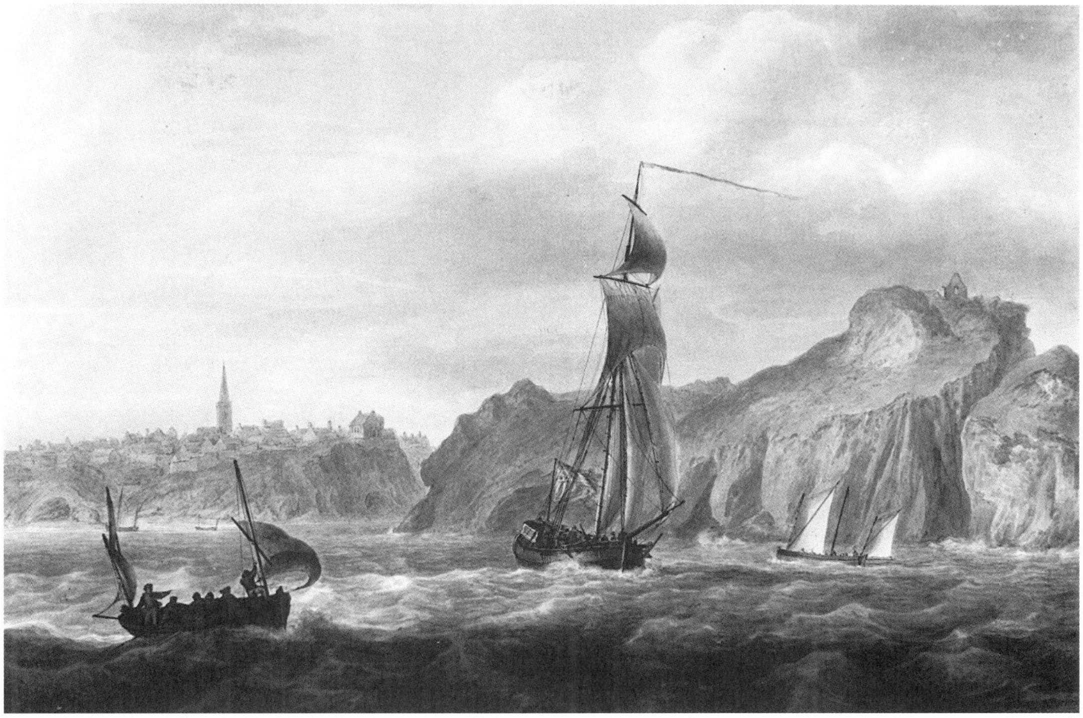

NICHOLAS POCOCK
A brig and other vessels off Tenby

As a result of his experience as a sea captain Pocock was continually commissioned to paint detailed canvases depicting sea battles, but he was at his best when painting less-demanding compositions. He worked most effectively in watercolours, and his finest pictures are his coastal scenes with beautifully drawn ships in the foreground.

Watercolour. Signed and dated 1789. Bristol City Museum and Art Gallery.

pay of His Majesties Navy.' He and his wife Sarah had three sons. The eldest, James, became a ship's carpenter and in this capacity travelled on Captain Cook's ship *Resolution* on his third voyage to the Pacific. The other sons were twins: John Cleveley the Younger became a shipwright and Robert was trained as a caulker.

John Cleveley the Elder is remembered today for his decorative and minutely detailed paintings of ship-building scenes in the royal dockyards on the Thames. John Cleveley the Younger went as a draughtsman on a voyage to Iceland organized by Sir Joseph Banks, and two years later accompanied Lord Mulgrave's expedition to the North Polar seas. Many of the watercolour illustrations he brought back from these two voyages were later engraved. Robert Cleveley outlived his twin by 23 years and painted naval actions and views on the Thames.

The prolonged period of naval warfare that began with the battles in the West Indies during the American War of Independence and ended with Napoleon's defeat at Waterloo in 1815 provided a succession of marine artists with commissions. Naval officers wanted paintings of their sea battles and their ships, publishers of books needed illustrations, and the public was keen to buy pictures of the stirring events taking place at sea. An artist who was well placed to take advantage of this market was Nicholas Pocock, who was born at Bristol, served an apprenticeship as a seaman, and spent ten years in command of merchant ships. He made 12 voyages across the Atlantic to Charleston, South Carolina, and to the West Indies before retiring from the sea and embarking on a second career as a marine painter. He gradually built up an impressive list of patrons, including Lord Barham, who was First Lord of the Admiralty, Lord Bridport and his brother Admiral Hood, and the Navy Board, which commissioned two paintings of the royal dockyards.

In 1789 he moved to London where he had a house in Westminster, and in 1794 he was present on board the frigate *Pegasus* during the Battle of the Glorious First of June. Like Van de Velde the Elder before him, he made numerous sketches of the four-day action and later worked these up into paintings and finished watercolours. Towards the end of a busy working life Pocock was commissioned to provide the key illustrations for Clarke and McArthur's *Life of Admiral Nelson*, his masterpiece being a jewel-like painting of all Nelson's ships anchored at Spithead.

It has to be said that many of Pocock's oil paintings are workmanlike but dull, and his talent was best suited to painting in watercolours. During his years at sea he had illustrated his logbooks with pen and wash drawings, and from tentative beginnings he became an accomplished watercolour artist, who was at his best when portraying coastal views with shipping. A great number of his paintings and drawings were engraved, and he contributed dozens of illustrations to early editions of *The Naval Chronicle*.

The most dramatic pictures of the sea battles of the Napoleonic era were made by P.J. de Loutherbourg, a German who trained as an artist in Paris and made his reputation in France before moving to England in 1771. His huge painting of the *Battle of the Glorious First of June* is one of the most powerful pictures of a naval action ever painted, but he also produced pictures of the battles of Camperdown and the Nile, which are almost as striking.

De Loutherbourg spent several years as chief designer at the Drury Lane Theatre, which helps to explain the theatrical air of many of his large-scale paintings. He was equally adept at working on a small scale, and during his extensive travels around the British Isles produced a large number of seaside studies and coastal views. Views of Brighton, Margate and Ramsgate are prominent among his drawings, many of which were engraved in aquatint and published in *The Picturesque Scenery of Great Britain*, which came out in 1801. A few years later a second volume of aquatints after his pictures was published by Bowyer, this time entitled *The Romantic and Picturesque Scenery of England and Wales*. This was full of subjects that reflected the taste of the Romantic movement, such as stormy sea shores, waterfalls and castles crouched on rocky cliffs.

The other recorders of naval actions who were working in England during the Napoleonic wars were more down to earth in their approach. William Anderson was

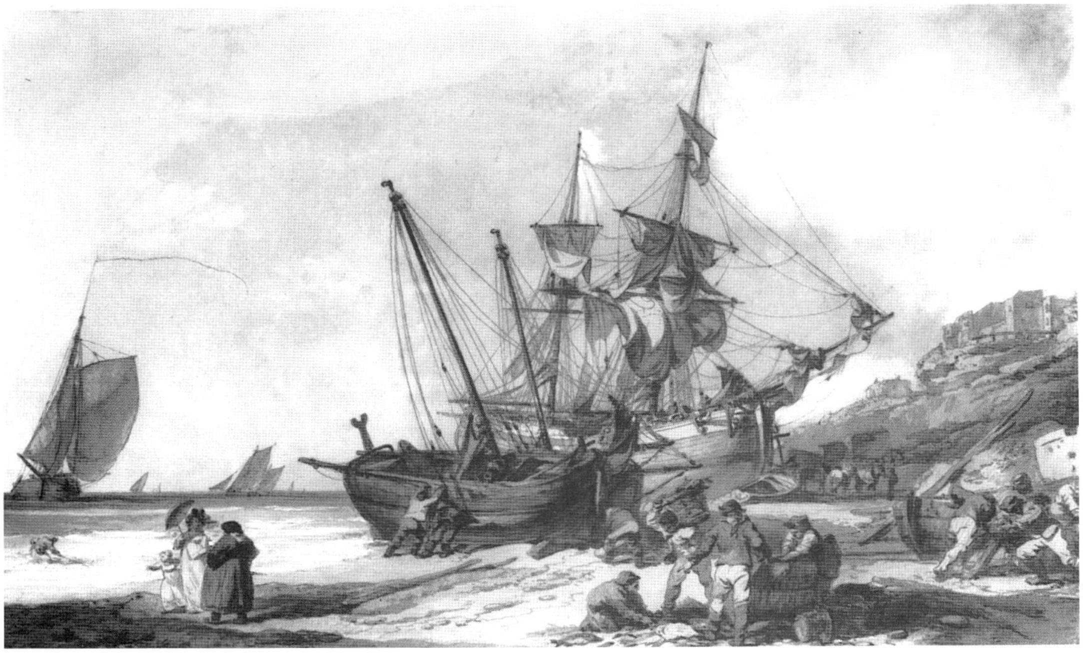

PHILIP JAMES DE LOUTHERBOURG
Shipping on the beach at Brighthelmston

This picture is one of many fine preparatory drawings of coastal views which the artist made in preparation for the series of aquatints entitled *The Picturesque Scenery of Great Britain.* In the 18th and 19th centuries it was common to see collier brigs and fishing boats drawn up on the beach at Brighton at low tide.

Pencil, pen and brown ink and watercolour with white heightening. Christie's Images, London.

a Scotsman, who trained as a shipwright but came south to London and established himself as a marine painter. He exhibited at the Royal Academy nearly every year from 1787 to 1834. A series of paintings which he made of the *Battle of the Nile* were engraved as aquatints and published by William Ellis in 1801, but it is his tranquil views of shipping on the Thames that are his finest works. A number of his sketch-books have survived, as well as some delicately rendered watercolours which are similar in style to those of Dominic Serres.

Of the same generation was Thomas Luny, a prolific painter of naval actions, ship portraits, shipwrecks and coastal views. According to a detailed inventory which he kept to record the pictures he painted, he produced more than 2,200 paintings between 1807 and 1835. The National Maritime Museum has 41 of his paintings and examples of his work frequently appear in the sale rooms. Luny was a pupil of the marine artist Francis Holman in London, but he moved to Devon around 1807 and acquired a fine house in Teignmouth. He suffered severely from rheumatoid arthiritis, which confined him to a wheelchair but in no way lessened his output.

An equally productive and accomplished recorder of the sea battles of the Napoleonic period was Thomas Whitcombe. Although 50 of his paintings were engraved for *The Naval Achievements of Great Britain*, published after the French Revolutionary Wars, and a further 100 of his pictures were published as prints, very little is known about the life of this artist. He appears to have been based in London and must have been in regular contact with naval officers because his sea battles are

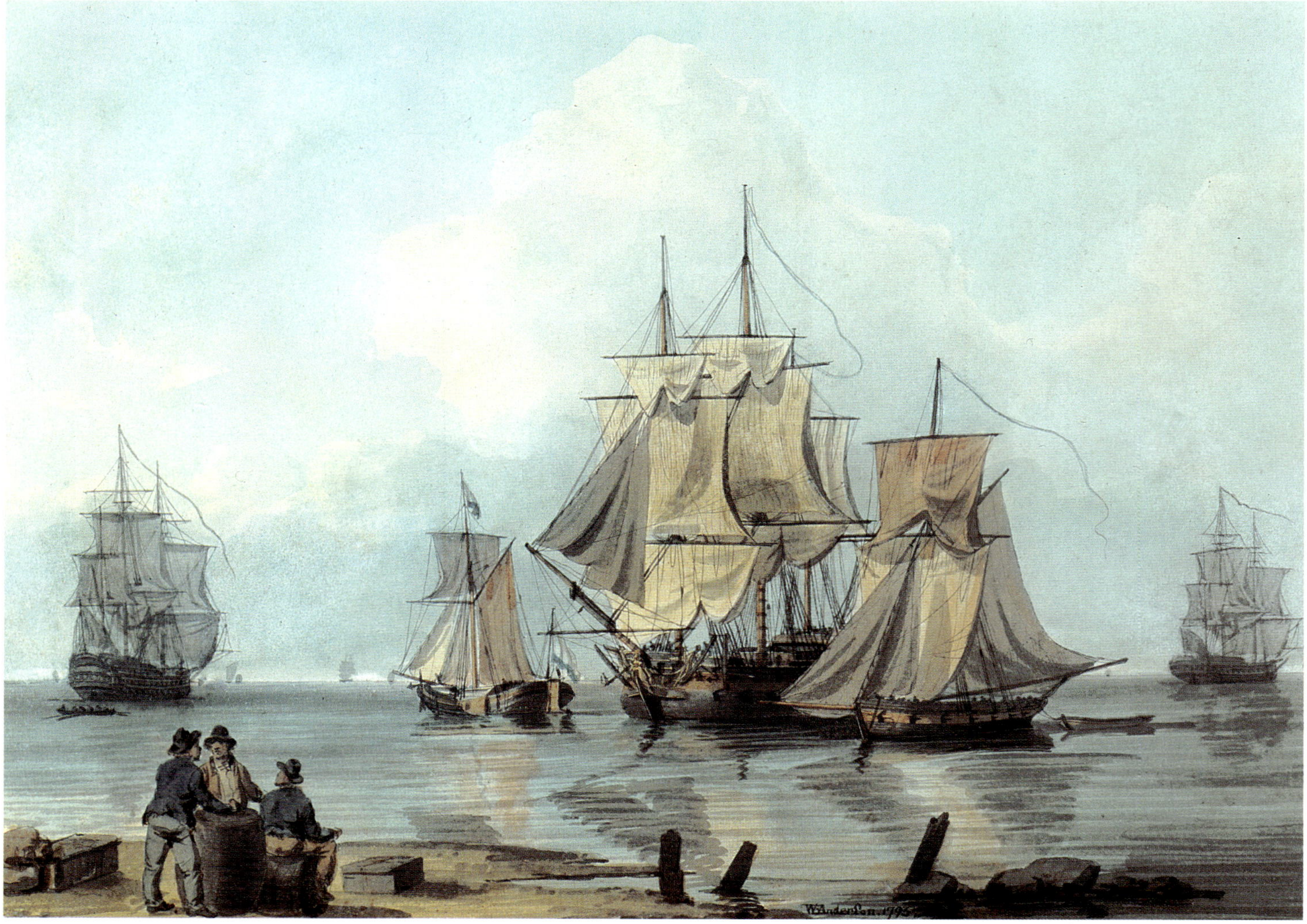

full of telling detail, with careful attention paid to flags, weather conditions and the amount of damage suffered by each ship.

One of Whitcombe's principal competitors for the market in prints was Robert Dodd, who exhibited regularly at the Royal Academy and had at least 100 of his pictures engraved, many in the form of aquatints. But unlike the paintings of Pocock, Luny and Whitcombe, who each developed a distinctive style and managed to inject a sparkle into the best of their naval actions, Dodd's paintings tend to be dull and laboured.

Voyages of exploration and discovery

There has been a long tradition of artists and seamen filling journals and sketchbooks with drawings during the course of their travels overseas. Some of thse drawings were

William Anderson
A quiet anchorage

Anderson took as his model the calm scenes of Van de Velde the Younger and replaced the Dutch boats and canals with everyday scenes on the Thames and Medway. He painted many variations on this theme, and although he had limited skills as a draughtsman his pictures have a homely quality about them that is very appealing.

Pencil and watercolour. Signed and dated 1795. Private collection.

for navigational purposes, some had a strategic and military purpose, and some were scientific observations of fauna and flora. Very often the sketches were subsequently published as engravings. Among the earliest and most famous of the engravings resulting from voyages were those published in the 1590s by Theodore de Bry. Prompted by the English geographer Richard Hakluyt, and working from information brought back by the explorers, De Bry produced a series of books which are now known as *The Great Voyages* and *The Lesser Voyages*. These were illustrated with his finely detailed copper engravings showing incidents in the expeditions led by Columbus, Pizarro, Drake and others. Despite the classical poses and histrionic gestures of the principal figures, the pictures provide a vivid commentary on the trials and tribulations of the explorers and the cruelty and savagery which accompanied the landings in the New World.

In the following century, Dutch and Portuguese explorers brought back illustrated journals, among the most interesting being the series of pen and ink

SAMUEL ATKINS
Careening a brig on a beach

In tropical waters ships rapidly accumulated a growth of weed, worm and barnacles below the waterline and often had to be careened. In this detailed picture, seamen are shown burning and scraping the weed off a beached vessel, caulking the seams, and applying a mixture of tallow, oil and brimstone as a form of antifouling.

Pencil, pen and watercolour. Signed. 1790s. Private collection.

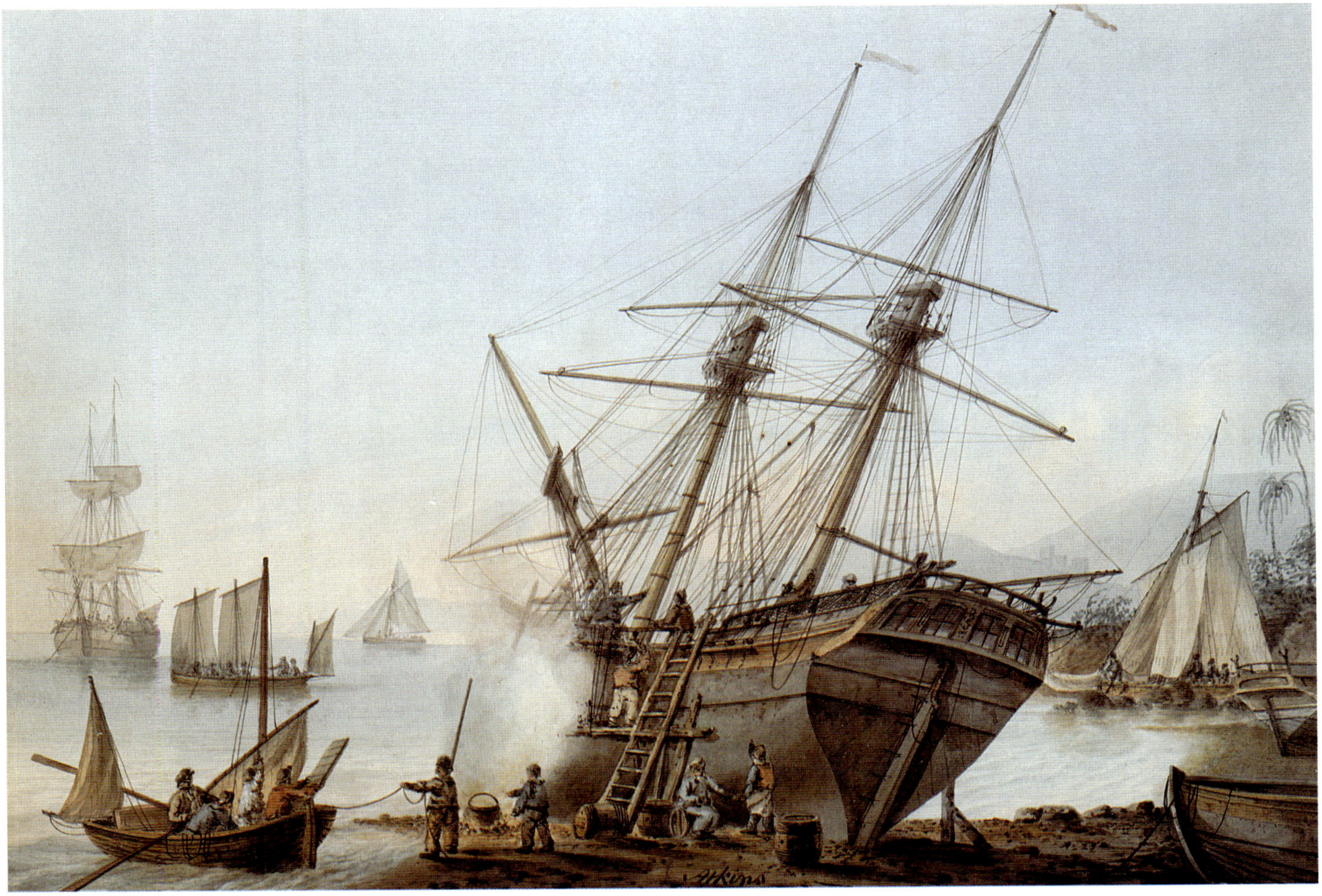

drawings made by the great Dutch explorer Abel Tasman during his Pacific voyage of 1642, when he became the first European to land in Tasmania and New Zealand. One hundred years later, when Commodore George Anson sailed around the world between 1740 and 1744, his second lieutenant Piercey Brett made a series of drawings of coastal profiles and harbour entrances which were subsequently engraved and published in the official account of the voyage.

But it was Captain Cook's three voyages that brought back the most comprehensive pictorial record of their kind. When Cook set off on the first of his voyages in 1768, the wealthy young naturalist Joseph Banks took with him two artists, Sydney Parkinson and Alexander Buchan. The Admiralty were so impressed by their drawings that on the second voyage they appointed the landscape artist William Hodges as official artist. Captain Cook was to give him proper accommodation and victuals and take care 'that he does diligently employ himself in making Drawings or Paintings of such places as you may touch at that may be worthy of notice...'.

On the third voyage to the Pacific, the talented watercolourist John Webber was appointed as the offical artist. Between them, these artists brought back hundreds of

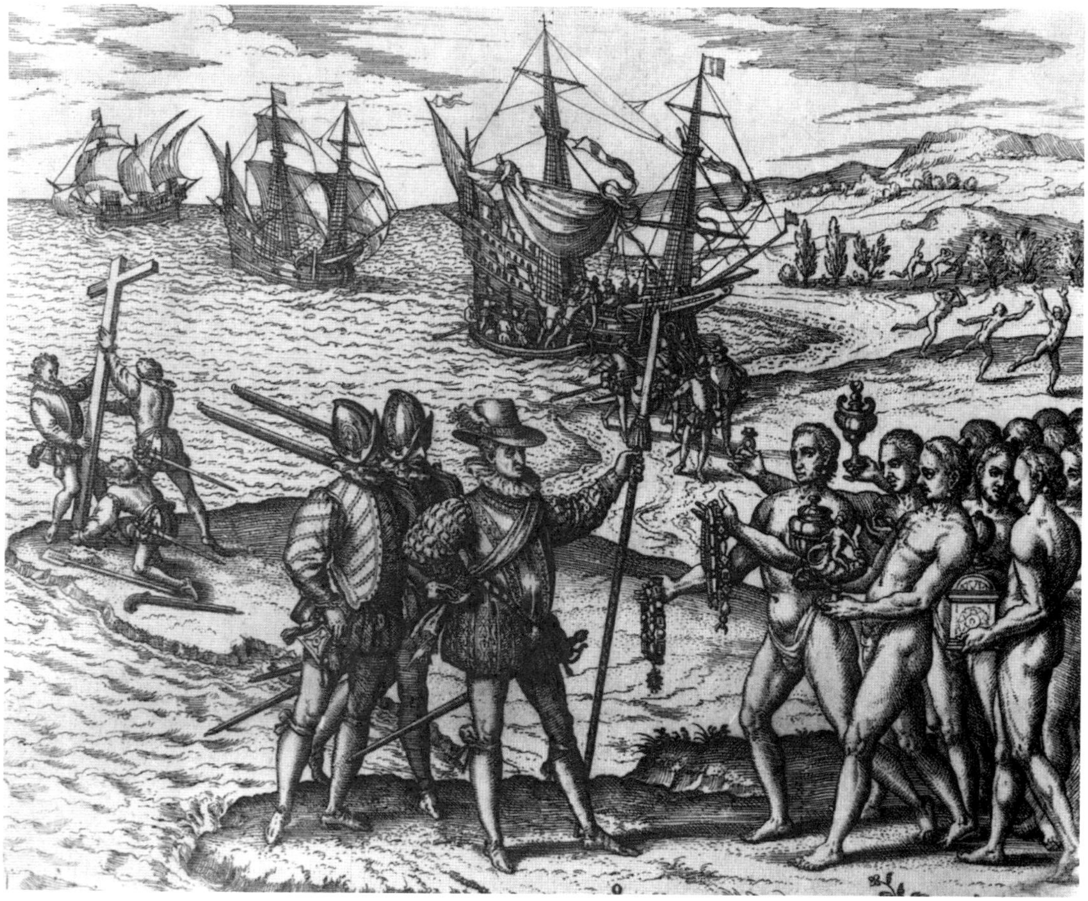

THEODORE DE BRY
Christopher Columbus is welcomed on his arrival in the New World

De Bry's copper engravings for his volumes of *Voyages* are one of the great achievements of print-making. The inaccuracies in the costumes, the ships and the landscape in this print can be explained by the fact that De Bry was illustrating a famous event which had taken place nearly a century earlier and that he had never travelled outside northern Europe.

Engraving. National Maritime Museum, London.

pictures, which ranged from Webber's depictions of Tahitian dancing girls to Parkinson's exquisitely detailed plant drawings. Everything of interest was noted: the tattoos on the faces of Maori warriors; the fishing boats of the Society Islands; the turtles and stingrays; the kangaroos and rare birds. At the conclusion of each of the three voyages, the drawings and paintings of the artists were handed over to a team of engravers and publishers. Sixty-one of Webber's drawings, for instance, were engraved and published with the official account of the third voyage.

Cook's artists gave the Western world the first detailed view of the South Pacific islands. Twenty years later William Alexander brought back a similar record of an expedition to China. In 1792 Lord Macartney, a former governor of Madras, led a delegation to Peking to meet the Chinese Emperor and open up trading links with Britain. Alexander was appointed as the official artist to accompany the embassy. He had trained at the Royal Academy Schools and was 25 years old when the expedition sailed from Spithead in two East Indiamen. During his two years in China, he made hundreds of drawings of the towns and villages, the people he encountered and the junks and small craft he saw on the Grand Canal and along the rivers and ports he passed through. In the words of John Barrow, comptroller to the embassy, 'Mr Alexander drew beautifully and faithfully in watercolours, and omitted nothing that was Chinese, from the human face and figure, down to the humblest plant, and so true were his delineations, that nothing before or since could be compared with them.' On his return to England, Alexander worked up his sketches into finished watercolours and many of these were subsequently engraved as aquatints.

The practice of sending artists to accompany scientific voyages, which had proved so fruitful in the case of Captain Cook's explorations, was continued when HMS *Adventure* and HMS *Beagle*, with the young scientist Charles Darwin on board, set sail in 1831. The artist selected was Augustus Earle, who had already spent many years abroad and had produced illustrated accounts of his travels in Australia and New Zealand. The watercolours he painted during the voyage on the *Beagle* are beautiful examples of their kind, carefully drawn and full of atmosphere [see page 94]. When he was forced to leave the expedition through ill health, he was replaced by the equally accomplished Conrad Martens.

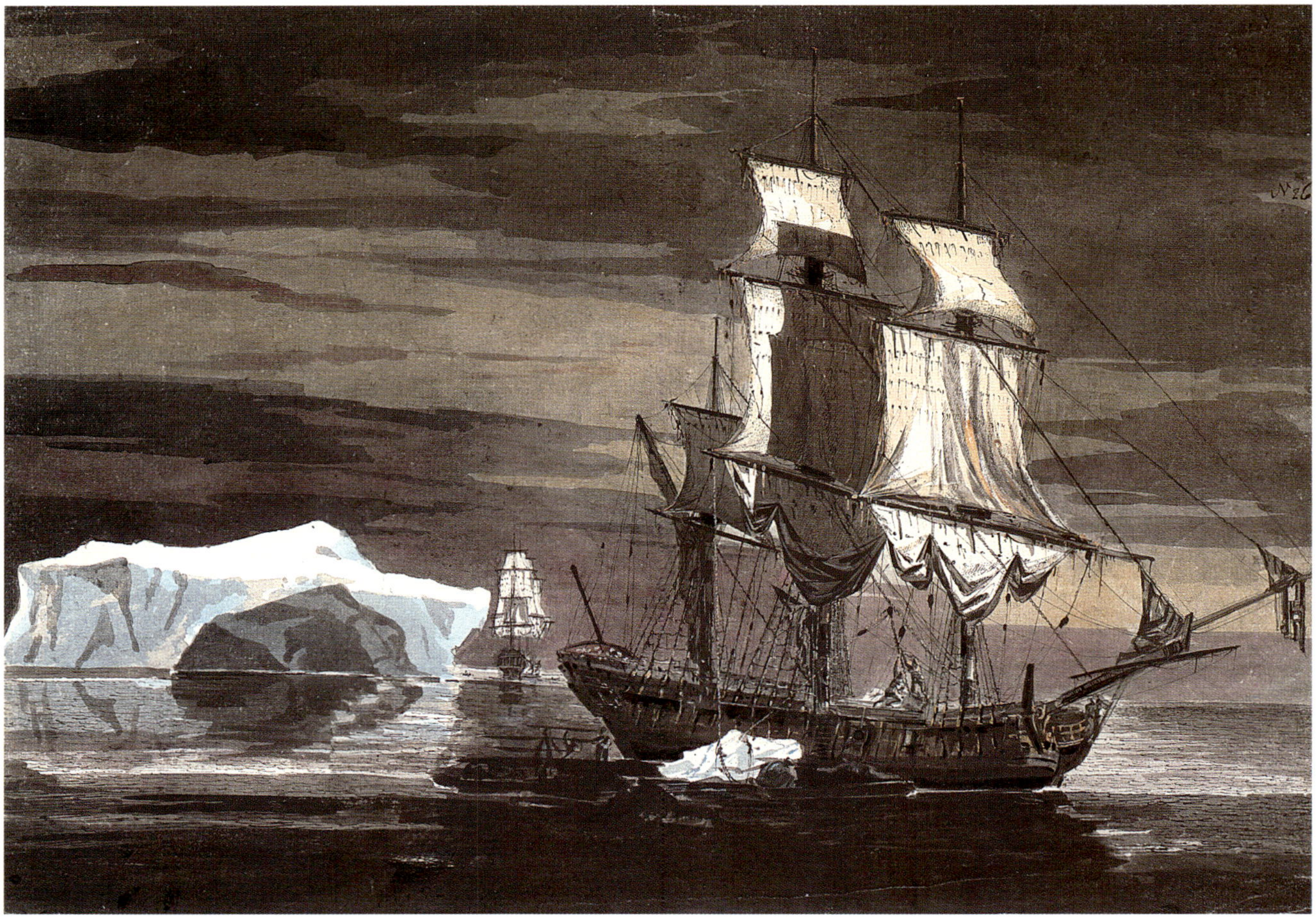

ABOVE

WILLIAM HODGES

Captain Cook's ships Resolution *and* Adventure *taking in ice for water, latitude 61 South, 4 January 1773.*

This graphic, on-the-spot sketch was made by Hodges during Captain Cook's second voyage of exploration, which took the two ships farther south than any previous expedition in the search for the Southern Continent.

Watercolour. Signed. The State Library of New South Wales,

RIGHT

AUGUSTUS EARLE

Raza (or Lighthouse) Island, with a distant view of the entrance of Rio de Janeiro harbour.

After 13 years spent travelling and sketching in Australia and South America, Earle returned to England and was appointed Artist Supernumerary to the surveying voyages of HMS *Beagle* and HMS *Adventure* led by Captain Fitzroy. When they reached Brazil he proved an excellent guide to the young naturalist Charles Darwin on his collecting expeditions.

Watercolour. Signed and dated HMS Beagle, July 1832. Christie's Images, London.

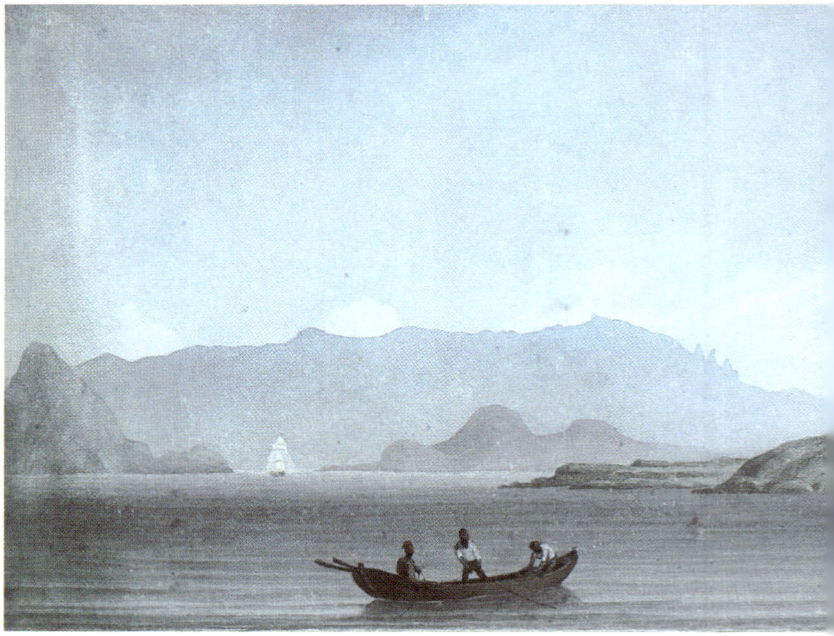

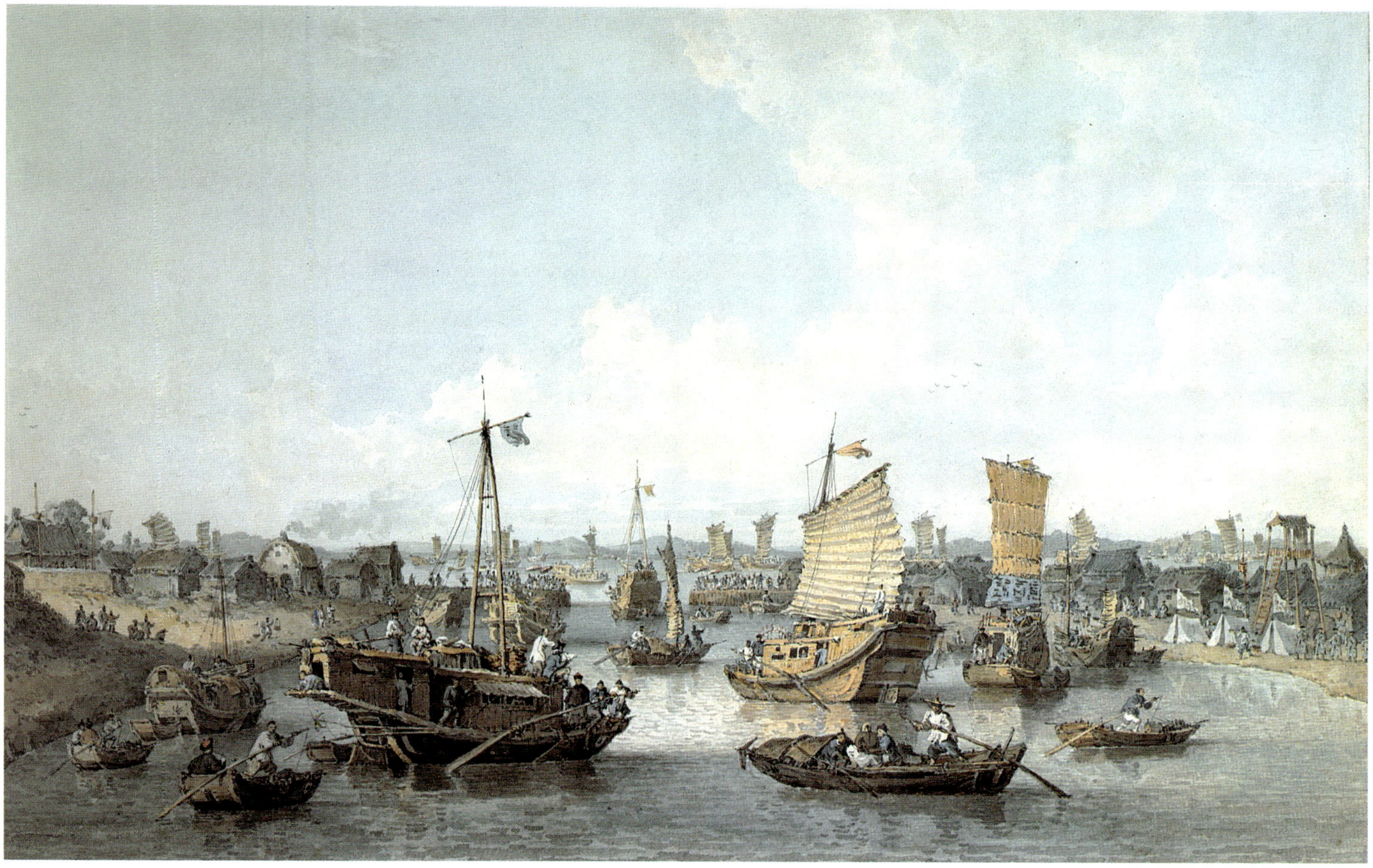

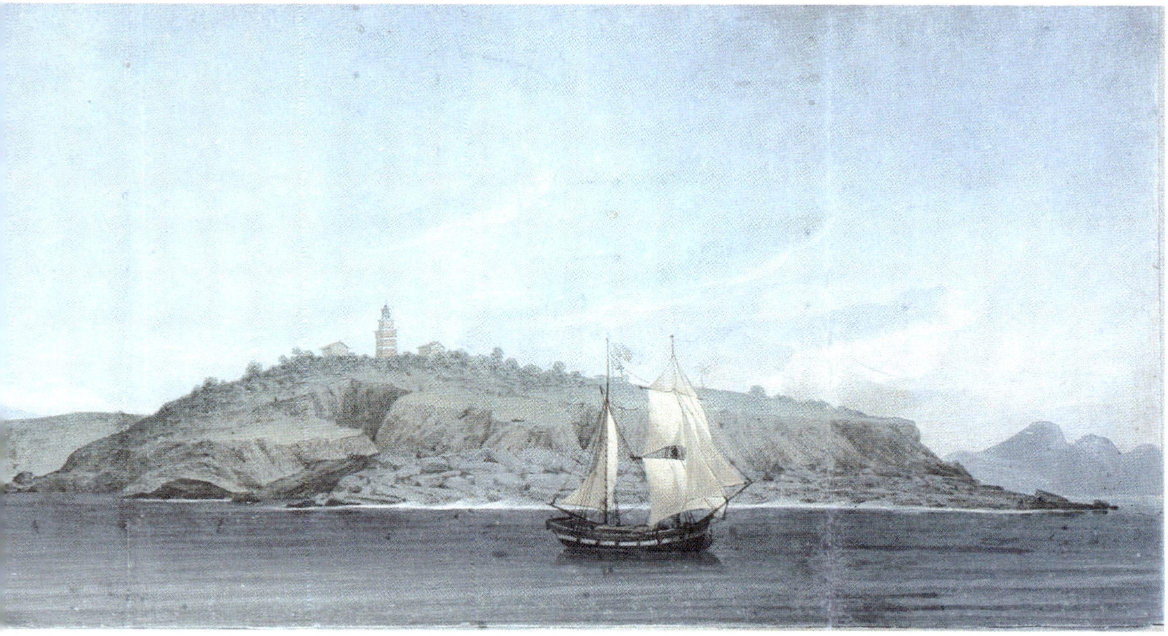

ABOVE

WILLIAM ALEXANDER

Lord Macartney's embassy entering the Hwang-Ho river

As official artist accompanying the British delegation to China in 1793, William Alexander made hundreds of drawings of the people and scenes which he encountered during his travels. He has included himself in this picture and can be seen in the left foreground, seated on the roof of the junk that is flying a blue flag. He is wearing a blue coat and has his sketch pad on his knee.

Pencil and watercolour. Signed. 1793. Martyn Gregory Gallery, London.

Chapter seven

Fishing boats, shipwrecks and coastal scenery

The 19th century saw a shift away from pictures of naval actions and warships. In Britain the demand for commemorative pictures of the Battle of Trafalgar and other conspicuous British victories continued for some years, but with peace established on the high seas for much of the century, it became necessary for marine artists to look elsewhere for subjects. The ending of several decades of naval warfare coincided with that change of mood in art, literature and music that became known as the Romantic movement. In the realm of marine art the mood was set by the poets and in particular by a long poem called *The Shipwreck* by William Falconer, a former seaman. This was a graphic account of a voyage in the Mediterranean which ended in disaster. Successive editions were illustrated by different artists and because the theme of man struggling against the forces of nature was a strong element in the Romantic movement, paintings of storms and shipwrecks became a regular feature on the walls of the Royal Academy and the Paris Salon. The sea was also a major preoccupation for Keats and Shelley, and played a central role in Lord Byron's hugely popular poem *The Corsair* and in Coleridge's *Rime of the Ancient Mariner.*

In the years around 1800, there was also a change of attitude towards the seashore. For centuries the seaside was generally regarded as an inhospitable place. Fishing villages were huddled behind shingle banks or were tucked away in coves and river estuaries. The major ports were positioned on rivers some way upstream, where they were sheltered from the worst of the winter gales. Nobody built a house with a sea view unless they were a fisherman or a sea captain, while swimming in the sea and sunbathing were almost unheard of. The taste for sea bathing is believed to have started in Scarborough, but it was Dr Russell of Brighton who recommended drinking sea water and swimming in the sea as a cure for various ills. With the arrival of the Prince Regent in 1783, the fishing village of Brighton rapidly grew into a fashionable resort. Visiting the coast changed from being a novelty to becoming a popular pastime, and other seaside towns followed Brighton's lead.

Artists visiting the seaside found picturesque subjects among the fishing boats and capstans on the shore. Landscape artists, as well as artists specializing in marine painting began producing pictures of beach scenes and harbours. There was a growing demand for illustrated books of coastal scenery. Some of these were simply bound volumes of engravings, others were in the form of guide books with a commentary on the views portrayed. By far the most ambitious undertaking in this area was an eight-volume set of aquatint engravings by William Daniell entitled *A Voyage Round Great Britain.* This was an illustrated survey of Britain's coastline. In spite of the title, most of the journey was undertaken on foot or on horseback, with occasional forays in boats to offshore islands. Daniell spent ten years in India with his uncle Thomas, travelling and making drawings. They returned to England in 1794 and took a house in London where they began work on the engravings for a six-volume publication *Oriental Scenery.* William later told Farington, the diarist, that 'the great facility which he had acquired in executing Aqua-tinta was obtained by the most severe application for seven years together afer he arrived in England from India – He said he had worked from 6 in the morning till 12 at night.'

Daniell began to exhibit regularly at the Royal Academy and it was not until 1813 that he began work on *A Voyage Round Great Britain.* While preparing the illustrations from his drawings and watercolours, he developed a new and more subtle technique for the aquatints. He told Farington that his method was to use 'at least two colours – warm grey and pale sepia, later adding a pale blue-grey.' These tints imitated the foundation washes or 'dead colouring' that were normally used in water colours at this period, and when the print was 'stained' or tinted with watercolour, the imitation of the original was exact. The result was a valuable record of Britain's coastline and a major contribution to print-making in Britain [see page 46]. The many drawings that he made for the work sometimes come up for sale and the individual plates are often to be found cut from the bound volumes.

We know from Farington's diary that Daniell, like so many artists of his day, was an enthusiastic admirer and imitator of the work of J.M.W. Turner, a prodigy who had entered the Royal Academy Schools in 1789 at the age of 14 and exhibited his first picture at the Academy the following year. After a quiet start with accomplished watercolours of architectural subjects, he turned to oil painting and was soon painting landscapes and seascapes that were deliberately intended to emulate and challenge the admired works of Claude, Cuyp, Ruisdael and Van de Velde. His progress as a marine painter was marked by one *tour de force* after another. With *Dutch boats in a gale,* which was commissioned by the Duke of Bridgewater as a companion piece to a Van de Velde sea-piece, he showed himself to be the equal of

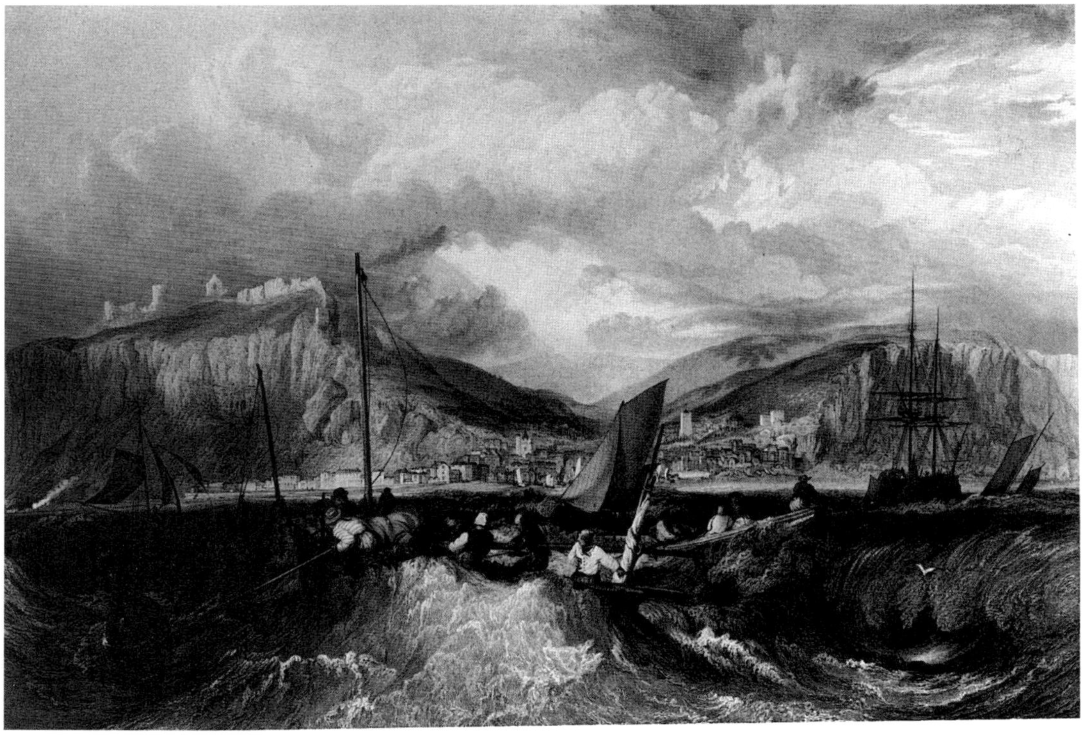

R. WALLIS after
J.M.W. TURNER
Hastings

Turner's maritime views placed unusual demands on the engravers because he was fond of depicting turbulent seas with breaking waves, complex cloud formations and a mass of detail in the shipping and shore scenery. He took great pains to oversee the work of the engravers, with the result that most of the prints made after his work are spectacular examples of the engraver's art.

Etching. Published in 1851 by E.Gambart. Private collection.

the Dutch master, and with *The shipwreck* of 1805 he produced what the art historian T.S.R. Boase has described as 'the most awe-inspiring struggle of man and ocean which had yet been depicted.'

But Turner was equally adept at calm scenes. Like Claude and Cuyp before him, he was able to flood a canvas with golden sunlight that is nowhere better demonstrated than in his magnificent painting *Dordrecht: the Dort packet-boat from Rotterdam becalmed,* now in the Yale Center for British Art at Newhaven, Connecticut. John Constable, who never achieved the popularity of Turner in his lifetime and was sometimes critical of Turner's wilder experiments, recalled this painting as one of singular intricacy and beauty 'and I think the most complete work of genius I ever saw.'

Turner painted some 20,000 watercolours and drawings during the course of his life. Many of his drawings were short-hand sketches intended as raw material for future paintings, but a large number of his finest watercolours were commissioned as illustrations for publication and were engraved. The first major series was inspired by the famous set of prints made by Richard Earlom after the drawings in Claude's *Liber Veritas*, published by Boydell in the 1770s. Turner planned to produce 100 engravings for publication to be entitled *Liber Studiorum.* He prepared drawings in pen and wash, etched many of the outlines himself and hired engravers to supply the areas of tone in mezzotint. Seventy-one prints were made and published between 1809 and 1819, when he abandoned the project due to lack of support.

In 1811 Turner was commissioned by the engraver and publisher W.B. Cooke to contribute 40 plates to a publication entitled *Picturesque Views on the Southern Coast of England.* The remaining 40 plates were made from drawings by Samuel Owen, Peter de Wint and others. Turner spent the summer of that year travelling along the south coast gathering material and on his return worked up his sketches into carefully finished watercolours. As always, he insisted on the highest standard from his engravers. On examining the first proof of the print of *Hythe*, he congratulated the engraver on his excellent work but thought one area was too coarse because the lines cut with the graver were too even in strength and width: 'The marsh is all swamp; I want light upon it up to the sea, and although I have darkened the sea in part, yet you must not consider it to want strength........get it into one tone, flat by dots or some means, and let the sea and water only appear different by their present lines.' The engraver in this instance was George Cooke, the brother of W.B. Cooke and father of E.W. Cooke, who was to become the leading British marine painter of the 1860s.

Turner carried out two more series of publications for W.B. Cooke. For *The Rivers of England* he produced 17 watercolours, which were engraved in mezzotint by Charles Turner and published in 1832. The sequel to this was *The Ports of England,* for which Turner made 12 watercolours. Only six of the engravings appeared in his lifetime, the remaining six were published in 1856, when the entire set was issued with a descriptive text by John Ruskin under the title *The Harbours of England.*

While the illustrations commissioned by Cooke resulted in some powerful images of ships and the sea, the most sustained expression of Turner's powers as a watercolourist was demonstrated in the series of pictures he made for the publication *Picturesque Views in England and Wales.* This was commissioned by Charles Heath in 1826 and was to have had 120 plates, but Heath went bankrupt before the project was complete and only 96 plates were made. The copper engravings were carried out by different engravers, but all convey the vigour and atmospheric effects of Turner's watercolours. Of the seascapes, the most memorable are the tempestuous views of Fowey harbour, Lowestoft and Lyme Regis, showing men in small boats struggling against the dreadful, heaving power of stormy seas.

Turner's later paintings baffled many of the critics and his place as the undisputed master of the sea-piece was taken by Clarkson Stanfield, a former merchant seaman who had first made his name as a scene painter at Drury Lane Theatre. Encouraged by his friends to abandon work for the theatre and concentrate on easel paintings, Stanfield rapidly established himself as a leading painter of landscapes and seascapes.

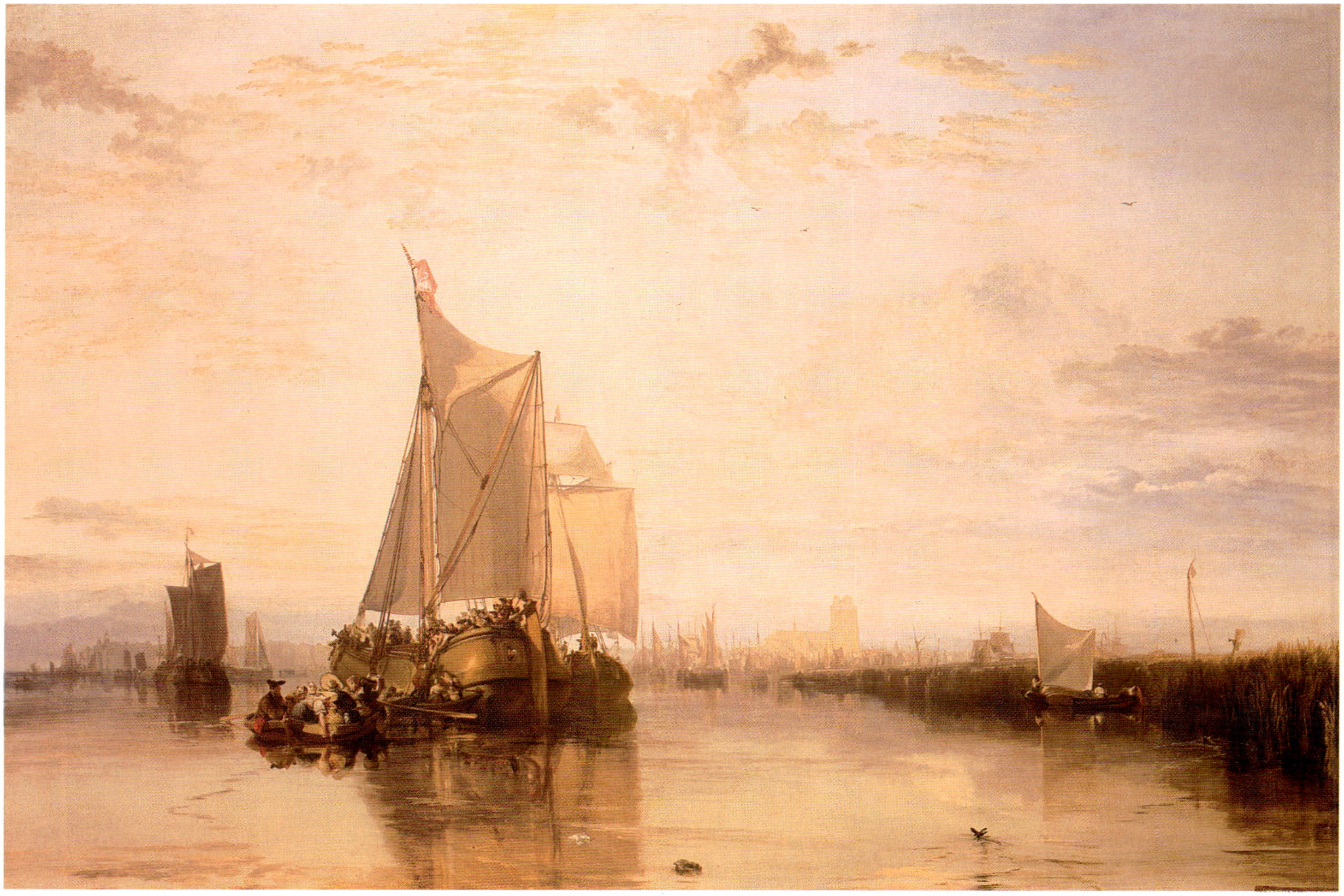

He painted similar subjects to Turner – fishing boats in gales and calms, shipwrecks, river estuaries with shipping, and coast scenes. He lacked Turner's original vision, but his seaman's background and his technical ability enabled him to bring an added realism to his depiction of ships and small craft. No artist equalled his ability to paint the surface of disturbed seas and to suggest the weight, the transparency and the movement of waves, brilliantly demonstrated by his masterpiece *On the Dogger Bank.*

Like so many artists of this period, Stanfield was much in demand for providing illustrations to books of picturesque views. His first commission of this kind, to contribute ten watercolours for *Views in London and its Vicinity,* came in 1827 from George Cooke. This was a book of 48 plates printed from copper engravings, the other pictures being supplied by A.W. Callcott, Samuel Prout, John Sell Cotman and other distinguished artists. Between 1832 and 1834 Charles Heath published three *Picturesque Annuals,* all of which were illustrated by engravings after Stanfield's

J.M.W. Turner
Dordrecht: the Dort packet-boat from Rotterdam becalmed

The most impressive of all Turner's marine paintings of calms, this picture was inspired by his visit to Holland in August 1817. It was a direct challenge to the pictures of similar subjects by Cuyp and Van de Velde the Younger.

Oil on canvas. Signed and dated 1818.
From the collection of Mr and Mrs Paul Mellon.
The Yale Center for British Art, Newhaven.

watercolours. The subjects were views of towns and landscapes in Europe, made during the artist's trip to Italy. He had now established an impressive command of watercolour, and his picture of *The Church of San Salute, Venice*, seen across choppy water with a lowering sky beyond, is typical of his best work for the engravers.

In 1836 a book of engravings was published called Stanfield's *Coast Scenery. A series of views in the British Channel.* This was based on watercolours he had made of Channel ports such as Boulogne and Dartmouth, and was followed two years later by *Sketches on the Moselle, the Rhine and the Meuse.* In this instance, the prints were lithographs, which produced a more accurate representation of the original watercolours. Stanfield also contributed illustrations to many of the novels and biographies of the day, notably the sea stories by Captain Marryat and several short stories by Charles Dickens, who was a close friend.

When Stanfield was preparing his material for George Cooke's *Views in London*, much of the preparatory work was carried out by Cooke's son Edward William Cooke, who was then aged 15. He made sketches of ships and waterfront details and carried out some of the etching. Brought up in his father's workshop alongside talented apprentices such as Thomas Shotter Boys, and in regular contact with John Sell Cotman, Turner and Prout, who were supplying pictures for publication, the young E.W. Cooke learned fast. He proved to be a precocious draughtsman and an

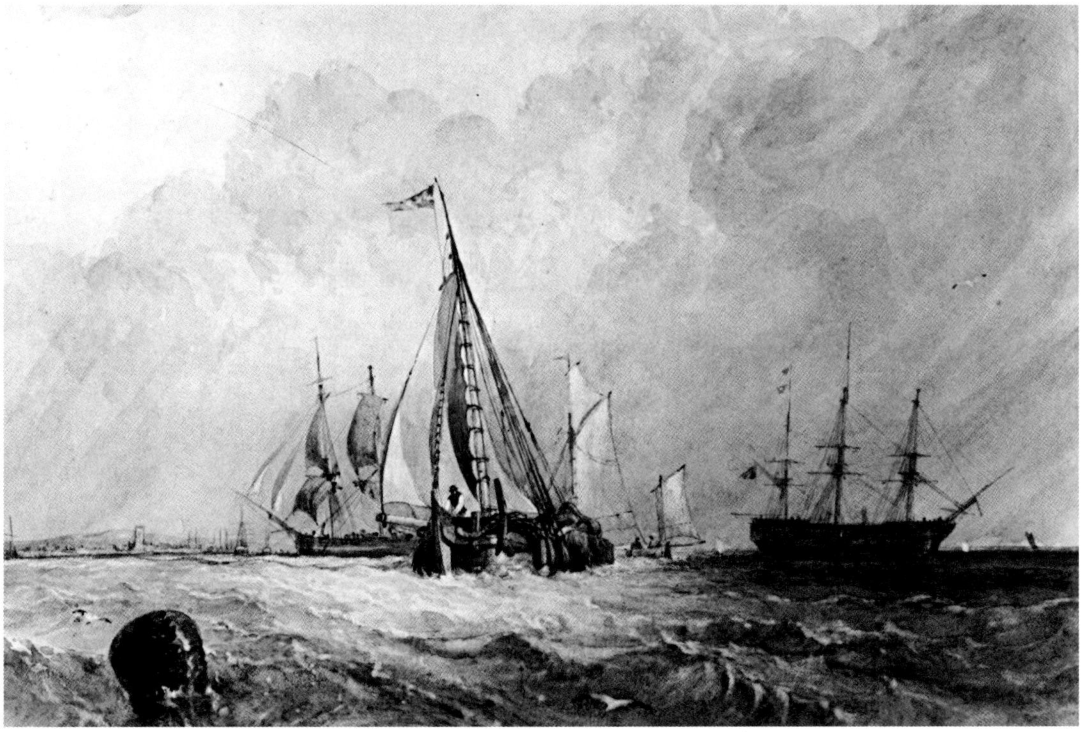

CLARKSON STANFIELD
A Dutch boat and other vessels in a fresh breeze off a coast

Stanfield was as skilful at drawing ships and waves as Van de Velde and Turner, and this watercolour is a typically accomplished example of his work. The anchored warship on the horizon was a favourite device of marine artists, for it provided a much needed vertical element in an otherwise featureless seascape.

Watercolour. Thomas Agnew and Sons, London.

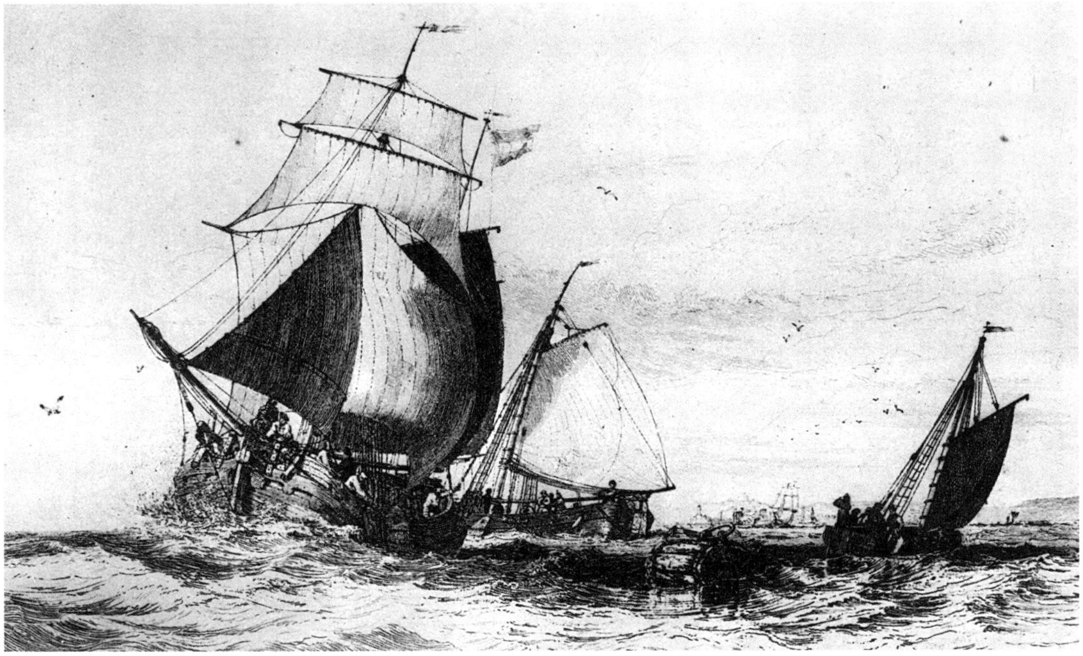

E.W. COOKE
Dutch boats beating to windward

This is one of the etchings from *Fifty Plates of Shipping and Craft* which was published in several parts in 1828 and 1829. The title page indicates that the prints were 'Drawn from the objects, and etched by Edward William Cook, under the superintendance of George Cooke.'

Etching. 1828. Private collection.

outstanding printmaker. In March 1828, at the age of 17, he published the first three etchings of *Fifty Plates of Shipping and Craft*, a series of prints depicting the wide range of sailing ships and small boats to be found on the Thames and around the coasts of Kent and Sussex. The best of these prints are minor masterpieces , exquisitely drawn and boldly composed, with a command of space and pattern which may have been inspired by Cotman.The series has become one of the classics of maritime prints, comparable with the best work of Groenewegen, Nooms, Le Comte and Wyllie.

Cooke went on to become a prolific and successful marine painter. He painted numerous pictures of Dutch fishing boats battling through the surf or beached on the sands at Scheveningen, as well as tranquil scenes on the waterways around Venice. The polished and minutely detailed style of his oil paintings is impressive but lacks the painterly quality of the seascapes of French artists such as Eugène Isabey, Charles Daubigny and Eugène Boudin, who were his near contemporaries. Cooke's work in watercolours was competent but dull, and the greatest contribution to marine art in this medium in the early and middle years of the 19th century was carried out by landscape artists, who occasionally turned to the sea for subjects. The best of these were Cotman, Richard Parkes Bonington and David Cox.

John Sell Cotman, who was born in Norwich in 1782, is now regarded as one of the great masters of the watercolour. The pictures he painted in the brief period between 1805 and 1810 sell for thousands of pounds and most are in museum collections. They include his famous views in the Greta valley, Yorkshire, and a few

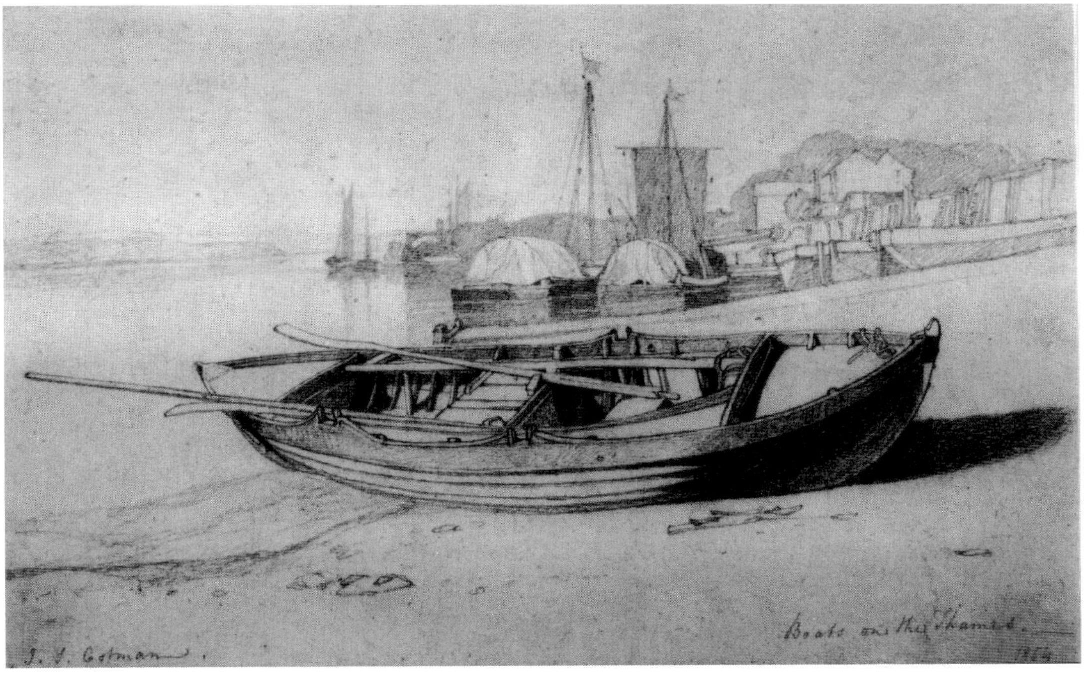

JOHN SELL COTMAN
Boats on the Thames

The boat in the foreground is a Peter boat which was used for fishing on the Thames. Clearly visible in the drawing is the wet-well amidships in which the fish could be kept alive until the catch was landed. In 1828, and again in 1831, Cotman made the coastal voyage from Norfolk to London in his own boat and made many drawings in the Thames estuary.

Pencil. Signed. Thomas Agnew and Sons, London.

memorable seascapes, notably *The dismasted brig*, *The Needles* and *The Mars riding at anchor off Cromer.*

After spending some years in London, where he exhibited at the Royal Academy, Cotman returned to Norfolk, which was his base for the next 30 years. Much of his time was spent working on volumes of etchings. His *Miscellaneous Etchings* was published in 1811; he made 60 plates for *The Architectural Antiquities of Norfolk;* and in 1822 he completed work on the two volumes of etchings, *Architectural Antiquities of Normandy*, which had been commissioned by his patron Dawson Turner. Preoccupied by his engraving projects, by his responsibilities as a drawing master and by the need to support six children, he failed to live up to the promise of his early years. He suffered periods of deep depression and when he died in 1842 not a single obituary marked his passing.

Cotman and his artist son Miles Edmund Cotman spent much of their time exploring the rivers and estuaries of East Anglia in a small boat called *The Jessie*, and on one occasion sailed from Norfolk to the Thames in her. Between them they drew and painted numerous seascapes filled with finely drawn fishing vessels. While his deceptively simple but carefully studied watercolours are his greatest legacy, Cotman was also a master engraver. He admired the work of the Italian engraver Piranesi, but developed a distinctive style of his own which enabled him to bring a grandeur and timelessness to a variety of subjects from ruined abbeys and massive castles to derelict windmills and groups of upended boats lying on the seashore.

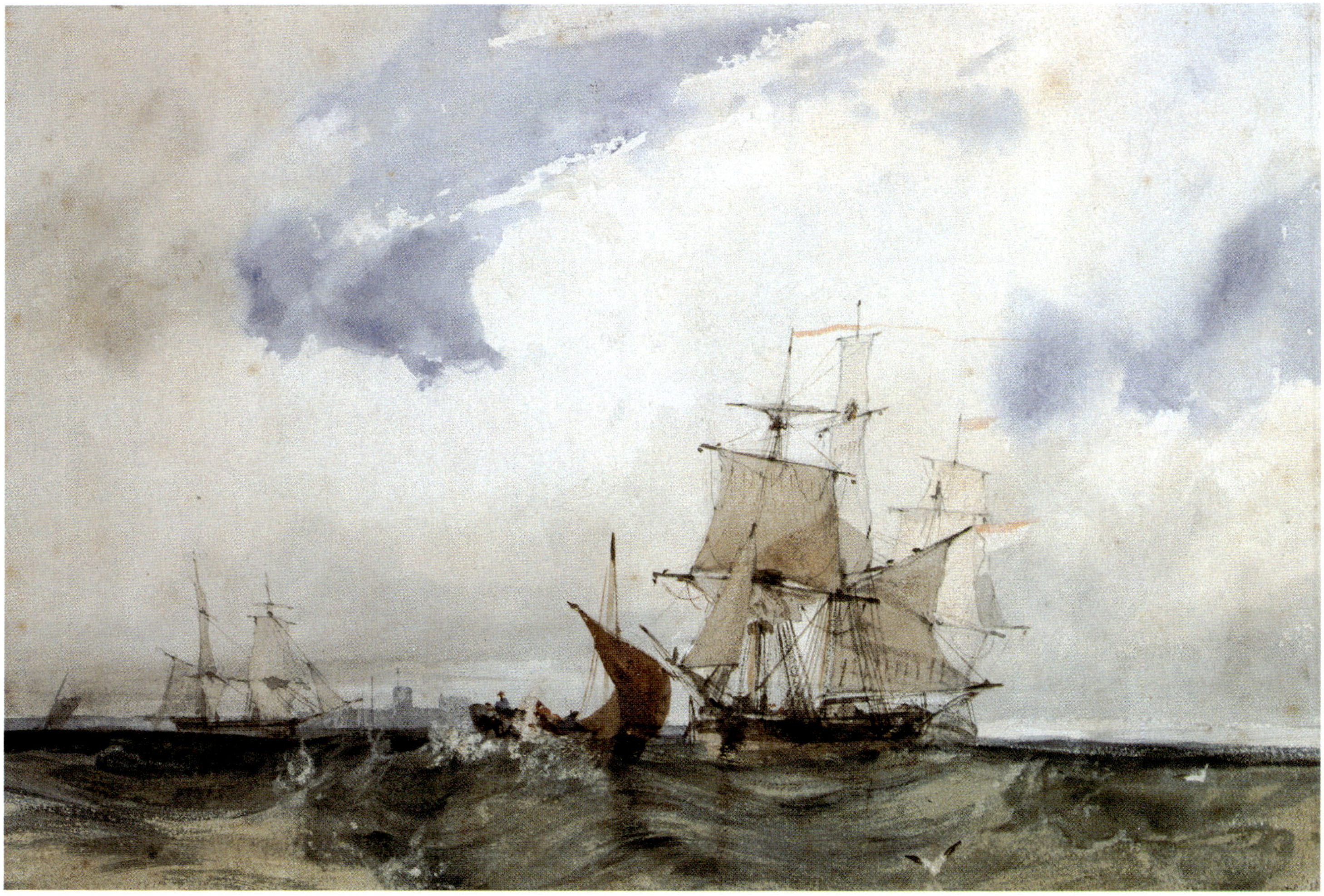

RICHARD PARKES BONINGTON
Dunkerque from the sea

Bonington's watercolour technique was the envy of his contemporaries. He could suggest a surging green sea and a cloudy sky with effortless ease. In this recently discovered watercolour the combination of fluid brush strokes for the waves and the delicate drawing of the ships is masterly.

Pencil and watercolour heightened with scratching out. Signed and indistinctly dated. Christie's Images, London

When E. W. Cooke was in his early twenties, he went to see a collection of Bonington's pictures in London. He thought them 'truly splendid and surprising works of Art!! Nothing in Art so much affected me before.' Bonington's precocious talent had a similar effect on other English artists. When he died a few months before his twenty-sixth birthday, his funeral was attended by the most distinguished Royal Academicians of the day. Clarkson Stanfield and Samuel Prout helped to organize a sale of his work at Sotheby's which realized £2,296 6s 0d, a considerable sum in those days. His work has continued to increase steadily in value and a fine example of one of his watercolours is likely to fetch around £30,000 in the sale rooms today. Richard Parkes Bonington was born in Nottingham, but when he was 15 his family moved to France. He was a pupil of F.T.L. Francia in Calais, studied at the École des Beaux Arts in Paris and became a friend of Delacroix. From his base in Paris he made several sketching tours of northern France, where the harbours and beaches provided him with material for a stunning series of watercolours and oil paintings. Many of his watercolours were engraved for a volume entitled *Excursions sur les Côtes et dan les Ports de Normandie*, which was published in 1824.

The other great painter of watercolours featuring beach scenes and coastal views was David Cox, the son of a Birmingham blacksmith, who spent some years as a scene painter. He became a drawing master, learned to etch on copper, and produced three drawing manuals, which he illustrated with soft-ground etchings and aquatints. The first, *A Treatise on Landscape Painting and Effect in Watercolour*, published in 1814, was followed in 1816 by *Lessons in Landscape*, and later by *The Young Artist's Companion*, which had the lengthy subtitle, *Drawing-book of Studies and Landscape Embellishments: comprising a great variety of the most picturesque objects required in the various compositions of landscape scenery, arranged as progressive lessons.* Cox's watercolour technique was characterized by vigorous brushwork and a rapid sketchy application of colour perfectly suited to the depiction of choppy seas and scudding clouds. His windswept views of Rhyl sands and Calais pier are typical, but he could also paint limpid calms with sailing vessels drifting beneath summer skies.

Other watercolour artists painting seascapes in the early years of the 19th century were Samuel Prout, Samuel Owen and Copley Fielding. Very little is known about Samuel Owen, who exhibited periodically at the Royal Academy. He produced a

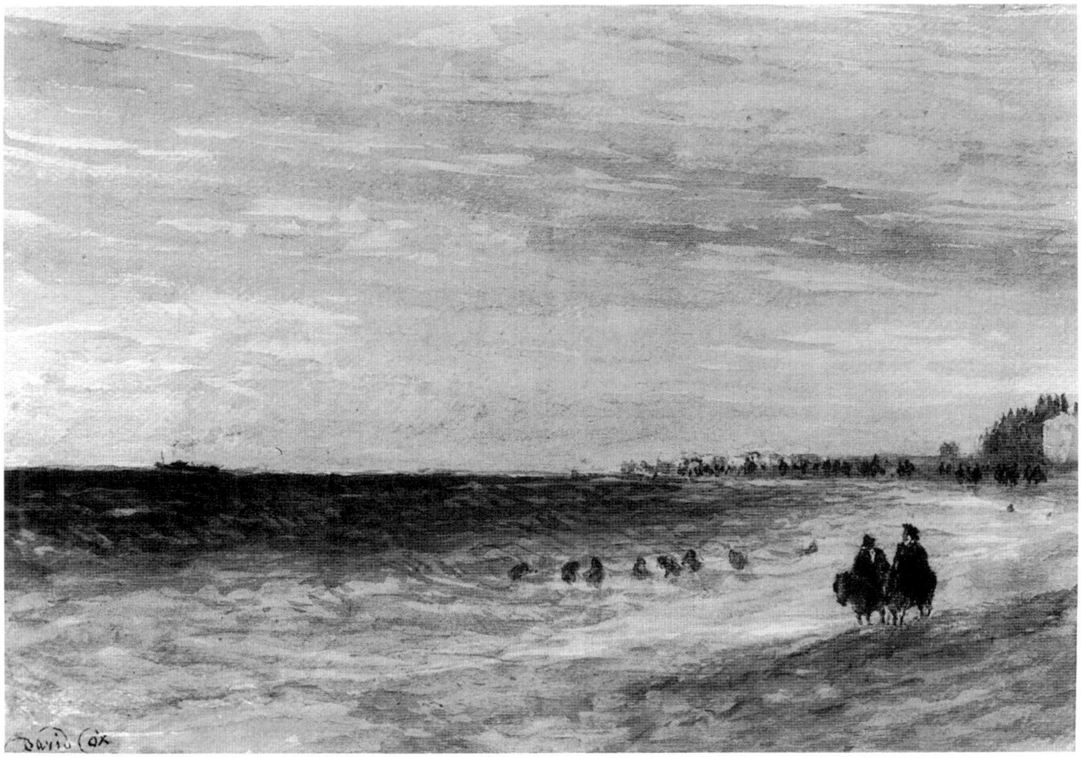

David Cox
Aldeborough

Cox painted several views in watercolours of windswept beaches, most of them at Rhyl Sands and Lancaster Sands. He was adept at capturing the exhilarating atmosphere of the seaside.

Watercolour. Signed. Thomas Agnew and Sons, London.

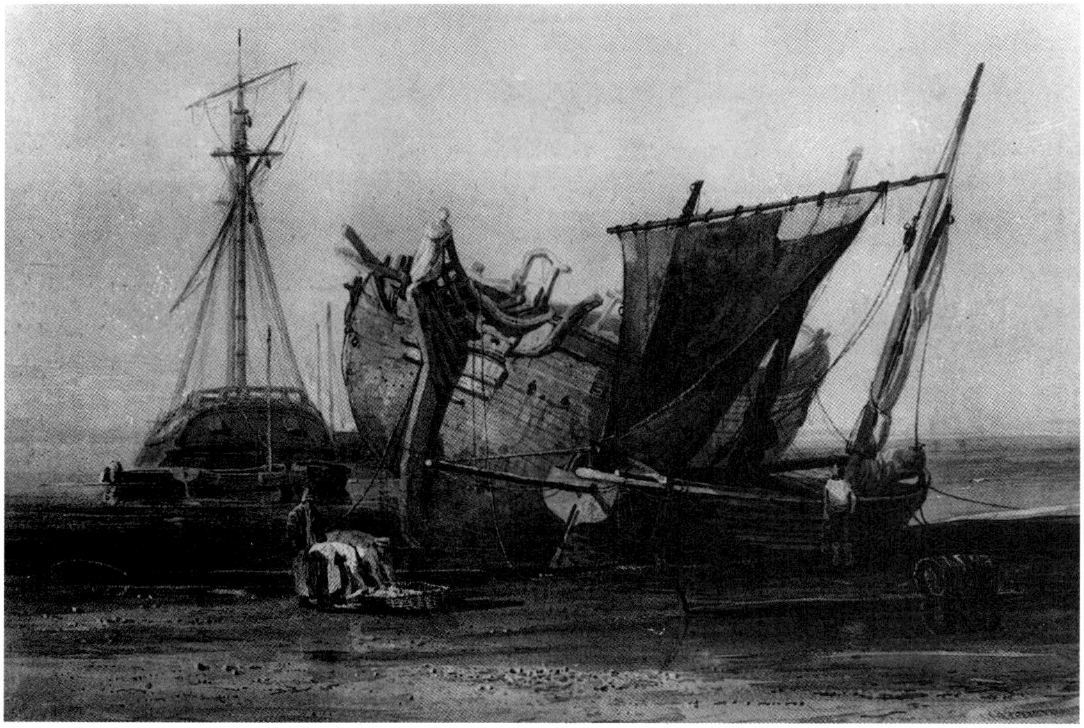

SAMUEL PROUT
A beached hulk and other vessels at low tide

Although he is better known for his picturesque views of medieval buildings, Prout made numerous studies of shipping. He preferred to paint ships aground or at anchor rather than sailing, and this is typical of his maritime subjects.

Watercolour. Martyn Gregory Gallery. London.

series of 84 watercolours, which were engraved by W.B. Cooke in 1811, and published a two-volume work entitled *The Thames, or graphic illustrations of seats, villas, public buildings and picturesque scenery on the bank.* He had an attractive and most accomplished technique in watercolours and drew ships with assurance.

Samuel Prout, the son of a Plymouth bookseller, made a name for himself with his pictures of street scenes and ancient buildings. In 1803 he was commissioned by the antiquarian John Britton to illustrate *Beauties of England and Wales* and, following a number of sketching tours in Europe, his picturesque views of ancient medieval towns were engraved. The subsequent publications reached a wide audience, as did his teaching manuals such as *A Series of Easy Lessons in Landscape Drawing*, 1820, and *Prout's Microcosm: The Artistic Sketchbook of Groups of Figures, Shipping and other Picturesque Objects*, 1841. In spite of his reputation as an architectural draughtsman, ships featured prominently among his drawings and engravings. In 1816 Ackerman published his *Studies of Boats and Coastal Scenery*, and conspicuous among his work are pictures of East Indiamen aground, influenced apparently by his witnessing the dramatic wreck of the *Dutton* in Plymouth Sound in 1796.

Anthony VanDyke Copley Fielding was one of the leading lights of the Old Water-Colour Society. In the space of seven years between 1813 and 1820, he showed no fewer than 327 pictures at the exhibitions, and from 1831 until his death in 1855 he was the Society's president. For most of his early life he painted landscapes but in 1817 he moved from London to the Kent coast and turned to the sea as a source of subject matter. He earned high praise from John Ruskin for his ability to paint calm water, as well as breaking waves and 'the race of a running tide under a stiff breeze'. Copley Fielding's finest works are technically impressive but he had a tendency to paint to a formula. He produced numerous variations on the theme of fishing boats sailing off a harbour mouth, usually showing the vessels heeling dramatically against a backdrop of storm clouds.

In addition to the landscape artists who sometimes painted sea-pieces, there was a group of early 19th-century artists working in Britain who specialized in marine painting. These included J.W. Carmichael, George Chambers, Edward Duncan, R.H. Nibbs and the brothers John and William Joy. They were all born within a few years of each other, were prolific in their output, and their work frequently comes up for sale in the auction rooms. The most talented of this group was George Chambers, whose reputation rests with his oil paintings rather than his watercolours. He came from the humblest of backgrounds and, like Charles Brooking, managed to pack into a short life of 37 years a succession of pictures which have secured him a place among the great names of British marine painting.

Chambers was born at Whitby in 1803, the second son of a seaman. He had minimal schooling, was working on the collier brigs at the age of eight, and was then apprenticed to the captain of a vessel trading between Whitby and London. Chambers escaped from life at sea by taking up scene painting in London and by painting seascapes on the side. He was plucked from obscurity by Admiral Capel, who saw his pictures in a shop window and gave him the first of a series of prestigious commissions, which culminated in Chambers being invited to Windsor to meet King William IV and Queen Adelaide.

Although entirely self-taught, Chambers developed a fluid and painterly style in both oil paint and watercolours. In the six years between 1834 and 1840, the year of his death, no fewer than 41 of his pictures were hung in the Old Water-Colour Society. Unlike the paintings of his fellow marine artists, only very few of his pictures were engraved.

J.W. Carmichael also had a maritime background. He was the son of a ship's carpenter in Newcastle-upon-Tyne and was apprenticed in the same trade for several years before deciding to earn his living as a marine painter. In 1835 he exhibited for the first time at the Royal Academy and continued to show there until 1859. He seems to have had no difficulty in finding patrons for his paintings, which were always workmanlike, and at their best were the equal of those of Chambers and E.W.

A.V. Copley Fielding
Shipping in a storm off Portsmouth

This is a fine example of the type of picture at which Copley Fielding excelled and for which there seems to have been a ready market. He painted numerous variations on this theme and proved particularly skilful at depicting sunlight and shadow moving across the surface of confused seas.

Watercolour. Thomas Agnew and Sons, London.

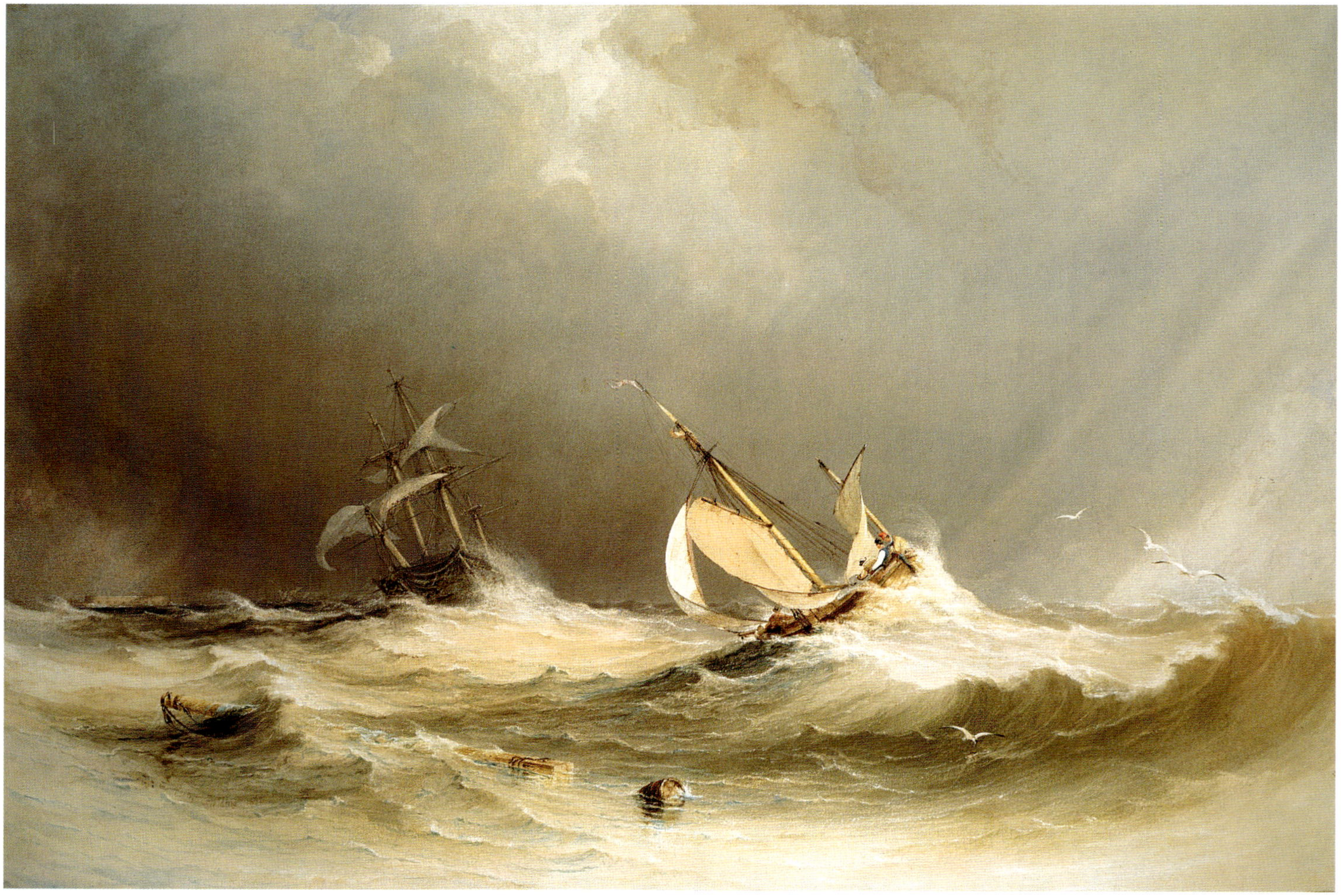

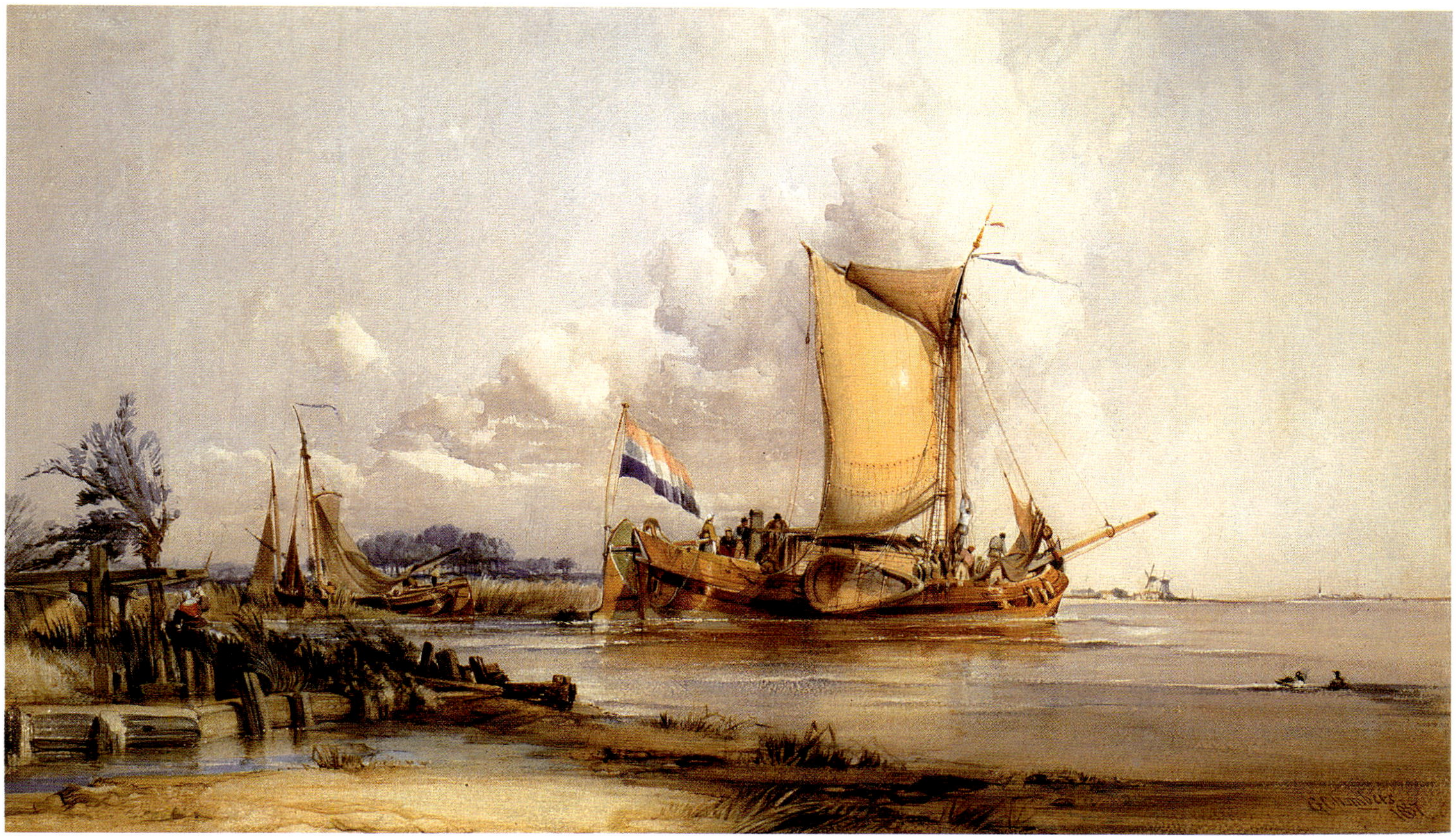

GEORGE CHAMBERS
A river scene with a Dutch barge in light breeze

In 1837 Chambers went on a sketching tour to Holland. It was his first trip abroad and it furnished him with the subject matter for several pictures including this one, which is an outstanding example of work in watercolour.

Watercolour. Signed and dated 1837. Thomas Agnew and Sons, London.

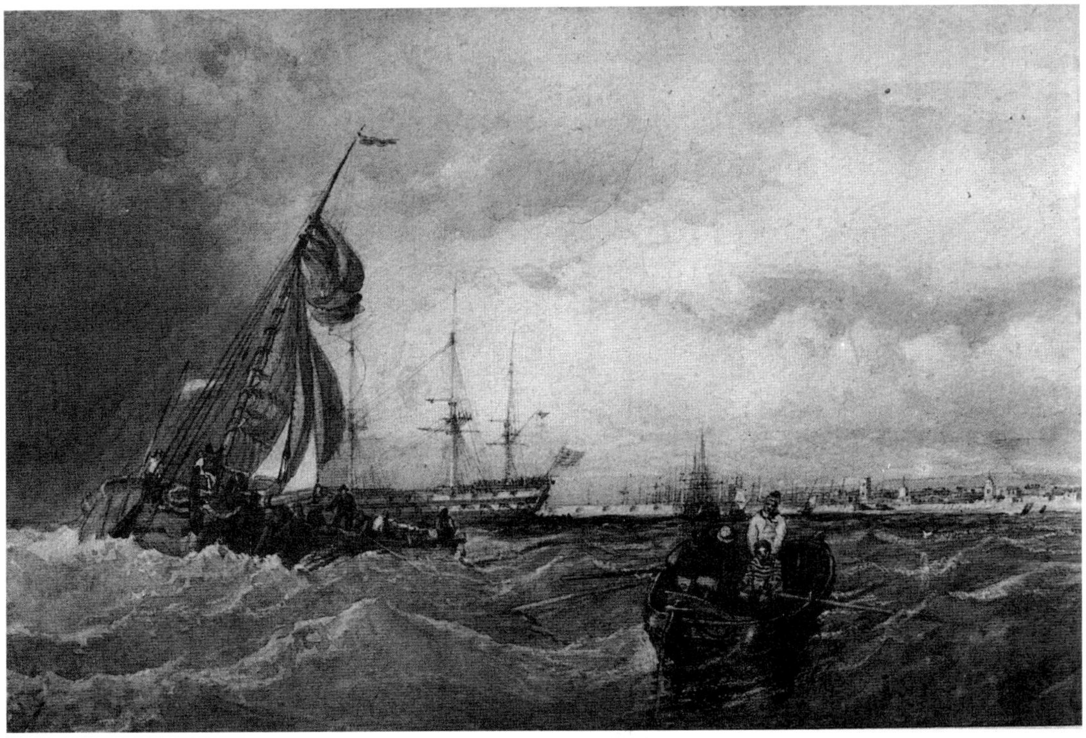

J.W. Carmichael
Hartlepool

Carmichael tended to work at speed and often finished a picture in a day. He once wrote in his diary, 'I always find a pure thought of a picture fully carried out turns out better with me than making many alterations afterwards.'

Watercolour. Laing Art Gallery and Museum, Newcastle upon Tyne.

Cooke. With the outbreak of the Crimean War in 1855, Carmichael sailed to the Baltic with the fleet and sent back a series of illustrations for publication in the *Illustrated London News*. He also produced two manuals of instruction for the aspiring artist: *The Art of Marine Painting in Watercolours*, which was published in 1859, followed a few years later by *The Art of Painting in Oil-Colours*.

There was evidently a ready market for teaching manuals because Edward Duncan was yet another marine artist who was involved in their production. He was commissioned to provide the illustrations for three titles in Vere Foster's series of watercolour books: *Simple Lessons in Marine Painting*; *British Landscape and Coast Scenery*; and *Advanced Studies in Marine Painting*. Duncan was born at Hampstead, in London, and was apprenticed to the publisher and engraver Robert Havel, who taught him the art of engraving in aquatint. In about 1826 he began engraving the work of William Huggins, a prolific painter of ship portraits and naval actions. Duncan subsequently married Huggins's daughter and took up marine painting himself. His watercolours are beautifully drawn and elegantly composed, with fresh blues and greens predominating.

A marine artist who produced watercolours and etchings of ships and scenery on the Sussex coast was Richard Henry Nibbs. He lived in Brighton and divided his time between teaching the violin, playing in the orchestra of the Theatre Royal and

EDWARD DUNCAN
Yarmouth herring boat alongside a wharf

Duncan trained as an engraver but later took up painting in watercolour and developed a most attractive style in this medium. Although the picture shown here is simply a study of a three-masted lugger, Duncan has drawn every detail with such care that it would be possible to construct a rigged model from the drawing.

Watercolour. Signed and dated 1849. Martyn Gregory Gallery, London.

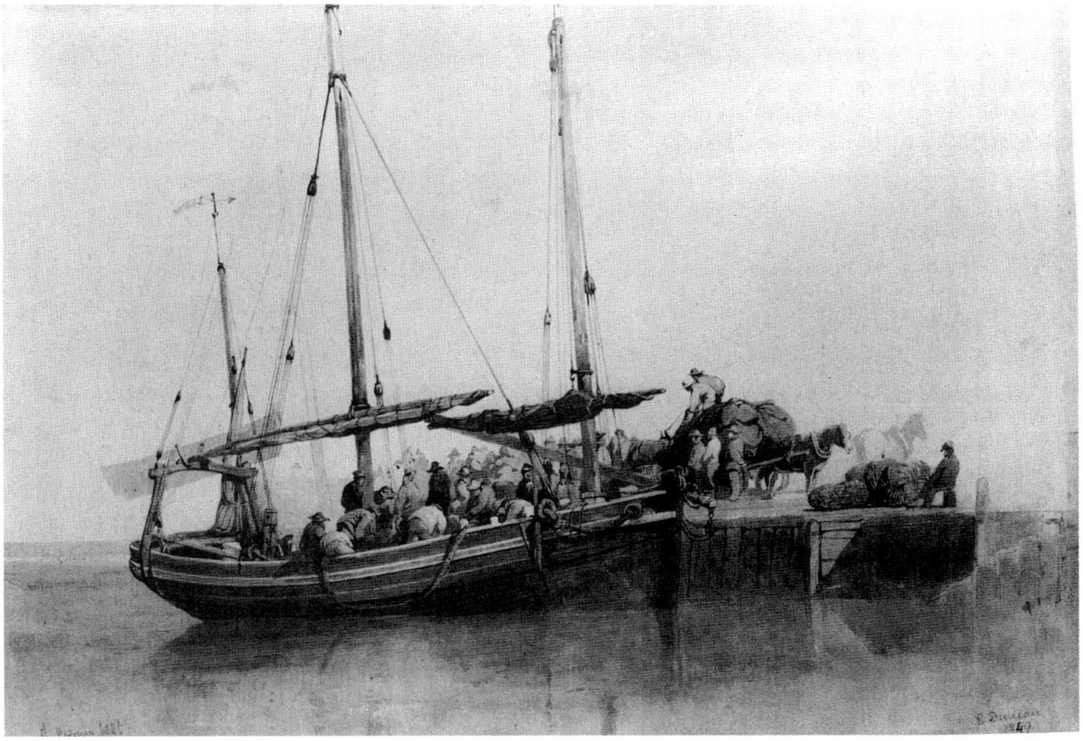

RICHARD HENRY NIBBS
A three-decker at anchor

Most of Nibbs's watercolours are highly finished and this is unusually broad and free in its treatment. The numerous small craft sailing around the warships suggest that the scene is a sheltered anchorage. Nibbs was a Sussex artist and the nearest place he was likely to see large warships at anchor was at Portsmouth.

Pen and wash. Signed and dated 1841. National Maritime Museum, London

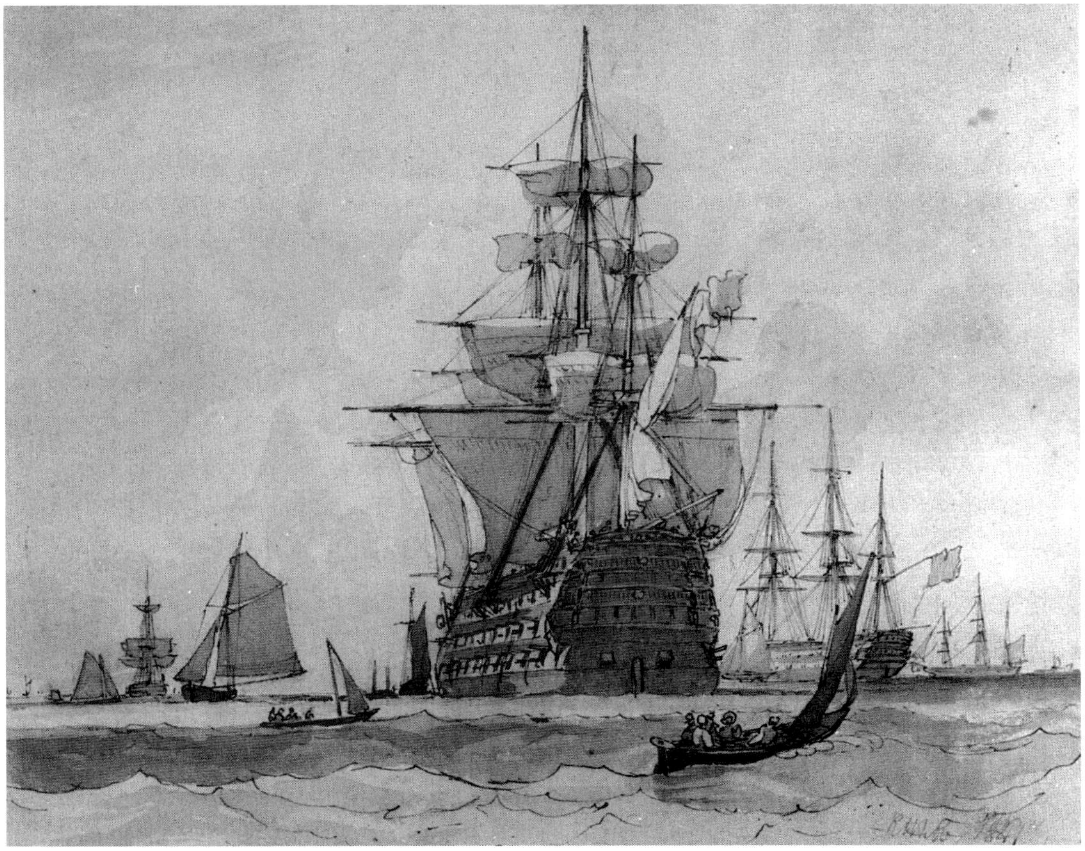

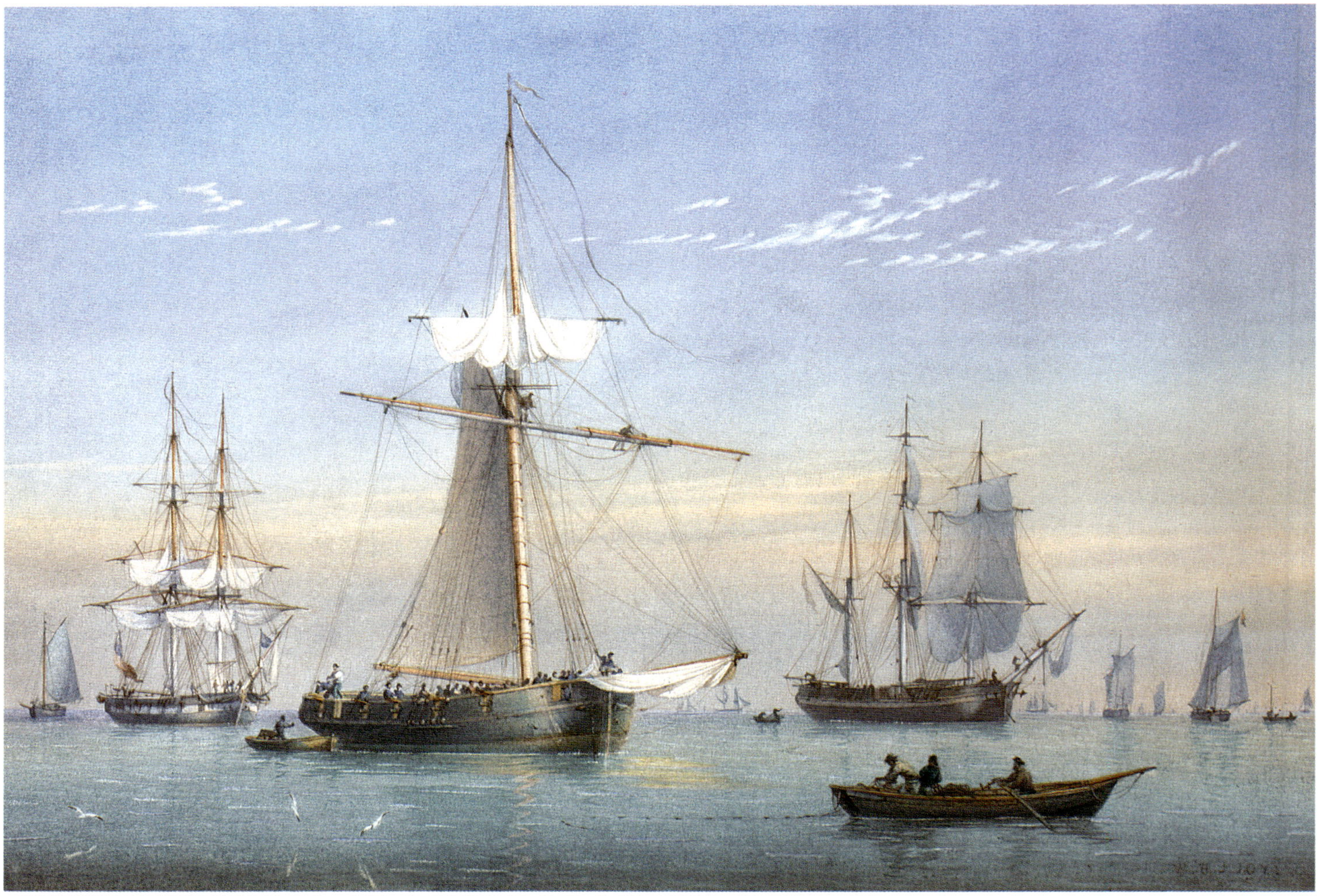

painting pictures. He seems to have been entirely self-taught, but exhibited fairly regularly at the Royal Academy betwen 1841 and 1888. His work is variable and some of his watercolours are spirited and free, others have a tendency to be dull and murky. He produced several albums of etchings, including a set of ten plates for *Marine Sketches,* published in 1836; 20 plates for *Marine Sketchbook of Shipping Craft and Coast Scenes,* 1850; and *Shipping, and Coast Scenes, and Antiquities of Sussex*, which contained 35 plates and was published in 1876.

The brothers William and John Joy came from Yarmouth and were fortunate to find an influential patron in Captain Manby, a pioneer in the establishment of life-boat stations and the inventor of a life-saving apparatus that was named after him. He was a keen collector of seascapes and encouraged the young artists to copy paintings in his collection. From 1819 onward they exhibited at the Norwich Society of Artists, sometimes working together on the same picture, and although it is often

WILLIAM JOY and JOHN CANTILOE JOY
Ferrying the crew ashore

This jewel-like watercolour is full of carefully observed detail. The focus of the picture is an armed naval cutter, her decks crowded with seamen. Left and right of her in the distance are a frigate and a merchant ship at anchor. In the foreground, three men in a small boat are busy with a net.

Pencil and watercolour heightened with white. Signed W & J Joy. Private collection.

impossible to tell their work apart, their joint style is distinctive. Their seas tend to be in cool shades of turquoise blue, with flickering wave crests picked out with a sharp knife. The ships are boldly placed and crisply drawn and show an expert knowledge of how sailing vessels of all types were handled in light and heavy winds.

LATE 19TH-CENTURY MARINE ART IN BRITAIN

Another shift in the subject matter of marine painting and drawings took place during the second half of the 19th century. The vogue for illustrated travel books and painting manuals continued, so did the demand for picturesque views of fishing boats, but several artists adopted a fresh approach to the treatment of seascapes. Shipping became a minor element in pictures and the emphasis was on the sea and the clouds, the moods of the weather and the effect of light on the water. This had been anticipated in the small oil sketches that Constable had made at Brighton and Weymouth, and by the work of Courbet in Europe. The leading exponents of this new approach were John Brett and Henry Moore.

While on a visit to Clovelly in Devon in 1857, the landscape painter Henry Moore wrote in his diary, 'There is one thing respecting the sea I never saw truly given in a painting – viz, its size and extent as seen from high cliffs – it is truly wonderful.' During the next 30 years he and his contemporary John Brett proceded to make good this deficiency. They painted vast panoramic views of the sea in which ships were incidental to the overall impact of the picture and were sometimes absent altogether. Henry Moore, who came from a family of artists, had spent his early years painting landscapes, but after his visit to Clovelly he devoted himself entirely to marine painting. He spent hours making studies of waves, and frequently went cruising in the English Channel in an 80-ton yacht owned by his friend Mr Burnett. His watercolours, like his later oil paintings, are freely handled, with loose trailing brushstrokes to suggest the waves.

John Brett's work is tighter and has a highly wrought finish, which can sometimes produce an effect of startling realism, as in his vast canvas *Britannia's Realm*, but at other times resulted in pictures that can appear repetitive and laboured. He made his name in his early twenties with two remarkable landscape paintings, *The Stonebreaker* and the *Val d'Aosta*, which were lavishly praised by John Ruskin. During the 1860s he moved away from landscape subjects and concentrated on coastal scenes and lonely seascapes. He used to take his family off to Cornwall or Pembrokeshire and spend the summer months painting meticulous studies of rocky shores. Later he purchased a large schooner and went cruising to the Channel Islands and around the coast of

Britain. Beatrix Potter met him in his house in Putney and noted in her journal, 'He goes sailing around the West Coast of Scotland in his sailing yacht in the summer, making small oil sketches which he uses for the colour in his pictures which he paints in the winter months, chiefly from memory, though also assisted by photographs, for he is a successful photographer.' Although Brett's paintings, and particularly his small oil sketches, frequently appear in the sale rooms, his watercolours are comparatively rare. They tend to be bright in colour and highly finished in the style of the Pre-Raphaelite artists whose work he emulated in his early years.

Of the many other artists who were painting watercolours of ships and seascapes in late-Victorian Britain, there is one who should receive a mention here. Charles Napier Hemy was born and brought up in Newcastle-upon-Tyne and spent some years at sea on a merchant brig before settling in London. Like Brett and Moore, he was much influenced by the Pre-Raphaelites as a young man. The first painting

HENRY MOORE
Hastings Beach

In the 1850s Henry Moore turned his attention from landscapes to seascapes and concentrated on oil paintings dominated by large expanses of sea and sky. He also made a great number of on-the-spot studies in watercolour of waves breaking on beaches.

Watercolour. Signed and dated 1876. Royal Exchange Art Gallery, London.

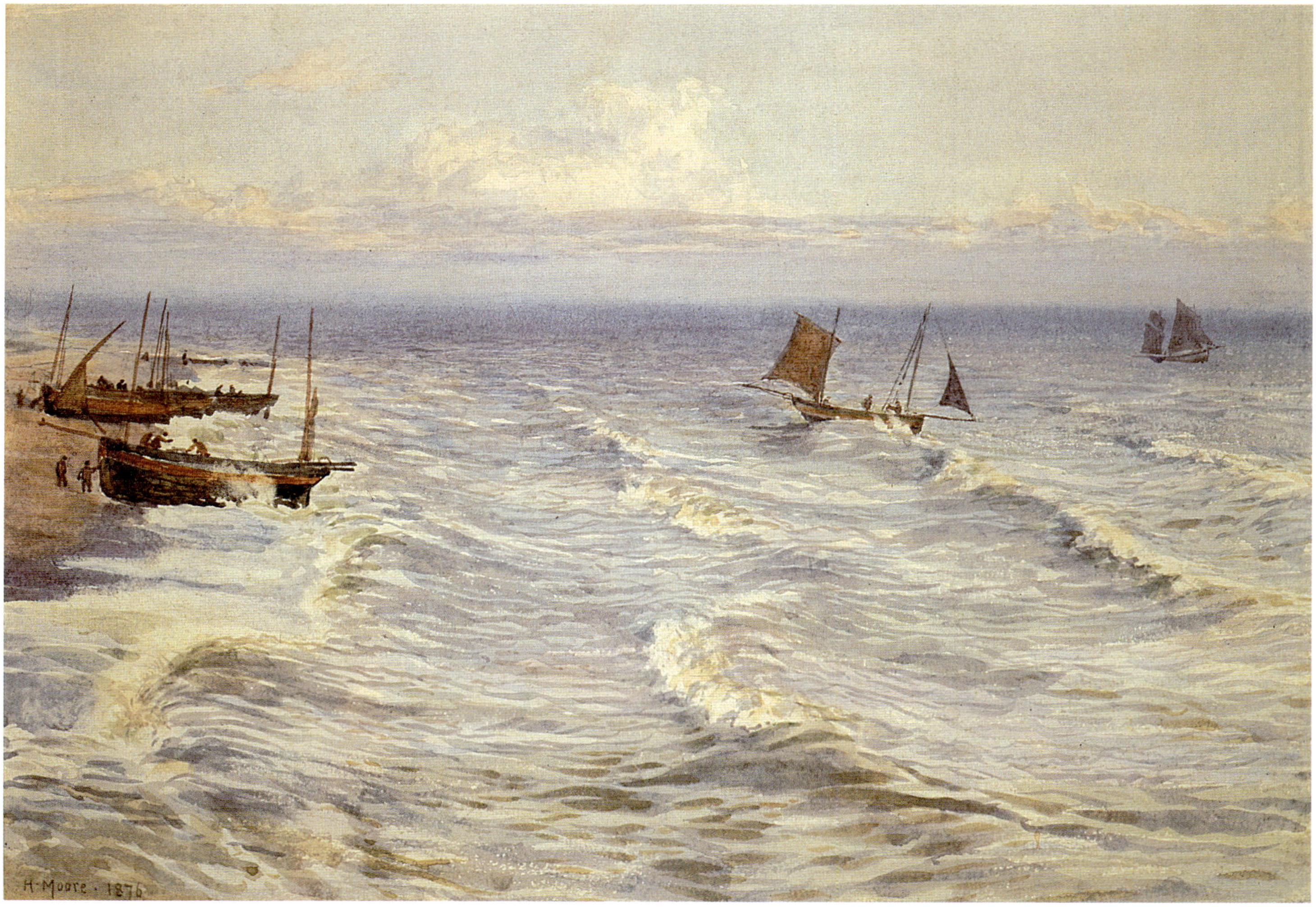

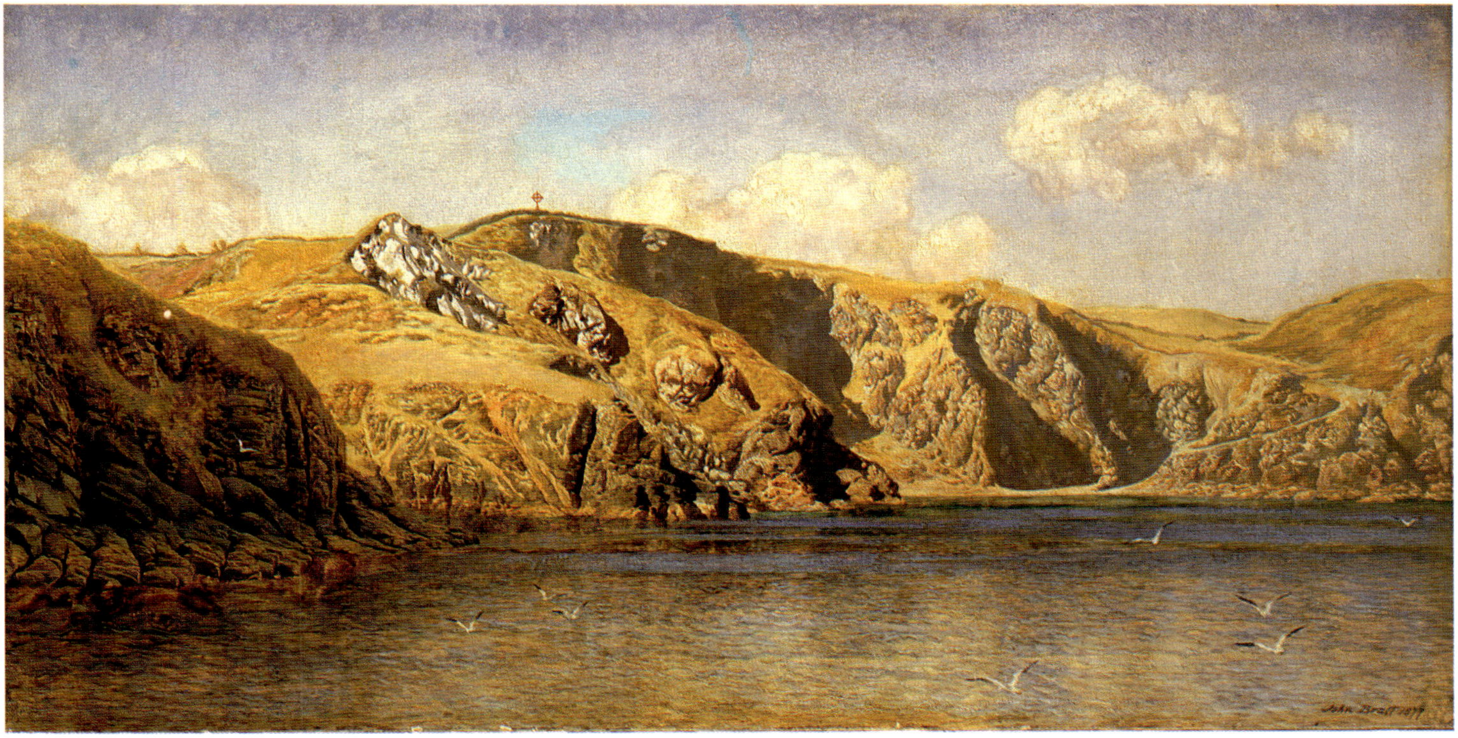

JOHN BRETT
A quiet cove at Cadgwith, near the Lizard in Cornwall

The coast of Cornwall was one of Brett's favourite sketching grounds. He made numerous oil sketches, watercolours and sketchbook studies of harbours and beaches during the summer months and then returned to his studio in London to work up his sketches into large and highly finished oil paintings.

Oil on canvas. Signed and dated 1877. Private collection.

Hemy showed at the Royal Academy in 1865, entitled *Among the shingle at Clovelly,* is an astonishing picture of a section of the beach with every pebble and flint minutely rendered. Over the years his style loosened up, and by the 1880s he was painting watercolours and oil paintings with an impressive assurance and freedom [see page 62]. In 1881 he moved to Falmouth, where he stayed for the rest of his life and had a boat fitted out as a floating studio.

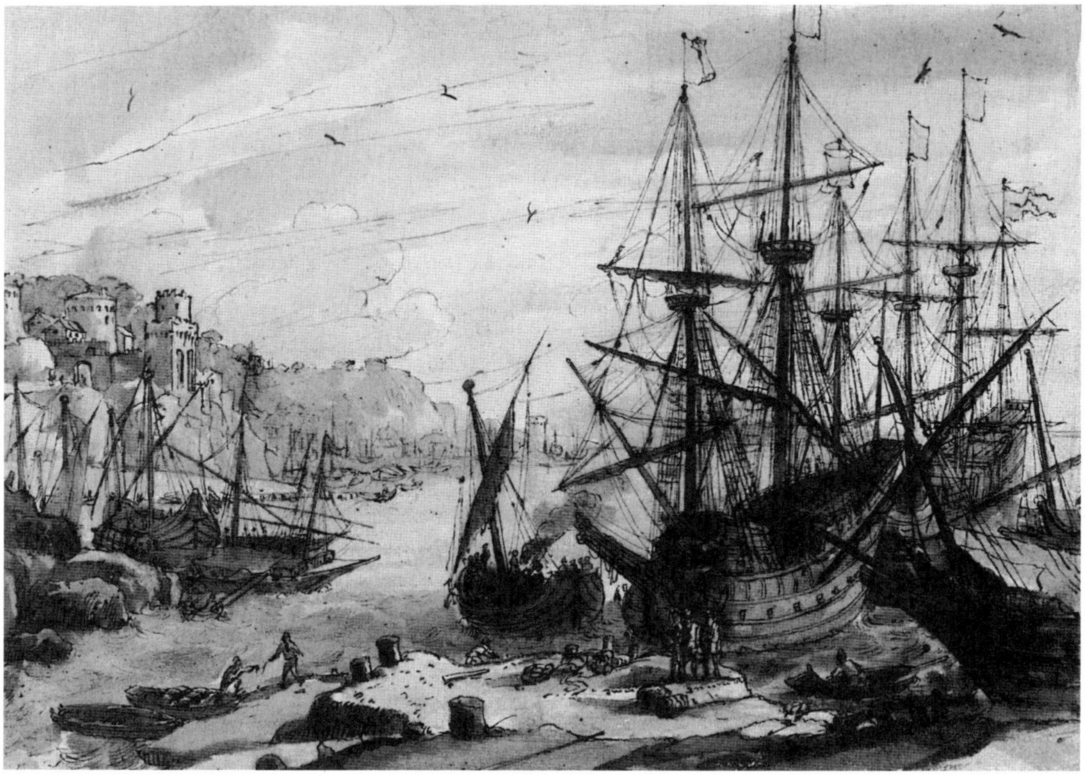

CLAUDE LORRAIN
Harbour scene

Claude's drawing is loosely based on a painting of a harbour scene by Paul Bril, the Flemish artist who was working in Rome many years before Claude arrived in the city. The drawing is a forerunner of the famous series of seaport pictures which Claude began painting in the 1630s.

Pen and grey wash. Plate 30 from *Liber Veritas*. The British Museum. London.

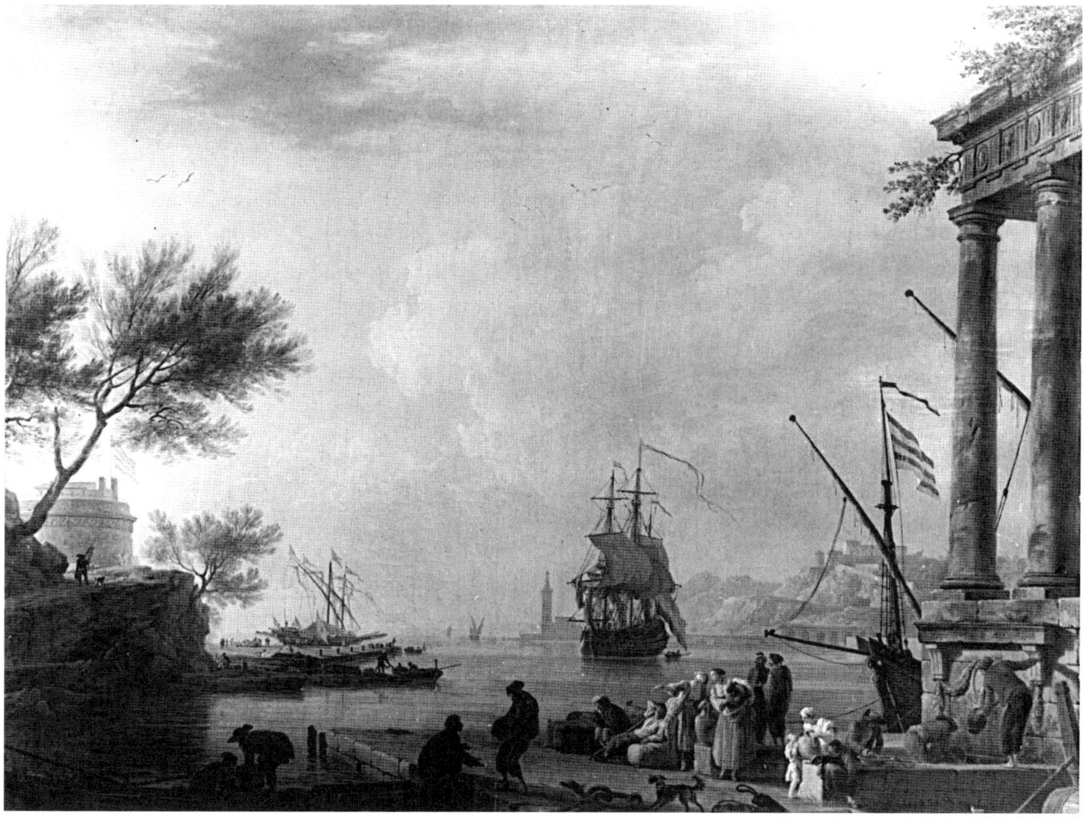

CLAUDE-JOSEPH VERNET
Seaport at sunrise

Vernet was the most celebrated marine artist of his day. He made his reputation with elegant harbour scenes and dramatic depictions of ships wrecked on stormy shores. His work was bought by English gentlemen on the Grand Tour and became well known through engravings.

Oil on canvas. 1759. Musée Calvet, Avignon.

Chapter eight

France and America

Because the subject of marine painting, drawing and prints is so vast, this books has concentrated on the work of two maritime nations, Britain and the Netherlands. It was the Dutch artists of the 17th century who created a market for seascapes and established the pictorial forms that subsequently inspired hundreds of paintings of ships and beach scenes. The British took over this tradition and, after years of imitating Dutch models, developed an individual style which reached a high point with the seascapes of Turner and the watercolour artists of the Romantic movement. But while Britain and the Netherlands probably produced more specialist marine painters than anywhere else, they did not have the field to themselves. Indeed, many of the greatest painters of the sea came from elsewhere, and particularly from France and America.

A survey of marine art, even one with a focus on watercolours and prints such as this, would be incomplete without a mention of Claude-Joseph Vernet, Eugène Boudin, Claude Monet, Winslow Homer and a number of other French and American artists who painted images of the sea that were as memorable and as evocative as any we have already looked at. Many of these artists have been the subject of major exhibitions and scholarly books and catalogues, so what follows is intended to do no more than draw attention to some of the names and to put the work of British and Dutch artists into perspective.

The first of a long line of French artists to turn their attention to maritime subjects was Claude Lorrain, who, after some early travels, settled in Rome in 1623. Acknowledged in his own day, and by many since, as the greatest of all landscape painters, he also painted pictures of seaports at sunrise and sunset. These beautiful dreamlike visions of Mediterranean harbours filled with classical buildings and elegant ships were imaginary settings for stories such as the embarkation of St Ursula. Claude made some lovely pen and ink sketches of shipping as studies for these pictures, but it was his ability to fill his seaport paintings with a golden sunlight that most impressed Turner and his fellow artists. Prints of his pictures ensured that his fame spread far beyond Rome, where he spent most of his working life.

One hundred years later Claude-Joseph Vernet established a name for himself as the leading marine painter in Europe and, as with Claude, his reputation was increased by prints made after his work. The British publisher Boydell remarked that 'In the course of one year I imported numerous impressions of Vernet's celebrated *Storm*, so admirably engraved by Lerpiniere.' Vernet painted a famous set of paintings of the principal ports of France, as well as a variety of coastal scenes which were entirely fanciful and were intended to illustrate themes such as the times of day. Morning would be represented by a harbour scene with the sun rising above a lighthouse; a shipwreck on a rocky shore would represent midday. Evening might be a sunset on a wooded stretch of coast, and night might take the form of fishermen gathered around a fire on the water's edge.

Vernet was followed by a number of specialist marine artists who recorded the naval wars of the Revolutionary and Napoleonic era. The first of these was Pierre Ozanne of Brest, who spent some years as draughtsman to the French navy. His pen and ink drawings are vigorous and assured, and he also produced a large body of prints, notably a set of 60 engravings of different types of vessel entitled *Vaisseaux et Autres Batiments de Mer.*

The other recorders of French ships were the numerous members of the Roux family of Marseille. The most successful member of the dynasty was Ange-Joseph Antoine Roux, usually known as Antoine Roux (*père*). He painted naval actions and

FACING PAGE
FRANÇOIS GEOFFROI ROUX
A Mediterranean tartan *and other vessels in a strong breeze offshore*

François was the youngest of Antoine Roux's sons and, like his father and two brothers, he devoted his life to painting ship portraits. In 1876, when he was in his sixties, he was appointed *Peintre Officiel de la Marine.* His pictures tend to be more realistic and less stylized than those of his father, although he usually kept to the traditional formula of painting broadside views of his ships.

Pencil, pen, brown ink and water-colour. Signed and dated 1879. Private collection.

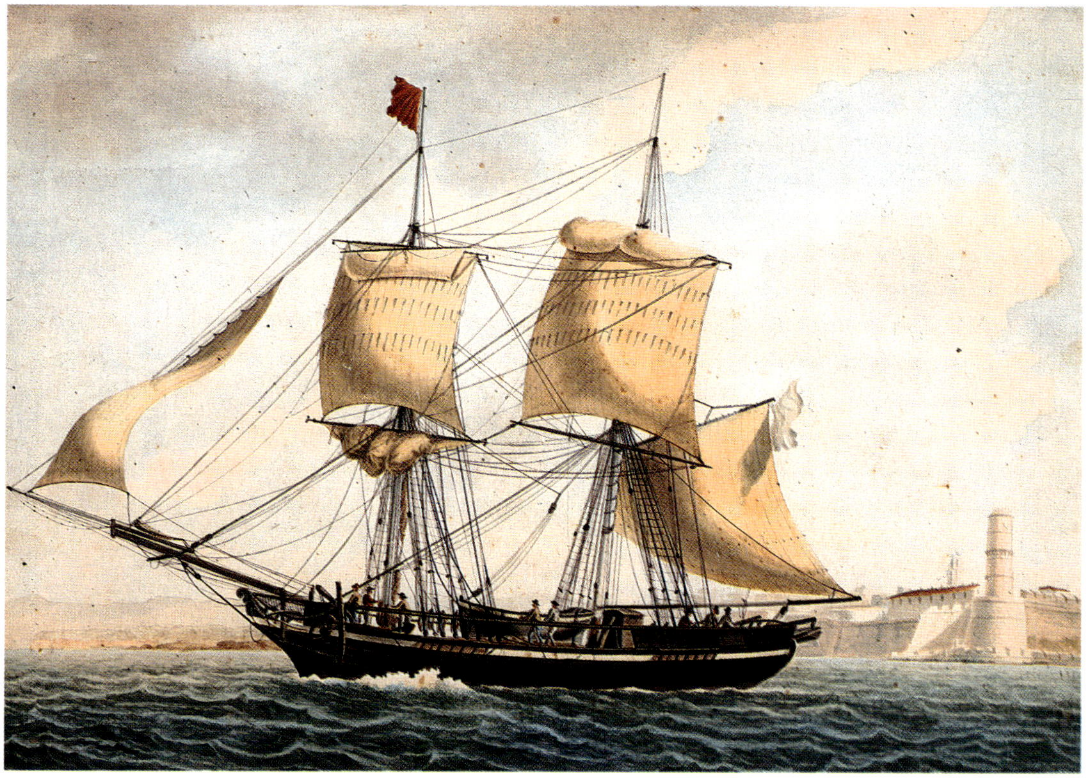

ANGE-JOSEPH ANTOINE ROUX
L'Aventurier

This is a characteristic ship portrait by the most admired member of the Roux family of artists. Although his work is curiously stylized, Antoine Roux painted his ships and their crews with such loving attention to detail that each picture repays the most careful study.

Pencil, pen, black ink, watercolour and bodycolour. Inscribed as title and dated 1816. Private collection.

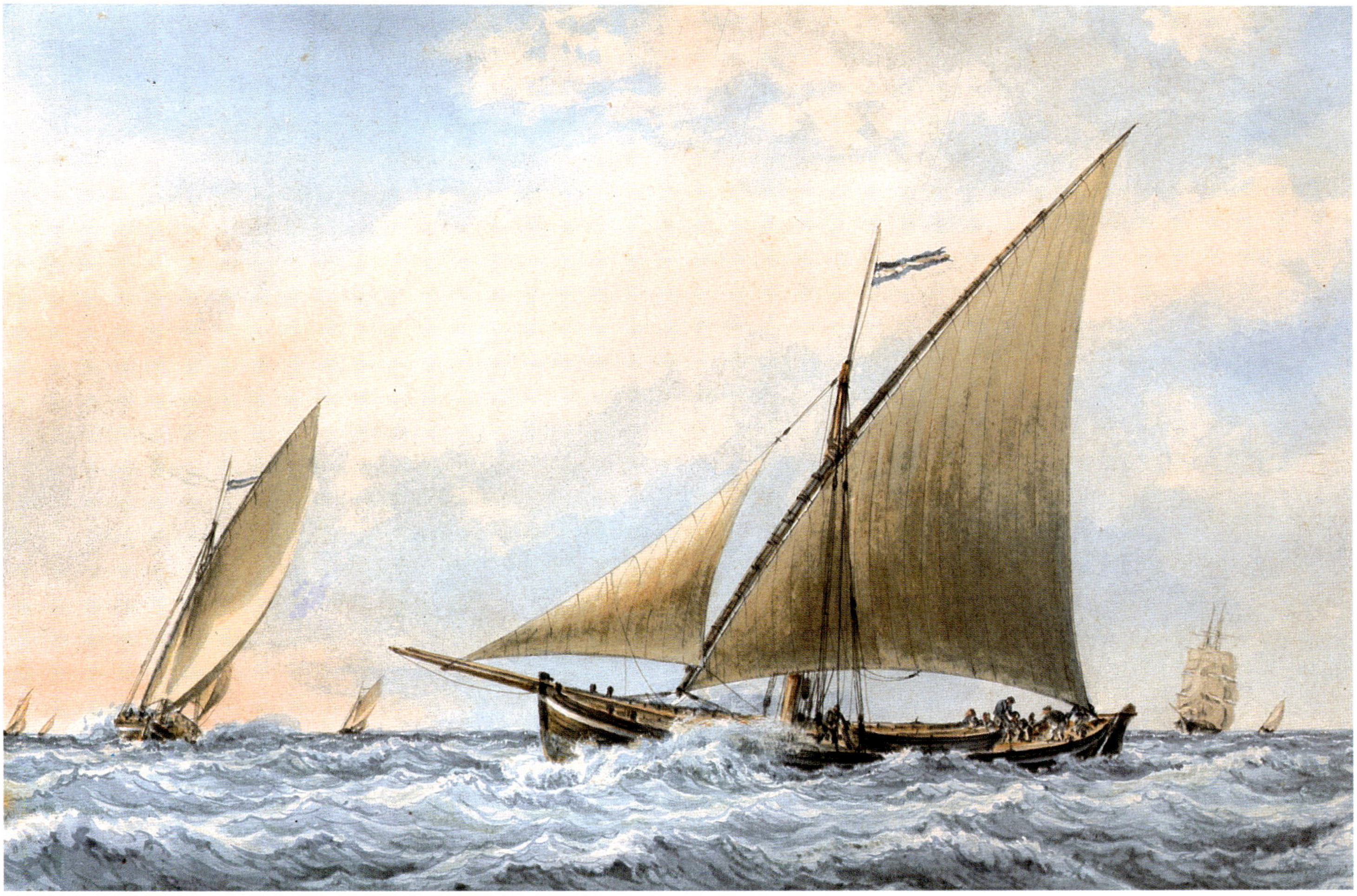

ship portraits and mostly worked in watercolours. His three sons were his pupils and also worked extensively in watercolours. The eldest son was Mathieu-Antoine Roux, also known as Antoine Roux (*fils*); the second was François Joseph Frederic Roux, usually called Frederic Roux; and the youngest was François Geoffroi Roux, usually called François Roux. Their ship portraits are exquisitely drawn and observed. There are large numbers of Roux drawings in America, where they are rightly prized for their quality.

Very different from the meticulous work of the Roux family were the dashing painterly seascapes of Daubigny, Isabey and Boudin. Charles Daubigny, who was born in Paris, spent much of his early working life making reproductive etchings and wood engravings for commercial publishers. In 1849 he met Corot and, much influenced by his work, took up the painting of landscapes and river scenes. He had a small boat in which he explored the rivers of the Seine and Marne, and which he used as a floating studio, as Monet was to do later. It enabled him to make his

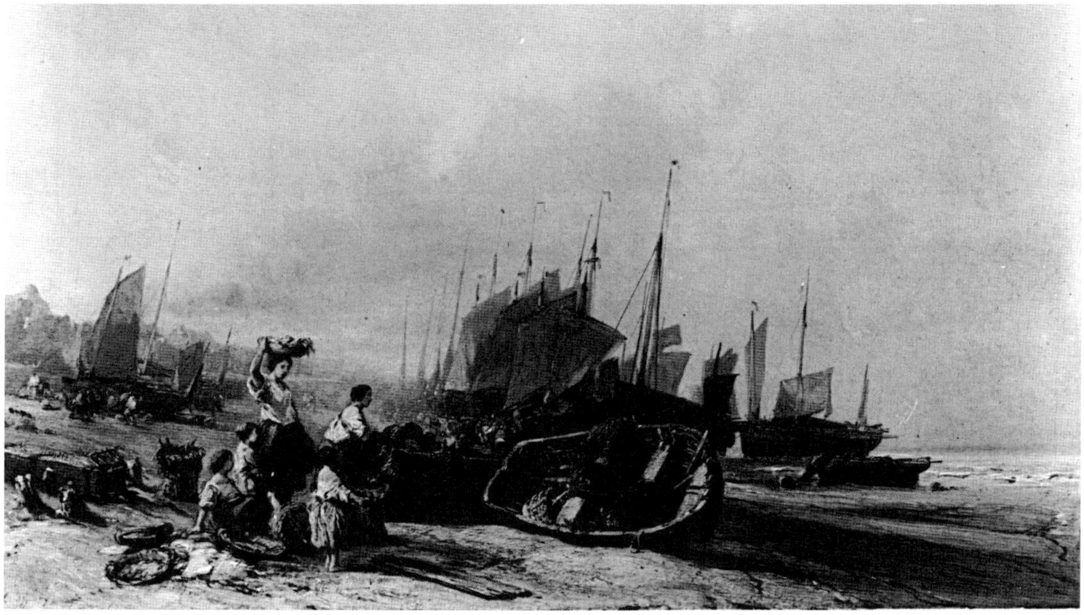

EUGÈNE ISABEY
A beach scene

The sparkling beach scenes of Richard Bonington, who was living in France and painting along the coast of Normandy in the 1820s, evidently inspired this picture. His work was much admired by Isabey and other French artists. Isabey also painted sea battles and shipwrecks and ended his days as a *Chevalier* of the *Légion d'Honeur.*

Oil on canvas. Wallace Collection, London.

preliminary sketches and to complete his paintings in the open air. Visits to London in 1854 and 1865 resulted in a marvellous series of Thames views. Eugène Isabey was another Parisien who took up marine painting and made a successful living from it. With other artists of the Romantic movement, he shared a taste for pictures of storm-swept beaches, shipwrecks and sea battles, which he painted with dramatic realism.

Even the smallest paintings of Eugène Boudin now command impressive prices and it is not hard to see why. He chose attractive subjects and painted them with dash and a sense of atmosphere that has rarely been equalled. The son of a ship's captain, he was born in the port of Honfleur. In 1835 his family moved to Le Havre, where he set up as a picture-framer and seller of stationery. Artists on sketching expeditions used to visit him and persuaded him to take up painting professionally. After a slow start, he found a ready market for his sparkling views of fashionable crowds on the beaches of Trouville and began to travel widely in search of subjects. Like Daubigny, he believed in working as much as possible in the open air and once wrote, 'Everything painted directly and on the spot always has a strength, vigour and vivacity of touch that can never be attained in the studio'.

Claude Monet, who met Boudin in Le Havre, adopted a similar approach and spent much of his time painting in the ports and on the beaches of northern France. Vilified for the harbour scene *Impression: sunrise,* which gave its name to the Impressionist movement, he is now one of the most revered and popular figures in the history of art. Monet endlessly studied the effect of light over water at different times of the day, and the movement of waves on beaches. His pictures of the cliffs of

FACING PAGE
CLAUDE MONET
La Pointe de la Heve, Saint-Advice
This single example of a glittering beach scene by Monet serves as a reminder of his ability to capture the special quality of the light associated with the seaside. Although he is generally regarded as a landscape artist, a large part of his work was devoted to seascapes, harbour views, and river scenes with shipping.

Oil on canvas. Signed and dated '04. Thomas Agnew and Sons, London.

EUGÈNE BOUDIN
Bretagne: Rivière du Faou

Most of Boudin's watercolours are rapidly executed sketches. Like the seascape studies of Whistler and Wilson Steer, they are painted with a dash and freedom that still manages to capture the essential atmosphere of a place and the mood of the weather.

Watercolour. Signed with initials. Thomas Agnew and Sons, London.

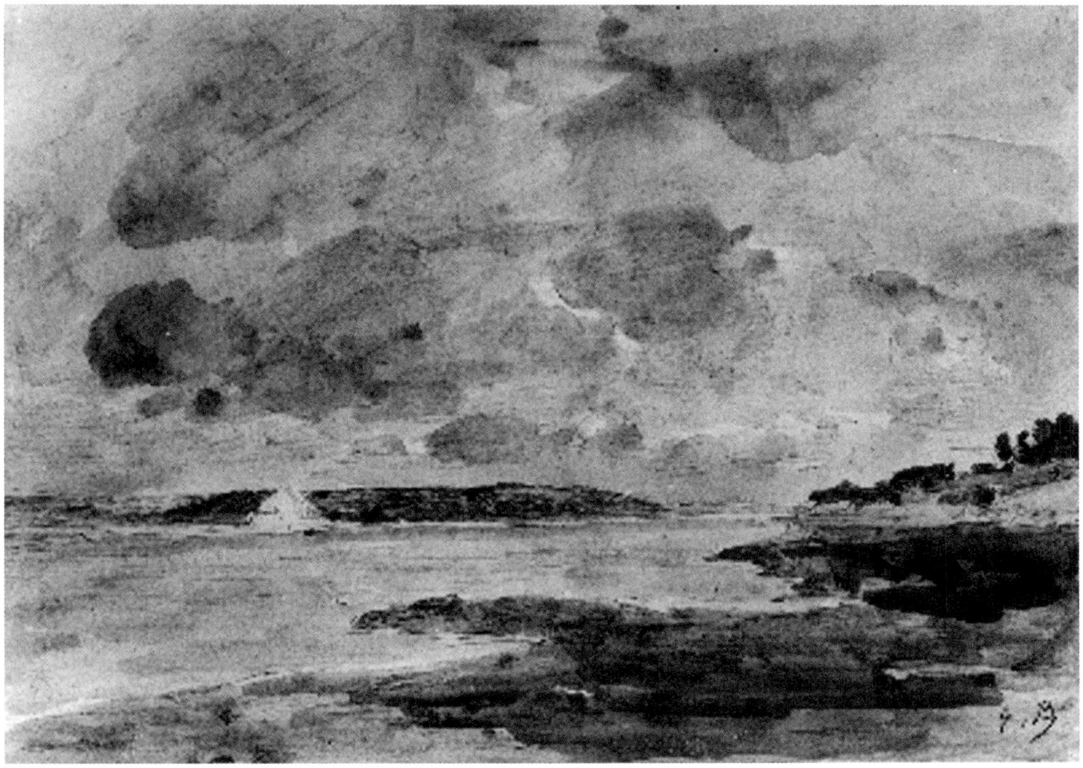

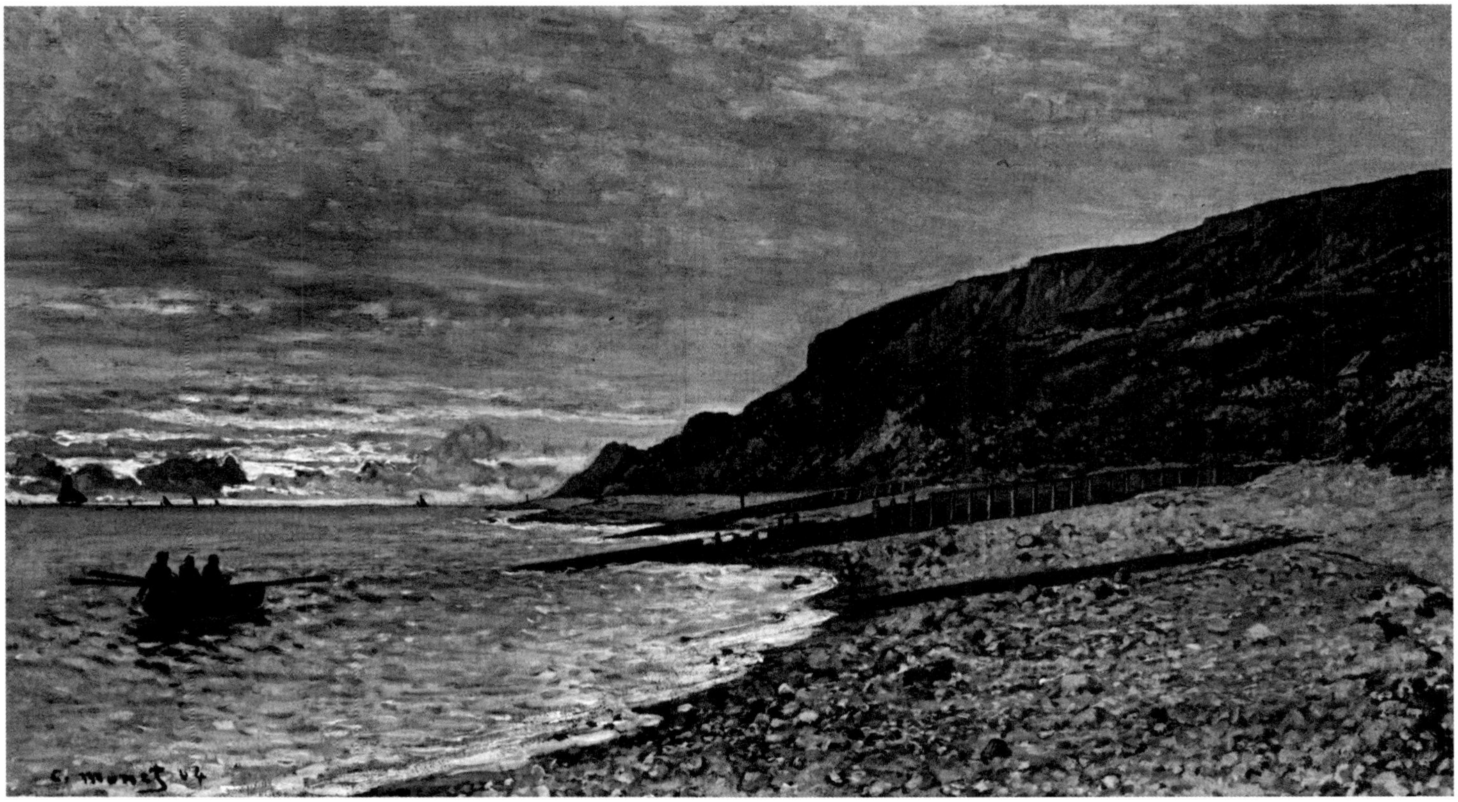

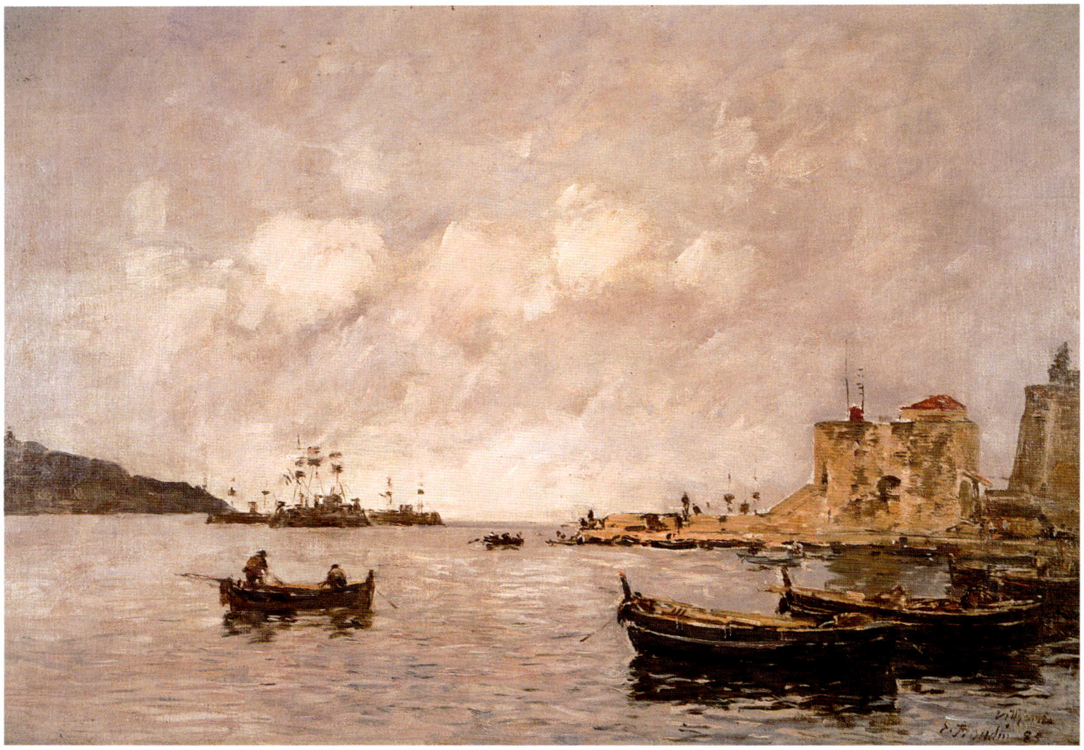

EUGÈNE BOUDIN
Villefranche

The son of a steamboat captain, Boudin served as a ship's boy for a while but then went to work in stationer's shop. His talent as a painter was recognized by visiting artists and he was encouraged to take up painting full-time. His pictures have a freshness and spontaneity that is partly due to his practice of working in the open-air.

Oil on canvas. Signed and dated '85. Thomas Agnew and Sons, London.

Etretat, the shipping at Honfleur, and the yachts and small boats on the Seine at Argenteuil are among the most beautiful of their kind.

And what of American marine painting? Apart from the work of a few 20th-century artists such as Jackson Pollock and Andy Warhol, the art of America has made little impact on Europe, while American marine artists are almost unknown outside the United States. And yet anyone who has stood in front of the astonishing painting *Storm over Narragansett Bay* by Martin Johnson Heade, or has walked through a gallery of drawings and paintings by Winslow Homer and Thomas Eakins, will be aware that America has produced some major artists who have made a significant and original contribution to the paintings of landscapes and seascapes.

Since the first American settlers came from Europe and were for many years dependent on Europe for a range of imported materials, it is not surprising to find that the earliest examples of marine art were painted by emigrants from Britain. The first of these were Thomas Birch, Robert Salmon and James Buttersworth. Birch's father was an engraver and painter of enamels who left England in 1794 and settled in Philadelphia when Thomas was 15. After some years helping his father in the production of engravings of views of Philadelphia and the surrounding area, he set himself up as a portrait painter. Inspired by paintings by Ruisdael and Van Goyen in his father's collection, he moved from portraiture to landscapes and then to pictures of

JAMES BUTTERSWORTH
The steam and sail ship Western Metropolis

Buttersworth was brought up in London but emigated to America with his wife and four children in about 1847. For the next 40 years he devoted himself to recording every type of vessel to be found in the vicinity of New York. His pictures are remarkable for their meticulously drawn ships and dramatic skies.

Oil on canvas. South Street Seaport Museum, New York.

sea battles, storms and shipwrecks.

The British artist Robert Salmon arrived in Boston in 1828 and established himself in a studio at the end of Marine Railway Wharf, overlooking the harbour. He had already painted many marine subjects in Liverpool and Scotland and had exhibited at the Royal Academy. He found a ready market for his ship portraits and harbour views, which are attractive but curiously stylized. His finest paintings, like his tranquil view of *Boston Harbor from Constitution Wharf* have a timeless quality about them, summed up by the *Boston Daily Advertiser*, which noted that 'his views are always correct, seeming like the present reality of the thing represented.'

The same could be said of the prolific output of James Buttersworth, who arrived in America between 1845 and 1848. He settled in Manhattan and during a long working life produced several hundred paintings and drawings of warships, tea clippers and a variety of steam ships, as well as some exhilarating views of yacht races.

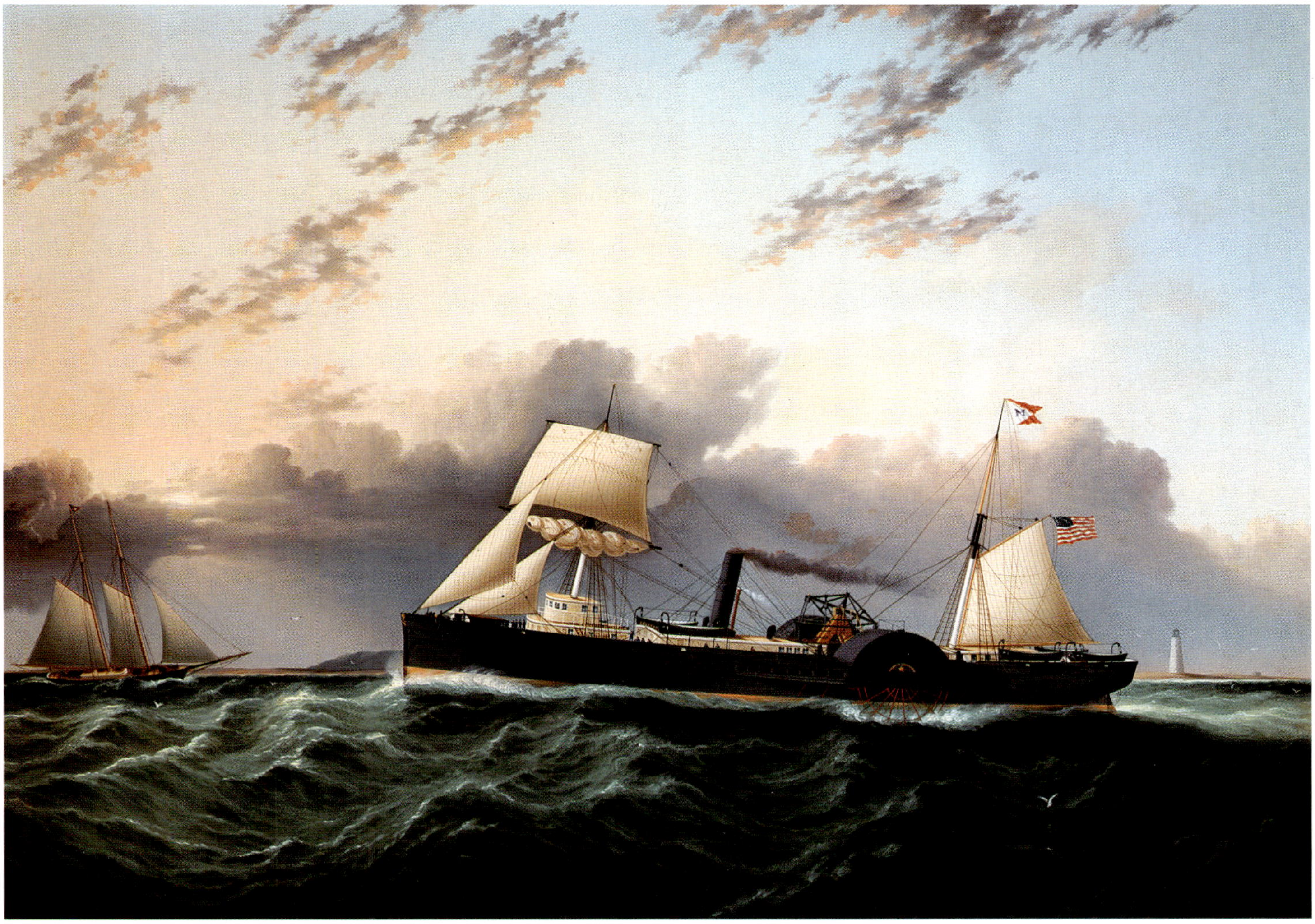

He shared with Robert Salmon an ability to draw shipping with masterly assurance and he, too, developed a distinctive style which is easily recognizable.

Thomas Cole was born in Lancashire and emigrated to America in 1825 when he was 18 years old. In spite of his British roots and the fact that he spent some years studying the Old Masters in France and Italy, he was the first painter in America to create a style which grew out of the New World rather than the Old. He associated with a group of writers, poets and artists who saw America and her vast landscape as a new Eden and the proper source of inspiration for artists. Cole's friend Asher B. Durand wrote, 'Go not abroad then in search of material for the exercise of your pencil, while the virgin charms of our native land have claims on your deepest affections.' Cole proceeded to paint a series of remarkable visionary paintings, some based on views of the mountains and valleys he knew, and others created from his imagination. Among these was a set of four pictures called *The Voyage of Life*, which depicted the ages of man and showed a boat travelling on a river towards the sea.

In 1844 Cole took on Frederick Church as a pupil. Church, who came from Hartford, Connecticut and was the son of a businessman, proved to have formidable gifts as a painter of landscapes, coastal views and seascapes. He travelled extensively in North and South America making studies for future paintings. On his return to New York he embarked on a series of large canvases which attracted popular acclaim. When he exhibited his painting *Niagara Falls* in a commercial gallery in New York,

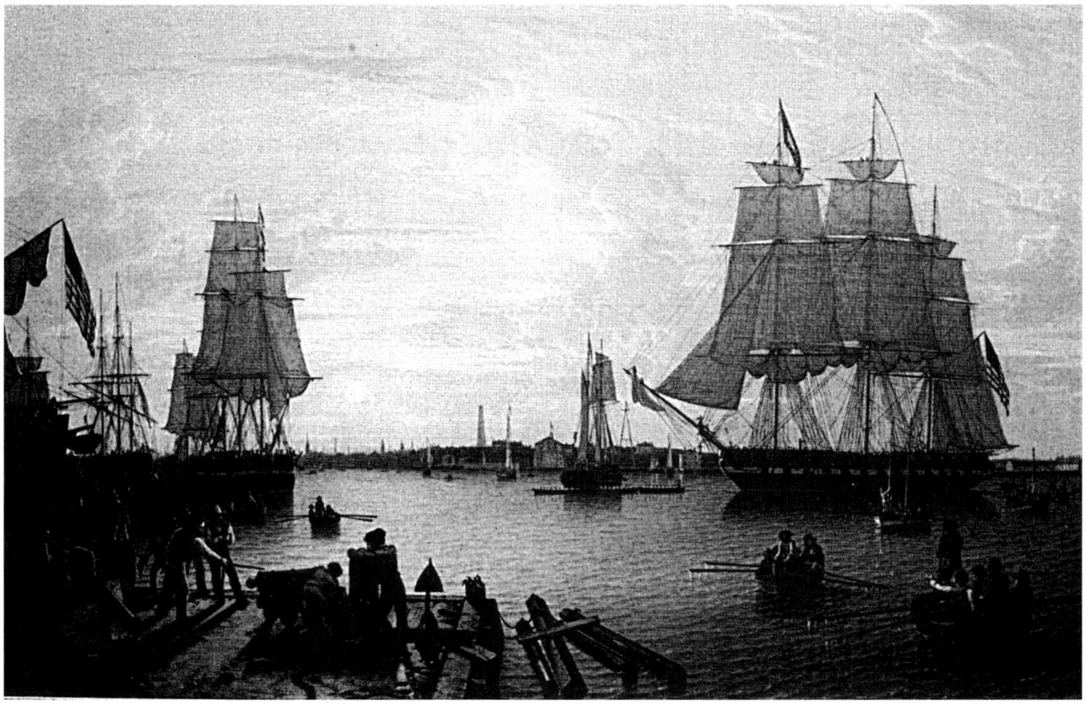

ROBERT SALMON
Boston harbour from Constitution Wharf

Salmon lived in Boston for some 14 years and had a studio overlooking the harbour. He frequently filled his tranquil scenes with a golden light reminiscent of the seaport paintings of Claude Lorrain. He was fond of portraying all the details of life on the water-front and his paintings have a stylized and slightly naive quality which is most attractive.

Oil on canvas. *c* 1829. United States Naval Academy Museum, Annapolis, Maryland.

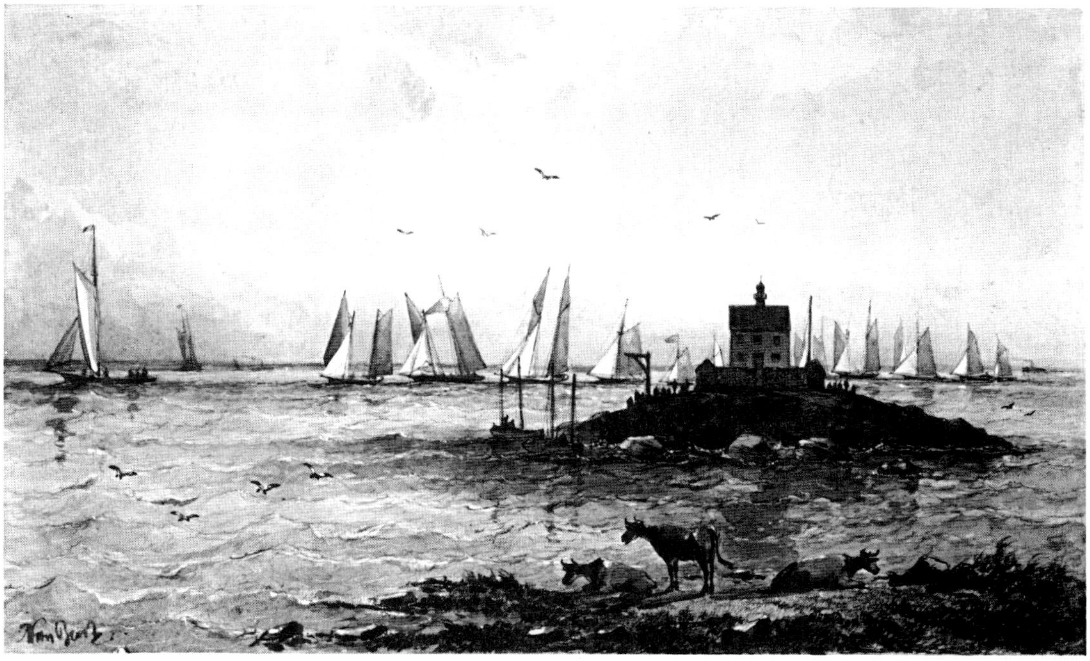

ALBERT VAN BEEST
Lighthouse

Van Beest was a Dutch marine artist who emigrated to America around 1845 and settled in Fairhaven where he painted local views along the waterfront.

Pencil and watercolour. 1850's. Signed. M. and M. Karolik Collection, courtesy Museum of Fine Arts, Boston.

huge crowds came to see it, and more than 1,100 people signed a subscription list for an engraving of the picture. It was hailed by the critics as 'perhaps the finest picture yet done by an American; at least that which is fullest of feeling' and was subsequently sent for exhibition in London and Paris, where it was greeted with similar enthusiasm. It captured the grandeur and immensity of a new nation on a vast continent.

Martin Johnson Heade, who had been encouraged to study art by his father, who was a farmer, met Church when he moved to New York in 1859 and they became lifelong friends. Unhappily, Heade never enjoyed the same public acclaim. When his masterpiece, *Storm over Narrangansett Bay,* was exhibited at the National Academy in New York in 1869, one critic condemned the 'hardness of colour and execution' and went on, 'It is to be regretted that so hard and chilling a painting as this should have been allowed to leave his studio.' Heade was so discouraged that he abandoned marine subjects and took to painting pictures of marshy landscapes. Like many other American painters of landscapes and seascapes, he travelled to Europe to study Old Masters, but on his return he pioneered a style of brooding landscapes and seascapes that show an entirely original vision.

Unlike Cole, Church and Heade, who were gifted landscape artists who also painted occasional marine subjects, Fitz Hugh Lane was a dedicated marine painter. He was born in the fishing port of Gloucester on the coast of Massachusetts, trained as a printmaker and much of his early life was spent making lithographs of topo-

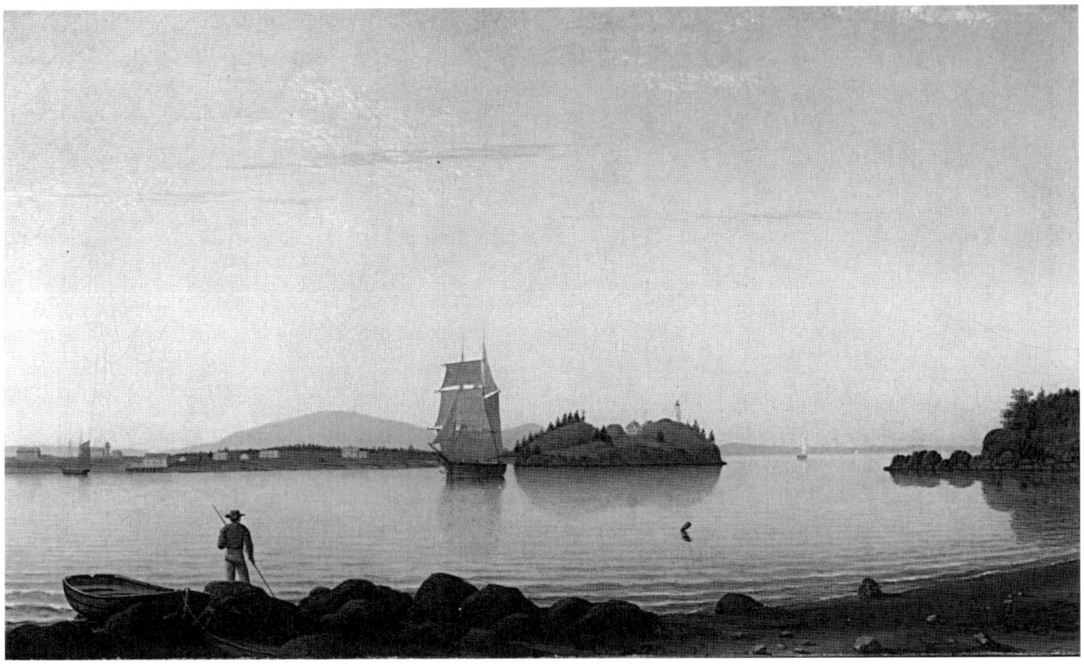

FITZ HUGH LANE
Owl's Head, Penobscot Bay, Maine

The finest paintings by this gifted artist have an extraordinary quality of stillness and calm.

Oil on canvas. 1862. Bequest of Martha C. Karolik Collection of American Paintings, Courtesy, Museum of Fine Arts, Boston.

graphical views. He took up painting in the 1840s and, since many of his pictures were painted in the vicinity of Boston, it was inevitable that his early work should be inspired by the paintings of Robert Salmon. The quality of his work was soon recognized and he was able to abandon print-making and concentrate on painting. He sailed up and down the East Coast seeking out subjects in the numerous ports and inlets. His beautifully composed and peaceful scenes of ships drifting in light airs have a luminous quality and a clarity of light that is reminiscent of the paintings of Van de Cappelle.

Two lesser but nevertheless interesting marine artists are Albert Van Beest and William Bradford who sometimes worked together and collaborated on the same picture. Van Beest emigrated to America from Holland around 1845 and settled in Fairhaven near New Bedford. There he met William Bradford who was a local resident and became his pupil. Both artists worked on oils and watercolours and painted ship portraits and local views with shipping.

The next generation produced three American artists of real stature: Whistler, Winslow Homer and Eakins. James McNeill Whistler had an unusually cosmopolitan upbringing. He was born in Lowell, Massachusetts, lived in Russia as a child, spent three years at West Point military academy and then went to Paris to train as an artist. In 1859 at the age of 25 he moved to London and took a house in Chelsea overlooking the Thames. He subsequently made many trips abroad but England remained his home for the rest of his life. Most of his work, including his

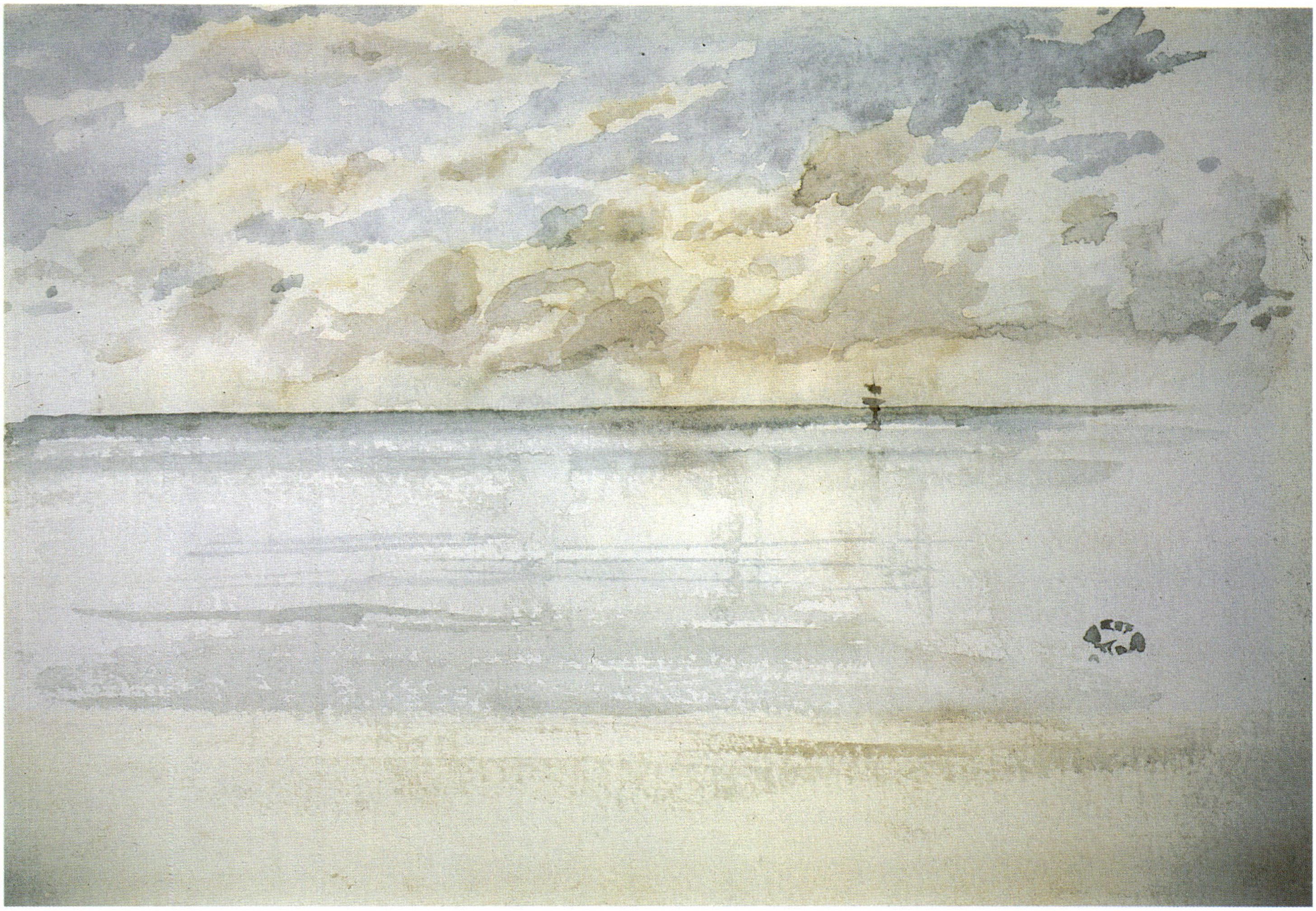

JAMES MCNEILL WHISTLER
Seascape

This is a watercolour version of the brilliant oil sketches that Whistler made of beach scenes and seascapes at Trouville in France and later at St Ives in Cornwall. He makes it look easy, but anyone who has attempted a similar seascape in watercolour will know that such an apparently slight sketch is the result of years of observation.

Watercolour. Signed with the artist's butterfly monogram. Thomas Agnew and Sons, London.

famous Nocturnes, his beach scenes and his seascapes with titles like *Grey and green: the silver sea*, were painted in oils and therefore fall outside the scope of this book, but he also painted some atmospheric beach scenes in watercolour and made a major contribution to the art of the etching. The latter included a series of 16 etchings known as *The Thames Set*, which depicted the moored barges and tumbledown buildings along the waterfront. They were exhibited at the Royal Academy in 1860 and are now regarded as masterpieces of etching. Many years later, following the libel action against Ruskin, which bankrupted him, Whistler retreated to Venice where he spent much time on pastel drawings and etchings. When he returned to London, the Fine Art Society published 12 of the 40 etchings he had carried out, and they became known as *The First Venice Set*.

The artists so far considered carried out their most important and significant work in the medium of oil paint and used drawings mainly as preparatory sketches for their canvases. Winslow Homer, however, was an artist, some would say America's greatest artist, who also worked extensively in watercolour and became one of the undisputed masters of this medium. Homer's life, like that of Turner was entirely devoted to his art. Born in Boston in 1836, he moved to New York in 1859 and spent several years producing illustrations for *Harper's Weekly*. It was on a visit to Gloucester in 1873 that he produced his first watercolours. These were colourful and cheerful studies of small boys sailing off the coast or making ship models on the beach. In 1876 he painted *Breezing up*, which was described by the critic of the *New York Sun* as the 'best sea-piece he had ever contributed to an Academy exhibition. It is painted in his customary coarse and nelige style, but suggests with unmistakable force the life and motion of a breezy summer day off the coast. The fishing boat, bending to the wind, seems actually to cleave the waters. There is not a truer or heartier work in the present exhibition.'

In 1881 Homer paid a visit to England and stayed for a year among the fishermen in Cullercoats, a fishing village near Tynemouth. This resulted in another fine series of watercolours, this time with a more serious subject matter. He had witnessed the local fishermen battling daily with an unforgiving sea, and had watched the lifeboat attempting in vain to rescue seamen from a shipwreck. In dozens of rapid sketches carried out in pencil or charcoal, or in watercolours, he recorded the work of the fishermen and the anxious wives who waited on the beaches for the return of the

OPPOSITE
THOMAS EAKINS
Starting out after rail

Two of the artist's friends are shown setting out across the Dela ware River to hunt the wading birds called rail which inhabit the hunting marshes in New Jersey.

Watercolour. 1874.
The Roland P. Murdock Collection, Whichita Art Museum, Wichita, Kansas.

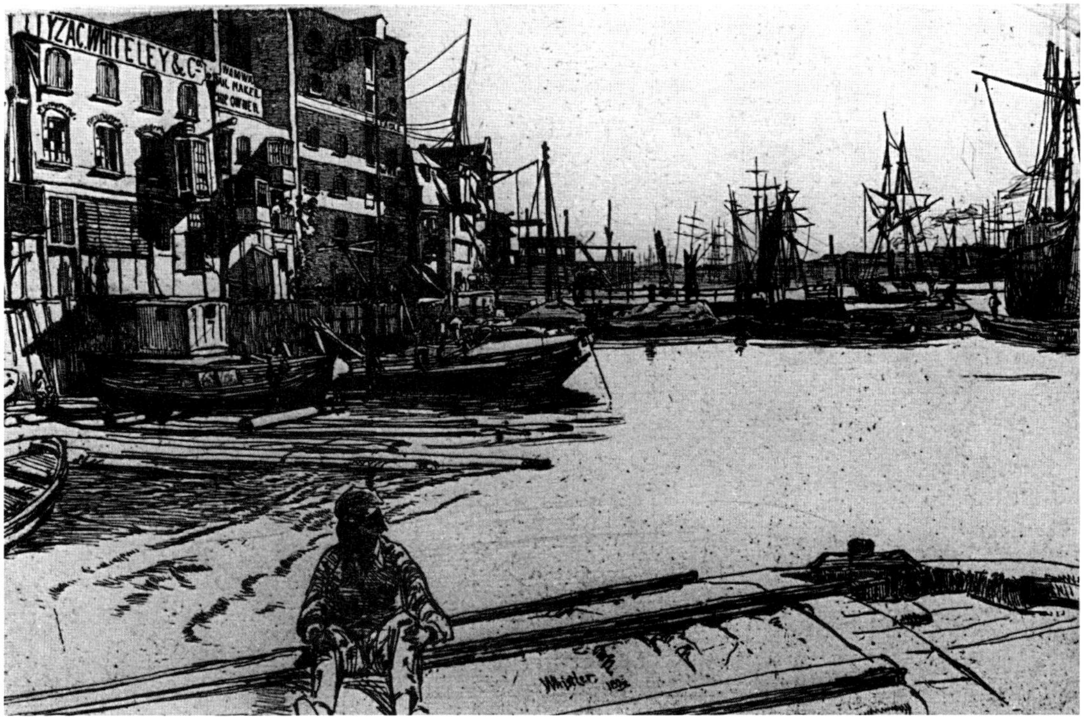

JAMES MCNEILL WHISTLER
Eagle Wharf

This is one of the 16 etchings known as *The Thames Set* which depict the barges, the merchant ships and the warehouses lining the banks of the river. The contrast between the mass of delicately drawn details of the waterfront buildings and the bold, empty spaces of water and sky reveals the artist's confidence as a draughtsman and printmaker.

Etching. Signed and dated 1859.
Private collection

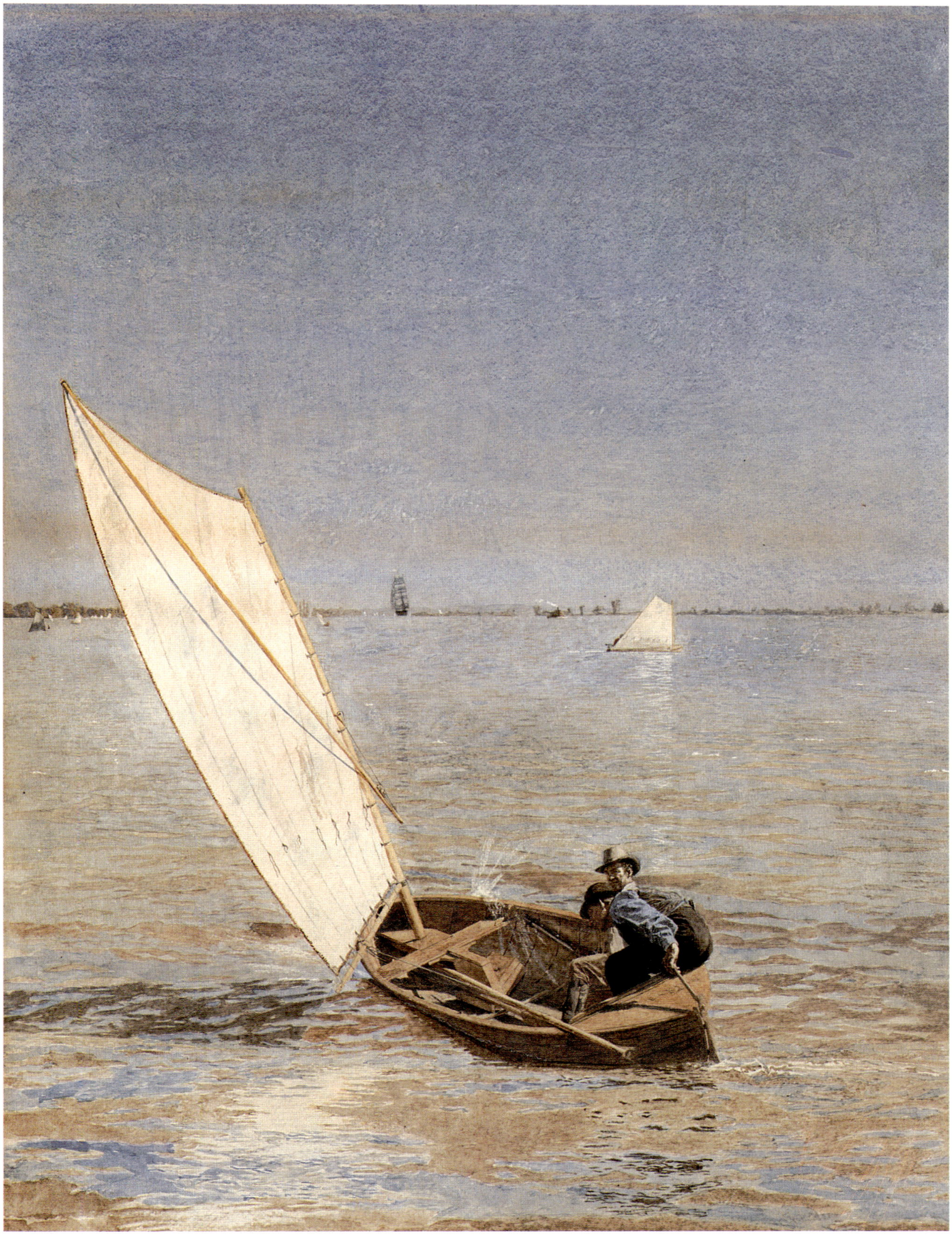

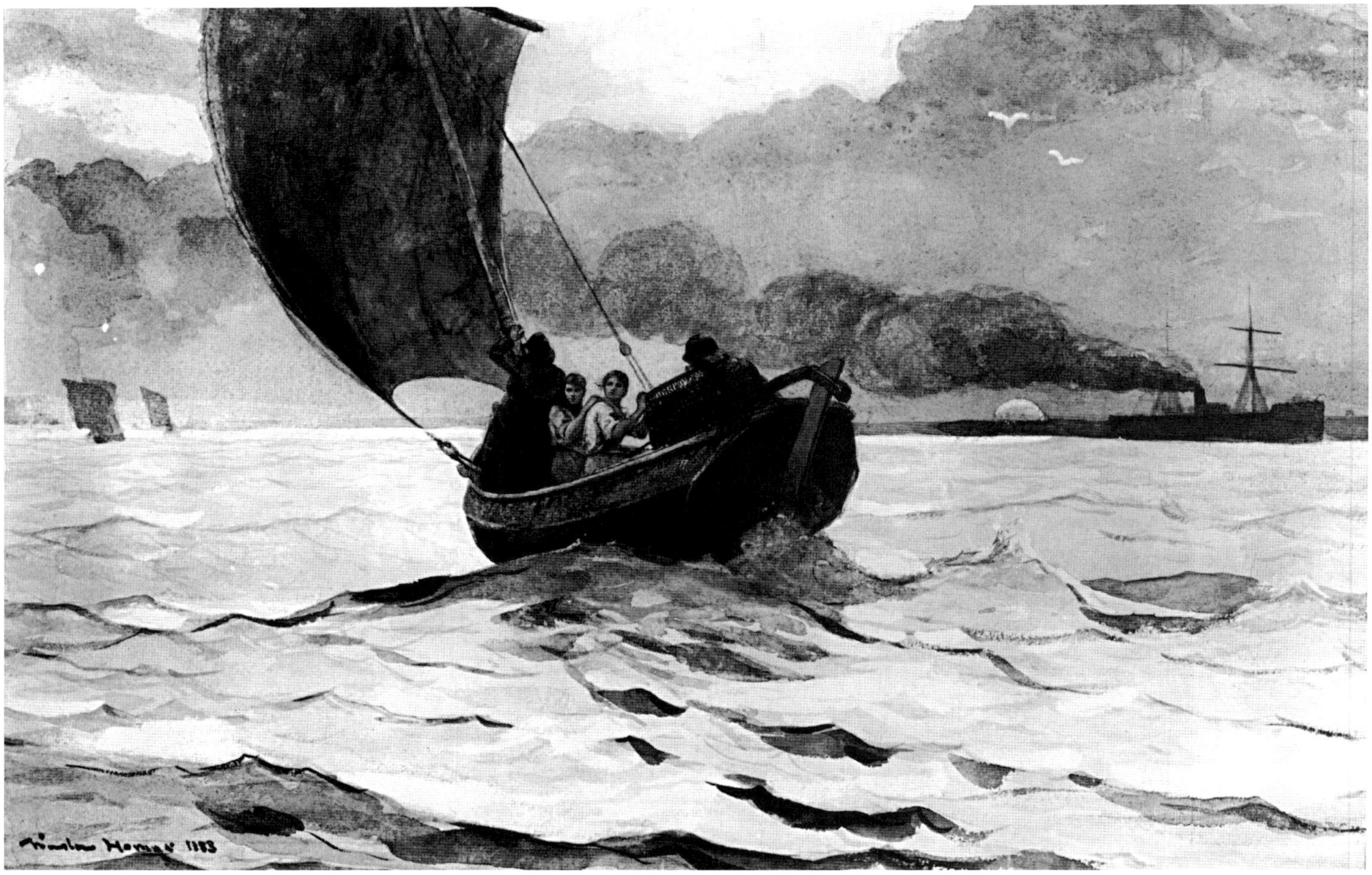

fishing boats. When he returned to America in 1884, he moved north to the isolated community of Prout's Neck in Maine, where he had a house on the cliffs overlooking the sea. His paintings from the 1880s were devoted to powerful pictures of the local fishermen. *The fog warning* is perhaps the most famous of these, but there were also the *Herring net*, *Eight bells* and *Lost on the Grand Banks*.

Thomas Eakins, who has a competing claim to be America's greatest painter, was not a marine painter but did paint maritime subjects. His painting *Starting out after rail* shows two men sailing a cat boat across the wide, lightly rippled surface of the Delaware river towards the hunting grounds in the marshes of New Jersey. Eakins said in one of his lectures to his students, 'I know of no prettier problem in perspective than to draw a yacht sailing.'

It is interesting to compare this painting with *Breezing up*. Homer's painting appears to have been dashed off in an afternoon, while Eakins' is a most carefully considered work, every detail refined and balanced, like a painting by Piero della Francesca. Homer's colours are bright and sunny, while Eakins uses cool blues and

WINSLOW HOMER
Returning fishing boats

In 1881 Homer crossed the Atlantic and spent a year living in the fishing village of Cullercoats on the northeast coast of England. In this picture he shows fishermen and fisherwomen returning to harbour at sunset. They are sailing a coble, the distinctive type of fishing boat used on the Northumberland coast.

Watercolour. Signed and dated 1883. The Fogg Art Museum, Harvard University Art Museums.

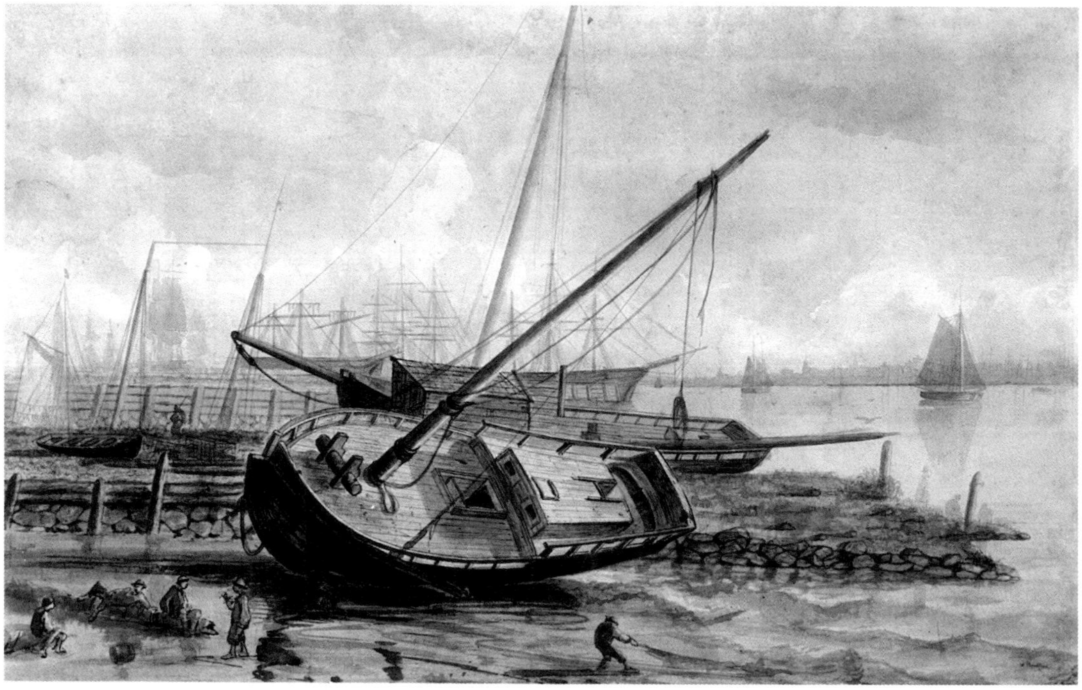

William Bradford
Study of the Fairhaven waterfront

Bradford was born and brought up in the small harbour of Fairhaven near Newport, Rhode Island. He painted ship portraits, coastal views and yacht races, and later in his life he travelled north to Labrador to paint and photograph icebergs.

Pencil and watercolour. 1850s. Museum of Fine Arts, Boston.

soft, subtle browns. Yet both are masterley. Among Eakin's most celebrated paintings is his series of rowing pictures, of which *Max Schmitt in a single scull* is the most famous. It is a subtle and intricate composition with beautifully observed reflections and is an almost perfect picture. Less spectacular but equally accomplished is *John Biglin in a single scull*, which was the final painting in a set of preparatory studies in watercolour. To ensure that he achieved the correct perspective, Eakins first constructed a complex grid of lines and vanishing points which enabled him to give a realistic three-dimensional effect to the picture and an increased sense of recession into the distance.

Twentieth century artists in America have continued the tradition which reached a high point with the work of Winslow Homer and Thomas Eakins. In the realm of watercolour fine examples of marine subjects appear among the work of Childe Hassam. John Marin and Andrew Wyeth. The lithographs of John Noble provide an evocative view of the ships and waterfront of New York. But perhaps the most memorable of all the seascapes produced by American artists in the last fifty or sixty years is Edward Hopper's *Ground Swell* of 1939. This painting which hangs in the Corcoran Gallery, Washington, shows a white yacht, with a group of young people aboard, sailing slowly past a rusty iron buoy. It is hard to think of another painting which so effectively captures the dazzling brilliance of summer sun at sea and the effect of a low swell rolling in from the vast expanse of the ocean.

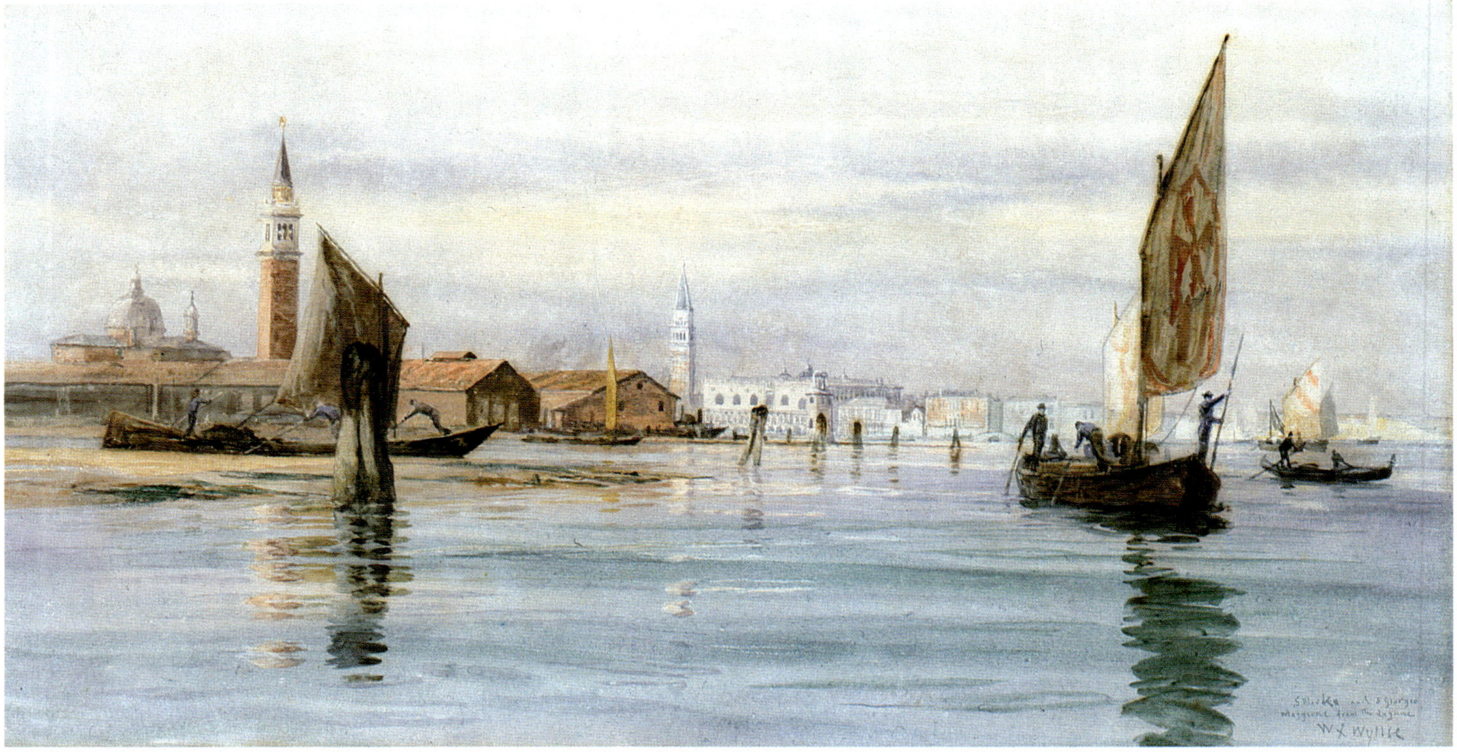

W.L.Wyllie
S. Mark's and S. Giorgio Maggiore from the Lagune

This beautiful watercolour shows Wyllie's ability to paint reflections and to fill a picture with a soft light, which is reflected in the calm surface of the water. The subject is an unusual one for the artist, who mostly painted shipping in the vicinity of Portsmouth and the Thames. He was in Italy in 1890 and exhibited a few watercolours of Venice in the following two years.

Watercolour. Signed. The Tryon and Swann Gallery, London.

Chapter nine

STEAMSHIPS, CLIPPERS AND TWO WORLD WARS

In 1838 Turner exhibited his celebrated painting *The Fighting Temeraire towed to her last berth.* It was a tribute to a ship which had fought at the Battle of Trafalgar but it also acknowleged the end of an era. The dominant feature of the picture is not the warship stripped of her sails, but the steam tug that is towing her to the breaker's yard. By the end of the 19th century, steam power had taken over from sail for passenger ferries, merchant ships and many fishing vessels. Tea clippers with billowing sails still raced across the oceans, but ocean liners now carried hundreds of passengers across the Atlantic, and the wooden warships of Nelson's day were being replaced by iron dreadnoughts. The profound changes in the design, construction and propulsion of ships were inevitably reflected in the paintings and drawings of marine artists. Pictures of the Pool of London or the East River in New York were no longer dominated by the masts of sailing ships, but by the sturdy iron hulls of steamships, with funnels belching forth black smoke.

The artists were also affected by the technical advances that had taken place in print-making and publishing. We have seen how several generations of artists were commissioned to supply drawings and watercolours which were then engraved and published as prints. The invention of photography in the 1840s led in due course to

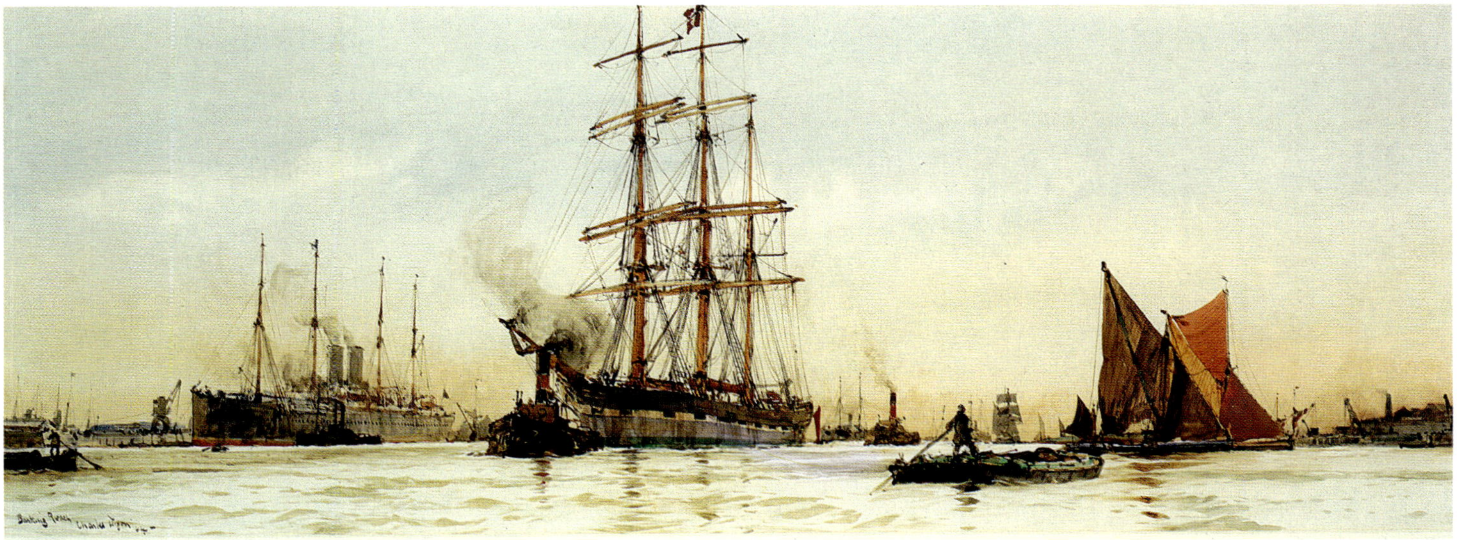

CHARLES DIXON
Barking Reach

Dixon frequently adopted an extended horizontal format for his watercolours. Here it has enabled him to provide a panoramic view of a busy scene on the lower reaches of the Thames around the turn of the 20th century. On either side of the square-rigger under tow can be seen a passenger liner, numerous steam tugs and the distinctive tan sails of two Thames sailing barges.

Watercolour. Signed and dated '04. Royal Exchange Art Gallery, London.

the use of photomechanical methods to reproduce pictures. Publishers no longer needed small armies of engravers laboriously converting pictures into prints. The demanding skills of engraving in aquatint and mezzotint were replaced by the relatively undemanding processes of photolithography and photogravure. It seemed likely that the arts of engraving and etching might likewise languish and die, but just as photography was seen as a useful tool by most artists, rather than a threat, so print-making by traditional methods simply changed direction. Instead of being used to produce an exact representation of a painting or drawing, the print was freed to become a means of self-expression. In the hands of Whistler, and subsequently of Degas, Rodin, Picasso and others, it became another form of art, as it had been for Rembrandt, Goya and Piranesi. In Britain, several marine artists produced prints, particularly etchings, alongside their other work in oil paints and watercolours. Foremost among these were W.L. Wyllie, Arthur Briscoe and Muirhead Bone.

Wyllie is one of the great names in marine art. His finest watercolours can stand comparison with any of the masters of this medium; he was also a highly accomplished printmaker, and although his oil paintings are variable in quality, the sheer range of his work and his ability to portray ships and the sea in all weathers places him in the front rank as a marine painter. His entire life was centred around the water. He came from a family of painters, was brought up by the sea at Boulogne, and from the moment he left the Royal Academy Schools made marine subjects the focus of his work. After his marriage in 1879, he concluded his honeymoon by sailing across the Channel with his wife in a 14-foot dinghy. After a few years in London he moved with his family into a house overlooking the Medway at Rochester in Kent and spent much of his time sailing the Thames and Medway in his yacht *Ladybird*, making drawings. For the last 20 years of his life he lived in a house on the waterfront at the entrance to Portsmouth harbour.

Wyllie exhibited his first painting at the Royal Academy in 1868, when he was 17 years old, and continued to show there regularly until 1931, but much of his early life was taken up with supplying illustrations for the *Graphic*, a magazine set up in competition with the *Illustrated London News*. He produced hundreds of drawings for it in black ink and Chinese white and this provided him with a grounding in monochrome work which he later applied to his print-making. Altogether he produced some 300 etchings and dry points, many of which were published by the Fine Art Society. According to his daughter Aileen, his method was 'to make the study straight from the subject in black paint on very thin paper & then stick the paper reversed on the window in front of him... . His etching tools lived in an old leather glove hung on the wall: a burin, a darning needle in an old paint brush handle, a chipped diamond, a burnisher, a little tin of Globe metal polish to rub into the scratches to get a black image.' Among the many images he produced perhaps the finest are his moody views of the Thames before the days of clean air acts, the surface of the river packed with shipping and murky with fog and smoke.

Wyllie's watercolours show a total command of that notoriously difficult medium. He never resorted to a formula and could convey with the lightest touch every variation from liquid calms to confused and turbulent seas. He set out his approach in a book entitled *Marine Painting in Water-Colour*, published in 1901, but a more vivid glimpse is supplied by his wife:

'With regard to his watercolours, they really were watercolours. He would take his pin board and sheet of paper to a basin or bath, soaking the paper at the back in the water, lay it on a pin board, the frame that fits on the top open, and walk back to his easel followed by a little trickle of water. While the board was still open he laid on the wash for the sky and sea, much darker than it would look when dry, holding the board upright so that the wash should run in the right direction while wet. All his lights, such as clouds, waves etc. were picked out at this moment with a big soft brush that he sucked into a hard broad point.'

Some 20 years younger than Wyllie, and somewhat overshadowed by him, was Charles Dixon. He, too, was a prolific and accomplished watercolour artist, and many of his pictures depict the shipping on the Thames. He first exhibited at the Royal Academy in 1889, when he was 17 years old, and became a regular contributor to the *Illustrated London News* and the *Sphere*. He became a friend of the millionaire yachtsman Sir Thomas Lipton and frequently sailed on board his famous yachts in order to record the races of the America's Cup. There tends to be a predictable sameness about many of Dixon's watercolours, but he was a skilful technician and every now and then he produced a very fine picture.

Altough Dixon and Wyllie painted a great variety of different types of ships and small craft, they rarely strayed outside European waters. Pictures of big ships on the oceans of the world were the preserve of an accomplished group of marine artists who were painting around the end of the 19th century and in the early part of the 20th century. They included Thomas Somerscales, Montague Dawson, Arthur Briscoe, John Fraser, Arthur Burgess and Frank Mason. Of this group, Somerscales and Dawson have become particularly associated with paintings of clipper ships under full sail. These have proved extraordinarily popular and command surprisingly high prices when they appear in the sale rooms.

Thomas Somerscales seems to have started the vogue for clipper ships. The son of a shipmaster, he went to sea but was invalided ashore at Valparaiso in Chile in

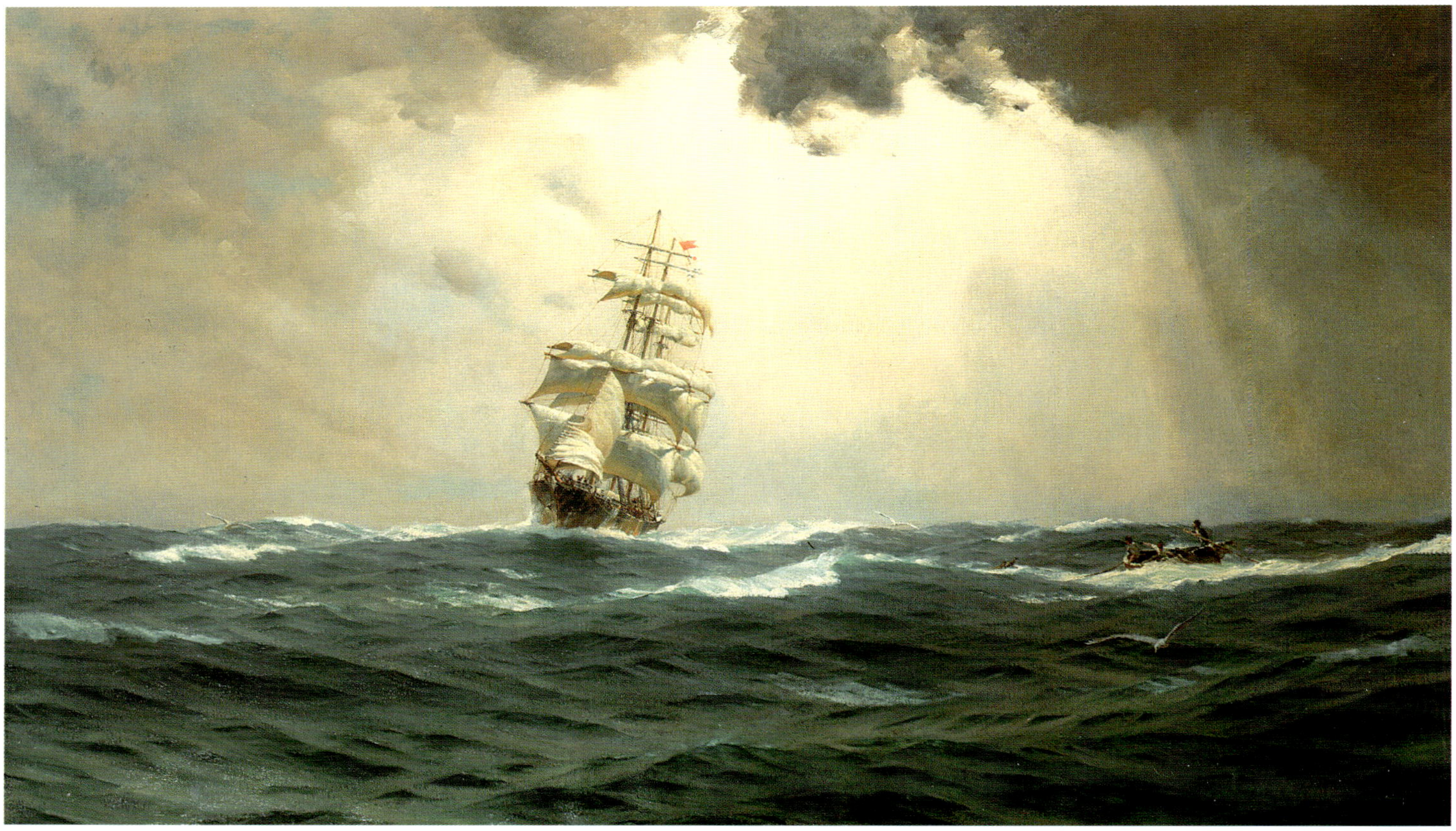

THOMAS SOMERSCALES
'I will not abandon you'

This oil painting, which has some claim to be Somerscale's masterpiece, is included here as a particularly striking example of the clipper-ship school of paintings, later made popular by Montague Dawson and Arthur Briscoe. On the rolling seas of the Southern Ocean a clipper ship turns to rescue three men in an open boat, while albatrosses glide over the surface of the waves.

Oil on canvas. Signed and dated 1916. N.R.Omell Gallery, London.

1874. It was there that he took up marine painting. In 1892 he returned to England and the next year exhibited for the first time at the Royal Academy. A few years later his powerful picture *Off Valparaiso* was bought by the Chantrey Bequest for the Tate Gallery. Somerscales painted with confident, open brushwork and used a low viewpoint so that his ships are viewed on a vast expanse of ocean as if seen from an open boat.

Montague Dawson based a great number of his pictures on a similar formula and painted clippers surging through deep blue seas, with the trade winds filling the clouds of white canvas aloft, or heavily reefed and ploughing through the southern ocean in heavy weather. But Dawson was more than a painter of windjammers. He was also an extremely competent painter of yachts and warships and worked in both oil and water colour. His father and grandfather were both marine artists and he was brought up in a house overlooking Southampton Water. He joined a commercial art studio in 1910 and spent much of his working life as a graphic artist, painting monochrome illustrations of marine subjects for the *Sphere* magazine. In the 1920s he was contracted to Frost and Reed, the art dealers, who subsequently handled all his sales. There has been a tendency to denigrate Dawson's work for its rather too obvious popular appeal and his tendency to stick to a winning formula. He was, however, a consummate technician and at his best he could paint battleships, as well as sailing vessels, with awesome realism.

Arthur Briscoe painted the big clipper ships viewed from afar, but unlike so many other marine artists he also produced dramatic images taken on board the vessels, showing the seamen at work. Many of his finest pictures of ships were carried out in watercolour and in the form of etchings, which are as beautifully drawn and as full of

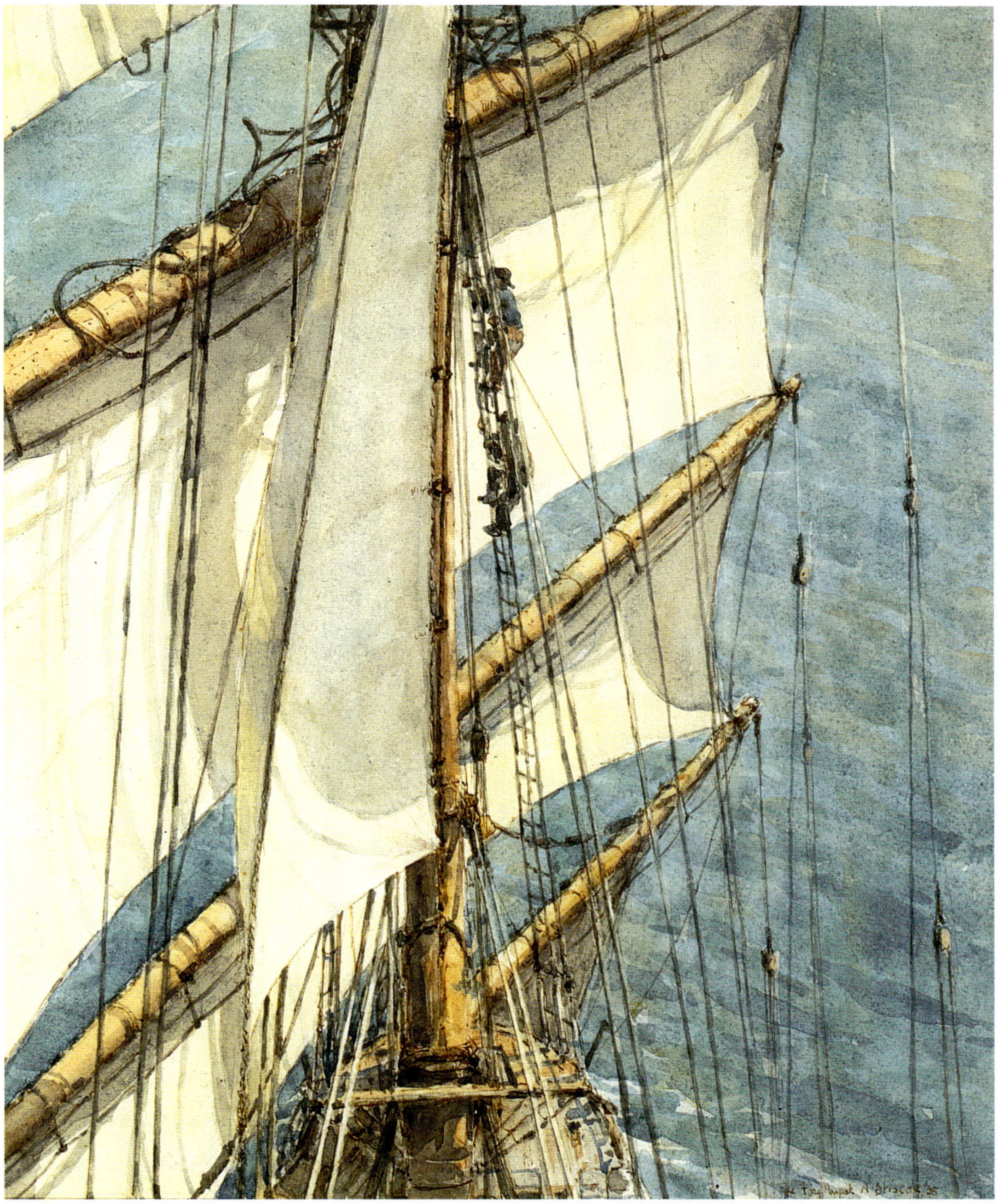

ARTHUR BRISCOE
Seamen aloft on the foremast of a square-rigger

While thousands of pictures have been painted of ships viewed from afar, there are surprisingly few pictures of life on board the sailing vessels. There are even fewer pictures of what went on aloft. Briscoe made good this deficiency and painted with the assurance of someone who understood the workings of a sailing ship.

Watercolour. Signed and dated '38'. Royal Exchange Art Gallery, London.

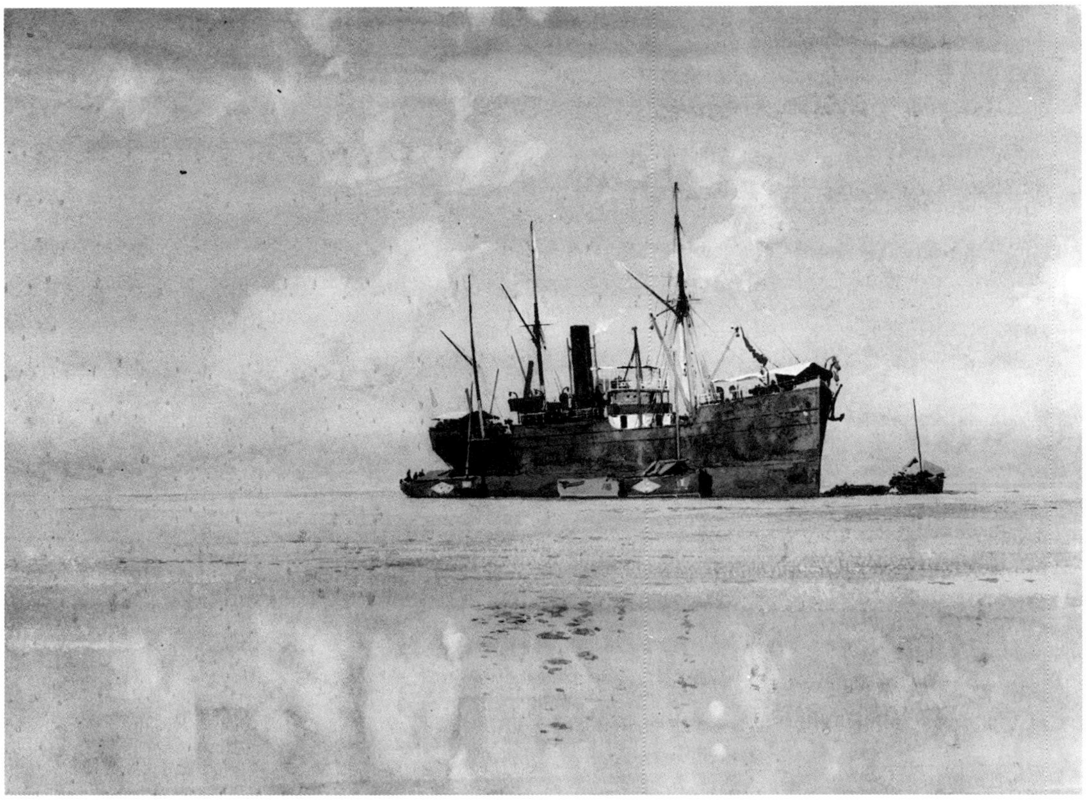

JOHN FRASER
The steamer Pickwick

Fraser is a little-known artist who deserves recognition. In this atmospheric picture he shows a weather-beaten tramp steamer at anchor off a tropical port surrounded by local craft.

Watercolour and some bodycolour. National Maritime Museum, London.

atmosphere as those of W. L. Wyllie. Briscoe was born at Birkenhead and studied art at the Slade School in London and at Julian's in Paris; he exhibited regularly at the Royal Academy and the other London exhibitions. He was a keen yachtsman and made frequent cruises along the East Coast and to Europe in his yacht *Golden Vanity* – at one period he lived aboard the yacht with his wife and son – and he wrote a *Handbook of Sailing* under the pseudonym Clove Hitch.

An artist who is much less well known than Somerscales, Dawson and Briscoe is John Fraser, whose seascapes deserve more attention than they usually receive. He was born into a family of seamen and two of his brothers were lost at sea during ocean voyages. He lived in America in the 1880s and then spent 20 years travelling the world, before eventually settling in England, where he kept a print shop in Westminster until his death in 1927. The contents of his studio were acquired by the National Maritime Museum, and among the pictures are some oil paintings remarkable for their vibrant colour and handling, and a number of very beautiful watercolours.

Two other marine painters of this period who painted big ships at sea were Arthur Burgess and Frank Mason. Like so many other painters of the time, they combined easel painting with commercial art. They both exhibited at the Royal

Academy but also made a reasonable living from illustrations for books, magazines and advertisements. Arthur Burgess, who was born in Australia and studied art in Sydney, came to England in 1901 and settled in St Ives. He provided illustrations for the *Illustrated London News*, the *Sphere* and the *Graphic*. Frank Mason, who received his educaton on the training ship HMS *Conway* and spent some years at sea, produced book illustrations and posters and made a memorable series of illustrations for Wills 'Senior Service' cigarettes, which for many years enjoyed a brand image almost as familiar as the Guinness posters in their day.

An artist whose work is very different in character from the professional marine painters of that time was Sir Frank Brangwyn. The son of a cathedral architect, he trained in the workshops of William Morris in the 1880s and made his reputation with huge fresco paintings, but also designed furniture and worked in stained glass and metal. He travelled widely and carried out a huge range of commissions before settling down in a lovely house in the Sussex village of Ditchling. One of the most noticeable shortcomings of artists who have specialized in seascapes is in the drawing of people; Brangwyn, however, could draw figures with assurance, and he used this ability to good effect in his vigorous portrayals of seamen at work. In addition to his paintings, he produced some fine lithographs and engravings and a great number of watercolours, which are unusually bright and colourful.

THE WAR ARTISTS OF THE TWO WORLD WARS

The National Maritime Museum and the Imperial War Museum in London contain remarkable collections of pictures that were drawn and painted by artists who witnessed at first hand the naval actions and associated activities of the wars of 1914–18 and 1939–45. Some of them were serving officers or seamen in the Royal Navy or the merchant navy, some were official war artists. Unlike the pictures painted by the 18th-century artists Pocock, Serres, Whitcombe and Dodd, all of whose paintings tend to be broadly similar in style and approach, the pictures produced by the war artists of the 20th century are notable for their extraordinary variety. Not only are the subjects and the techniques so various, but each artist responded to his subjects in an individual manner. The delicate and stylized drawings of Eric Ravilious, for instance, could not be more different from the broad-brush realism of Norman Wilkinson's battle paintings, and yet both artists witnessed action at sea.

The Willem van de Veldes had been paid by King Charles II to paint sea battles, and several subsequent British monarchs had given artists official titles, such as 'Marine Painter in Ordinary to the King', but it was not until the First World War that artists were granted some form of official status by the government. By 1916 a few artists such as Muirhead Bone and Charles Pears were designated Official War Artists, and their role combined the jobs of recording events and providing pictures which could be used for posters and propaganda purpurposes. There was also a group of artists, led by Norman Wilkinson, who were concerned with camouflage and, more specifically, with devising the system of dazzle painting that was used with some success to disguise the shape of ships and to confuse enemy submarines.

In the Second World War, the system of employing war artists developed a stage beyond providing propaganda pictures and camouflage. Sir Kenneth Clarke, who was then Director of the National Gallery, persuaded the Ministry of Information to set up the War Artists Advisory Committee, with the idea of making use of the skills of talented artists to record all aspects of the war. Naval and military actions were to be recorded, but artists were also sent out to document the effects of the Blitz on London and people sheltering in the Underground, life and work in the shipyards

FRANK MASON
Off Whitby

Mason's picture is a vigorous portrayal of shipping on England's northeast coast. The ruins of Whitby Abbey can be seen on the cliff tops, and beyond is the small seaport where Captain Cook learnt his trade as a young seaman.

Watercolour. Signed. Sotheby's, London.

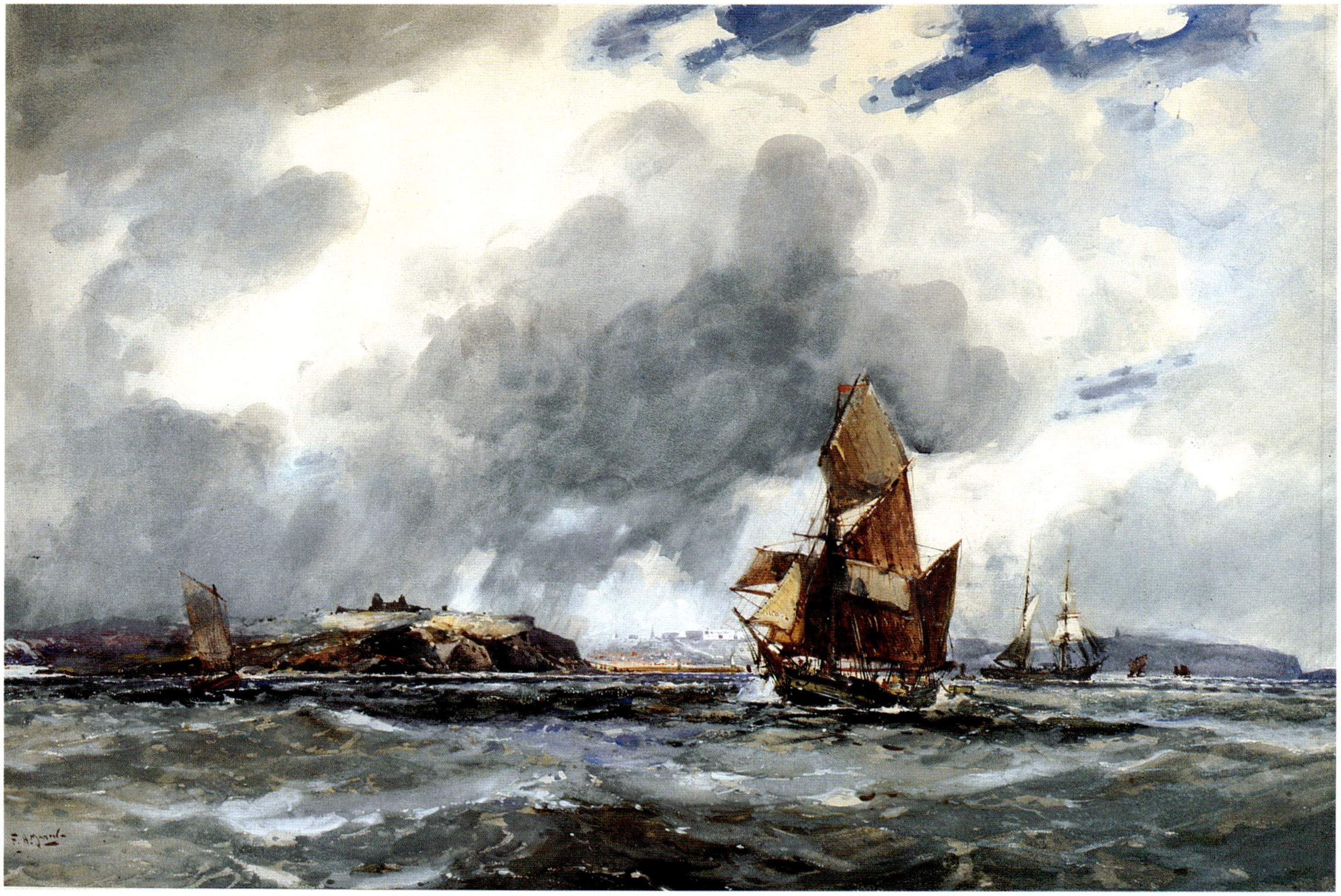

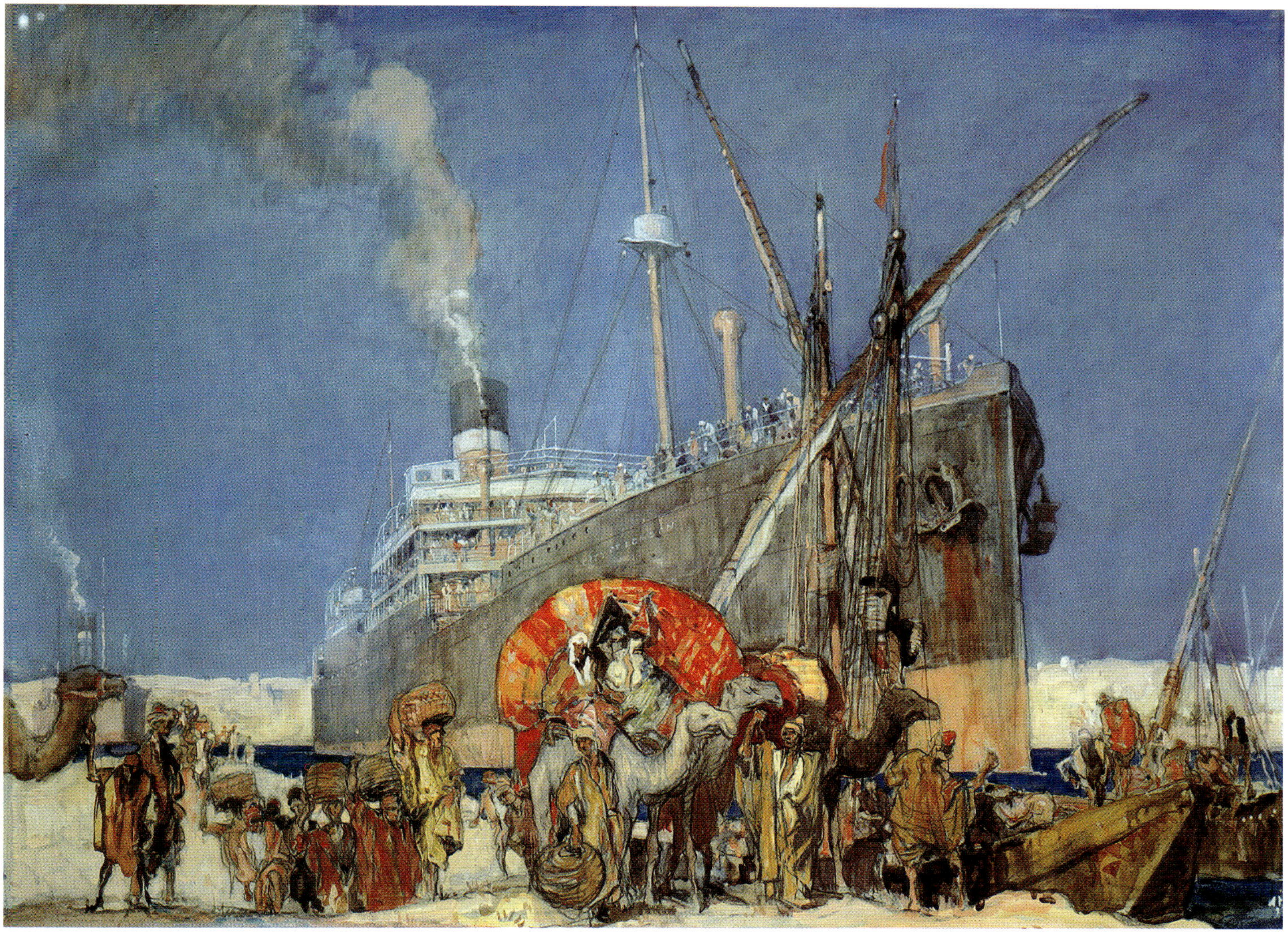

SIR FRANK BRANGWYN. SS City of London *on the Suez Canal*

It is characteristic of Brangwyn's individual approach that he should hide the great steamship behind the masts and sails of local dhows and an assorted crowd of Arab traders and camels laden with colourful goods.

Watercolour and bodycolour. Signed. Royal Exchange Art Gallery, London.

and docks, merchant ships in the convoys, and service men and women in training and in action. The result was a comprehensive pictorial record made by artists of the calibre of Henry Moore, Graham Sutherland, Anthony Gross and Paul Nash. On the maritime side, the official war artists included Eric Ravilious, Richard Eurich, Charles Cundall, Stephen Bone and John Worsley. A number of talented artists served as officers in the Royal Navy or RNVR (The Royal Naval Volunteer Reserve) and recorded their experiences at sea. Foremost among these were Rowland Langmaid, David Cobb and Claude Muncaster.

Three artists had offical positions in both world wars: Charles Pears, Norman Wilkinson and Muirhead Bone. Charles Pears developed a distinctive style in his oil paintings and watercolours, which may have been influenced by his early years as a graphic artist and illustrator. For many years he supplied illustrations for the

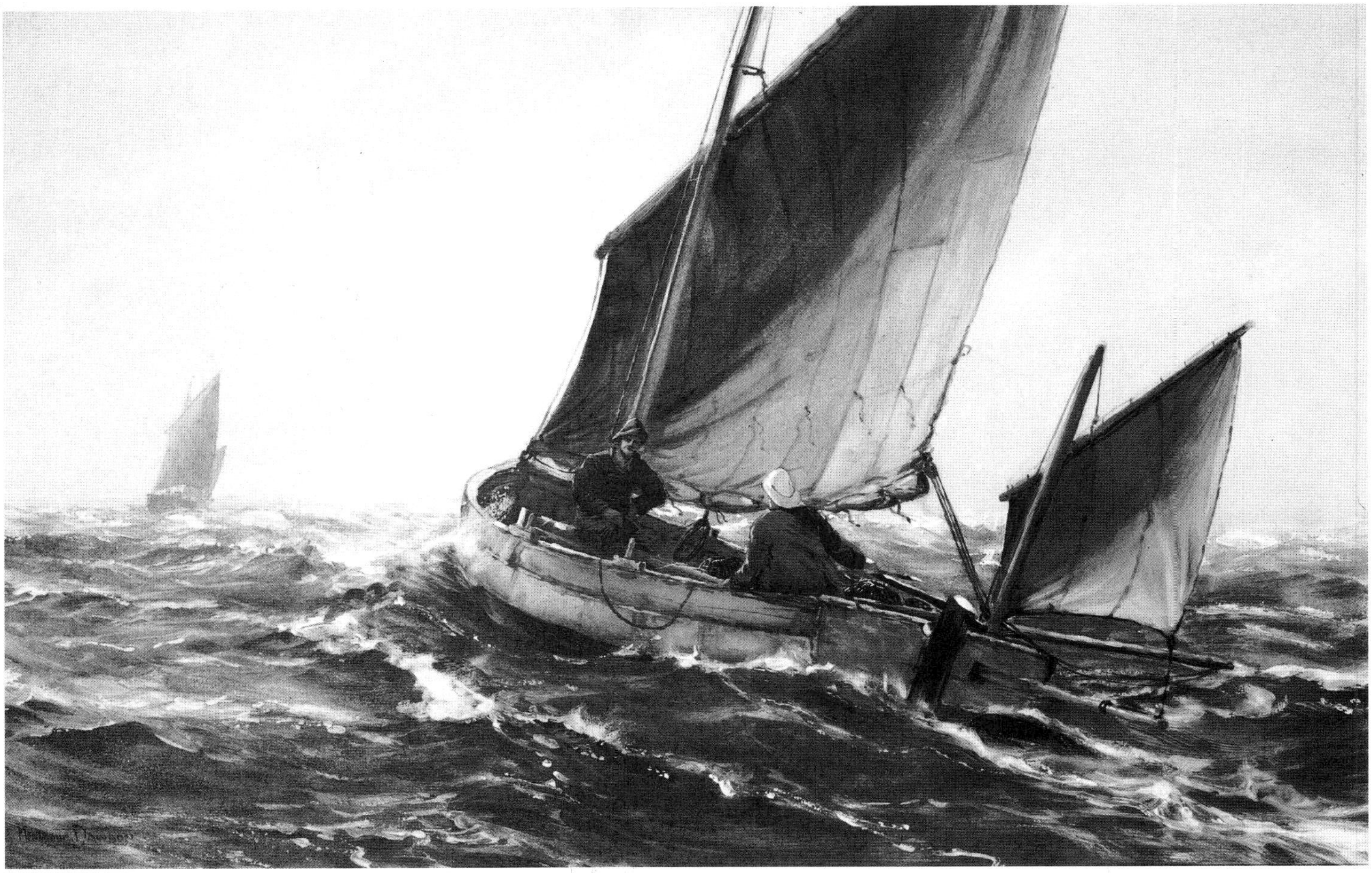

MONTAGUE DAWSON
A fishing lugger

With reefed mainsail, and several lobster pots in the bottom of the boat, two fishermen head out to sea, apparently unperturbed by the heavy weather.

Watercolour and bodycolour. Signed. Sothebys, London.

Illustrated London News, the *Graphic* and other magazines. He also illustrated R.H. Dana's *Two Years Before the Mast* and books by John Masefield and Charles Dickens. Like so many marine artists, he was a keen yachtsman, which was reflected in several books that he wrote and illustrated, including *From the Thames to the Seine*, *South Coast Cruising* and *Going Foreign*. In his pictures he frequently adopted an unusual viewpoint and created bold compositions in which ships and waves form striking, almost two-dimensional patterns. Far from detracting from his work, this poster-like style heightens the drama of his pictures, which is always underpinned by beautifully drawn ships and wave formations.

Sir David Muirhead Bone was an official war artist from 1916 to 1918 and soon after the start of the Second World War he was appointed to the War Artists Advisory Committee. He had trained at the Glasgow School of Art in its heyday and became a draughtsman and illustrator. He rapidly established a commanding position in the realm of print-making, particularly with etching and dry points. Much of his work during the first World War was published in a series of booklets issued by George

Newnes under the title *The Western Front.* His prints cover a wide range of subjects from shipyards to street scenes. Some are elaborate compositions on a grand scale, packed with a mass of carefully observed detail, others are sketchy and atmospheric. Muirhead Bone adopted the unusual practice of not only sketching out of doors but also making many of his engravings on the spot. He said, 'most of my country plates have been done direct on the copper plate from nature, as one works there under comforatble conditions, and the important thing to preserve is the feeling and freshness.'

Norman Wilkinson attended art school in Portsmouth and then spent nearly 15 years providing pictures of maritime subjects for the *Illustrated London News* and for railway posters. In 1915 he joined the Navy, and while on active service became convinced that merchant ships could be protected by a painting scheme which broke up their outlines and made it difficult for the enemy to identify the size of the ship and her heading. After some experiments at the Devonport Dockyard, the idea was taken up by the Royal Navy and Wilkinson was authorized to employ 25 women with art-school training to make ship models and paint different dazzle schemes. Initially 50 transport ships were painted, but the scheme was so well received that by 1918 Wilkinson was requested to visit Washington to give his advice. This resulted in 1100 American merchant ships being painted to designs orginating from London.

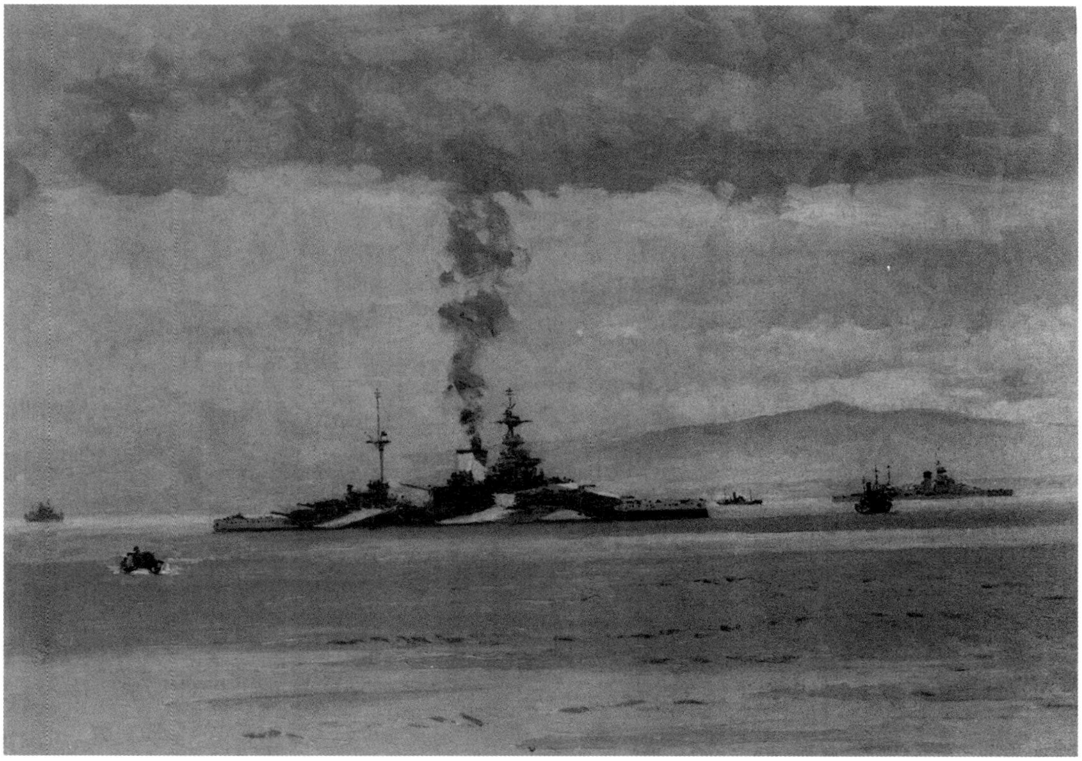

NORMAN WILKINSON
HMS Malaya

The *Malaya* took part in the Battle of Jutland in 1916, and during the Second World War was flagship at Gibraltar at the time of the Malta convoys. She is shown here painted in the dazzle camouflage scheme devised by Wilkinson.

Oil on canvas. 19423. National Maritime Museum, London.

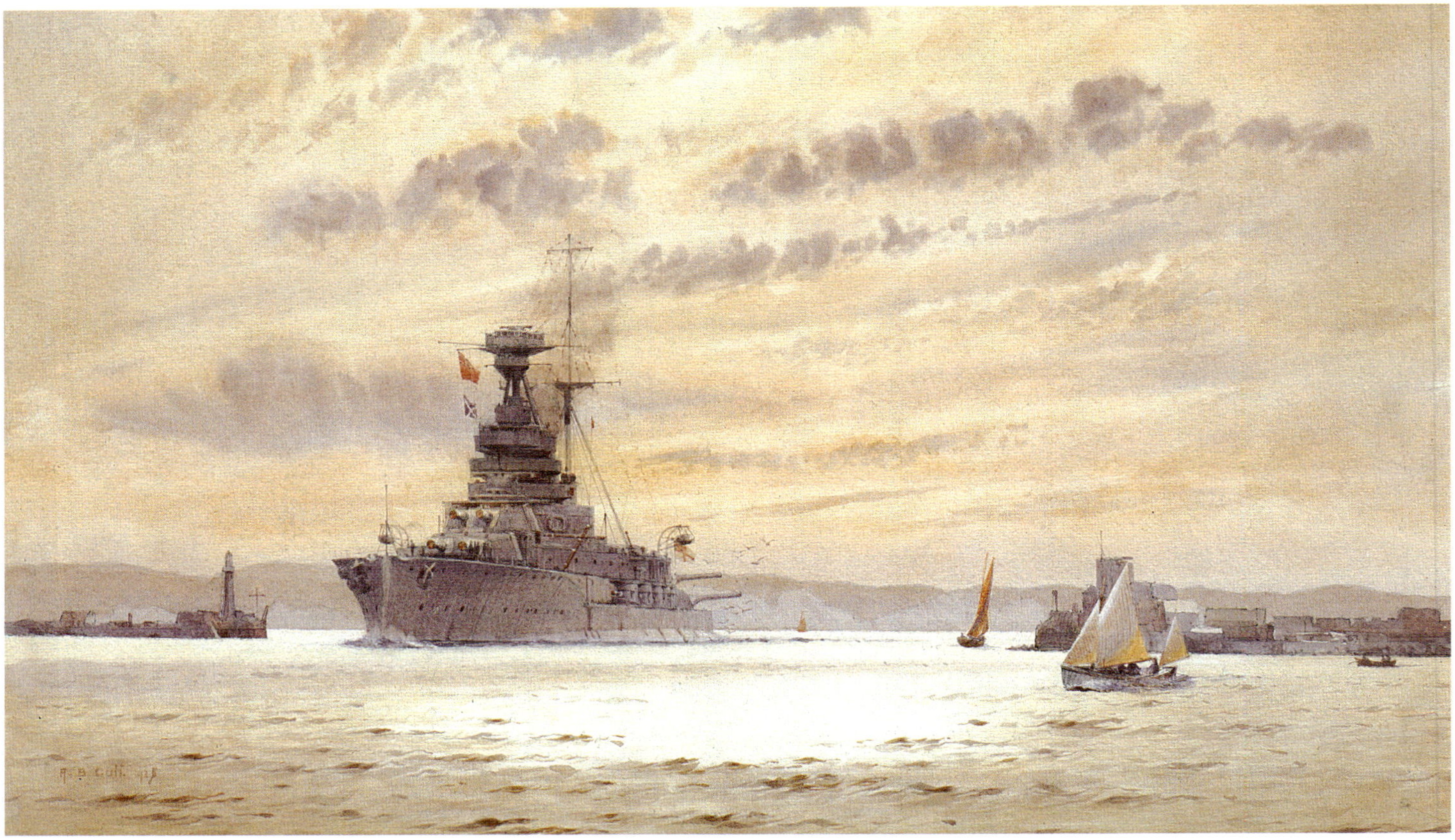

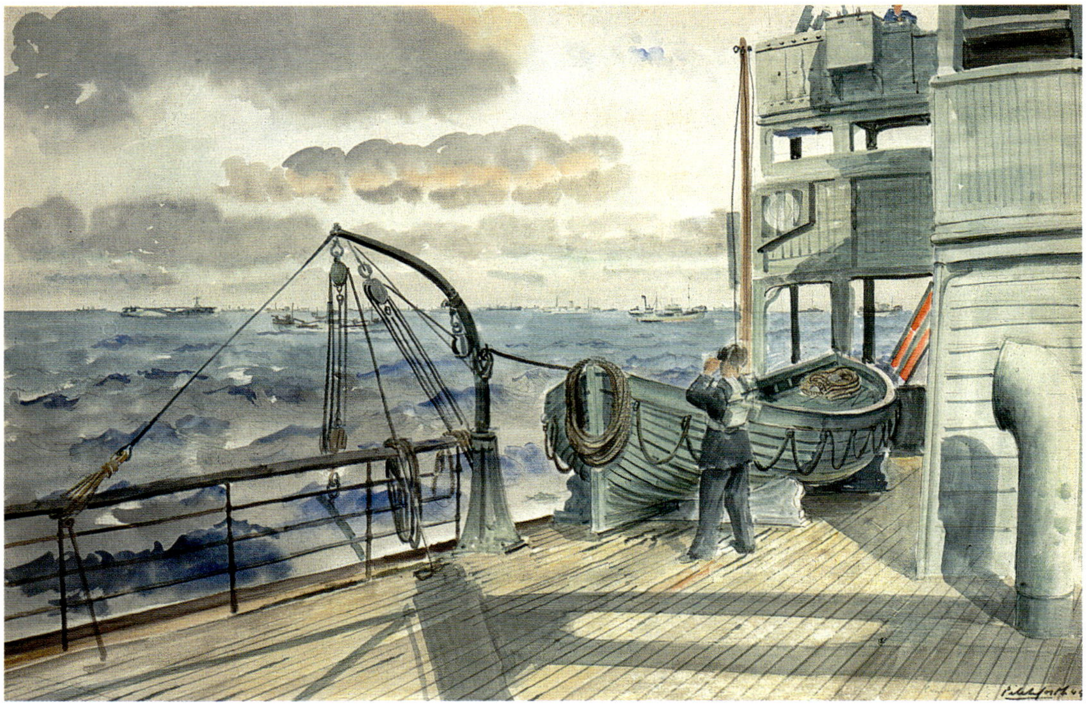

Roland Pitchforth
The convoy. 1944

Pitchforth was an official war artist from 1940 to 1945. His free, direct style of painting in watercolour was well suited to capturing aspects of life at sea in sometimes difficult conditions.

Watercolour. Signed and dated '44. Royal Exchange Art Gallery, London.

FACING PAGE
ALMA CLAUDE BURTON CULL
The Royal Sovereign *entering Portland*

This is an impressive picture by a marine artist whose work deserves to be better known. Many of Cull's oil paintings were put into storage in Portsmouth during the Second World War and were destroyed by enemy bombs, but the National Maritime Museum has 70 of his watercolours. Other examples frequently appear in the sale rooms.

Watercolour. Signed and dated 1928. N.R. Omell Gallery, London.

While experts still debate the effectiveness of dazzle painting, there is no doubt that it made a lasting mark on the marine art of the period.

Other artists were fascinated by the decorative quality of dazzle-painted ships. John Everett painted them with evident relish and so did Edward Wadsworth, both of them exploiting the Vorticist effect of the painting schemes. Dazzle painting was not pursued in the Second World War, but Wilkinson was called upon to advise the Air Ministry on the camouflage of airfields. During the course of a long and productive career, Wilkinson painted a huge variety of naval actions in oil and watercolour, his most impressive legacy being a series of 56 paintings of *The War At Sea*, now in the collection of the National Maritime Museum. One of the most interesting artists to be involved in Sir Kenneth Clarke's scheme was Eric Ravilious. He received his training as an artist at Eastbourne School of Art and then at the Royal College of Art, where Paul Nash and Edward Bawden were among his tutors. He specialized in wood engraving and in fine pen and ink drawings with the most subtle and restrained use of colour. In 1940 he was appointed an official war artist, first with the Royal Marines and then with the Royal Air Force; he was killed on a flight off Iceland in 1942. Ravilious's war drawings are of great distinction. He had a flair for creating patterns and textures from the most unlikely material. Aircraft carriers, minesweepers, tugboats and submarines were converted into images as memorable as the exquisitely drawn wheelbarrows and garden tools he produced for the Wedgewood pottery.

CHARLES PEARS
Cargo steamer in a heavy sea

Against a backdrop of ominous grey clouds, the rusty hull of the steamer is surrounded by a seething mass of white foam as she ploughs through the steep, rolling waves. Although Pears' poster-like style is distinctive he never resorted to a formula but constantly searched for new ways to depict the sea under different weather conditions.

Gouache. Signed. Royal Exchange Art Gallery, London.

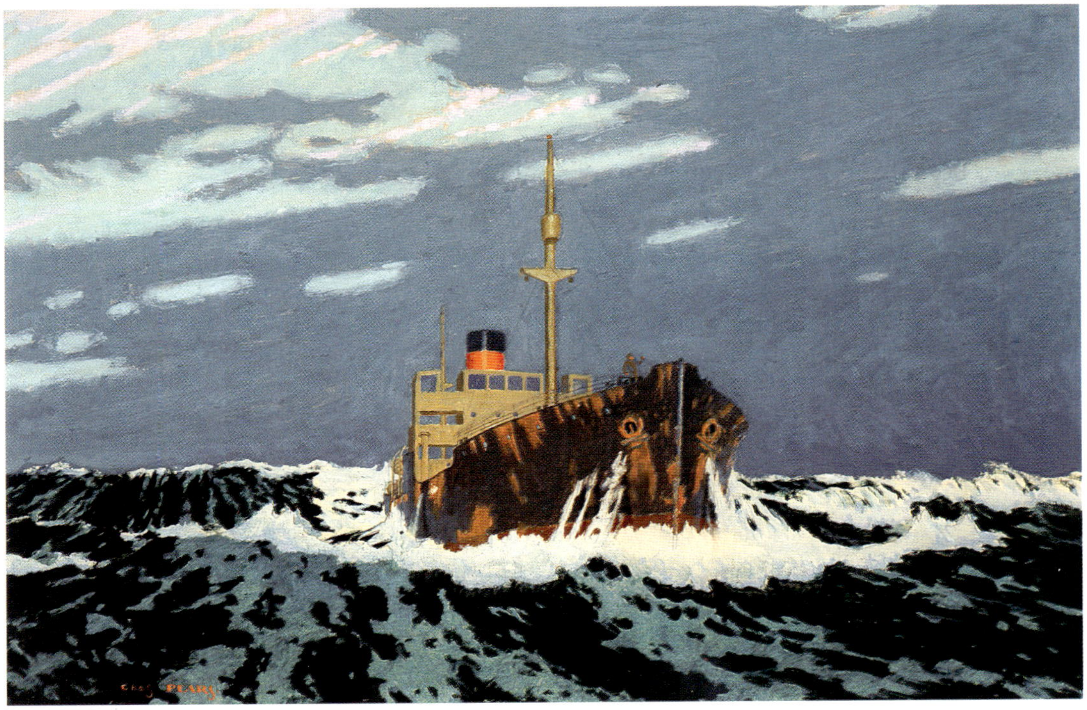

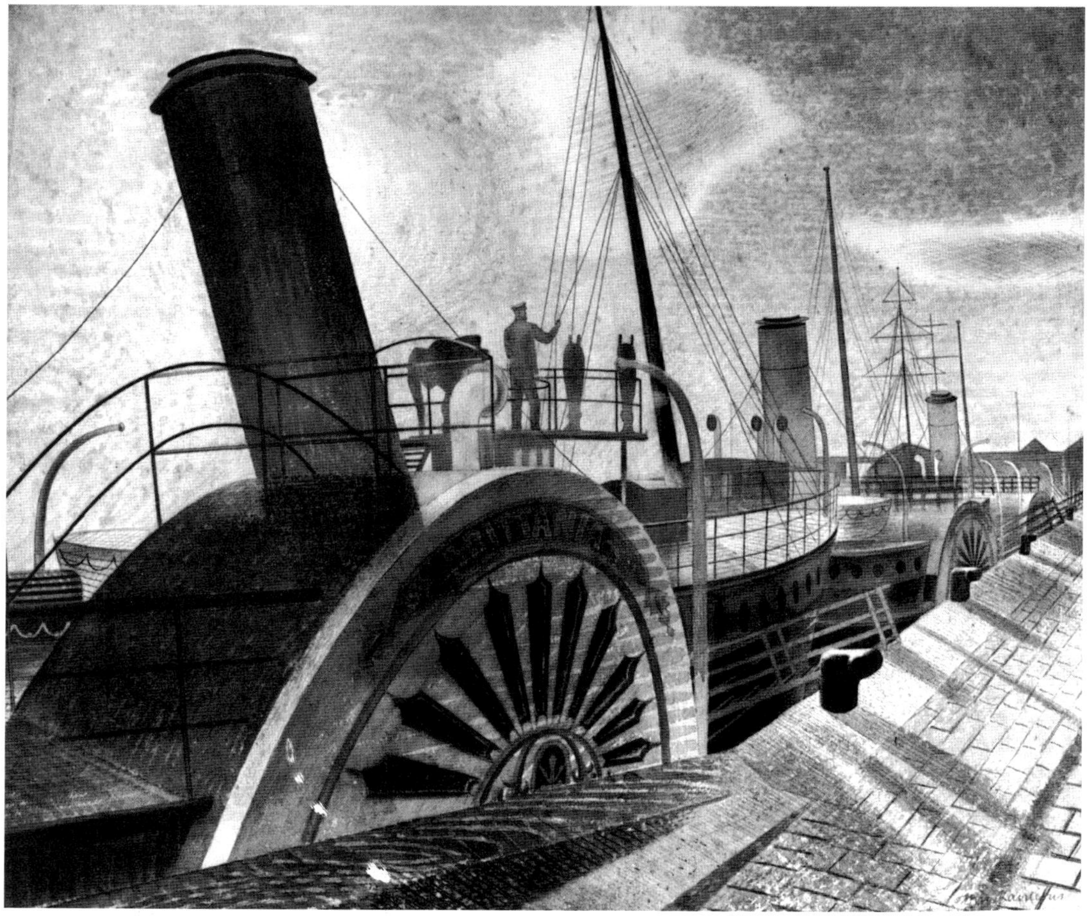

ERIC RAVILIOUS
Paddle Steamer

A line of paddle steamers moored alongside a quay is converted into a wonderfully decorative composition by an artist with a distinctive vision and an ability to create patterns and textures out of the most unlikely material.

Watercolour over pencil. Signed. Phillips, London.

Another war artist with an original vision was Richard Eurich. His painting *Withdrawal from Dunkirk, June 1940* is the most evocative of the many pictures that have been made of the famous scene on the beaches. He managed to combine an amazing amount of detail with a quirky viewpoint and an almost childlike drawing of the ships and people. The result is a curiously dreamlike vision and a frozen moment of history. Many of his other war paintings have a similarly arresting quality, which differentiates them from the more conventional portrayals of ships and harbour scenes. Eurich went to Bradford School of Art and then studied at the Slade. In 1934 he married and moved to a house near Portsmouth, and in 1941 was appointed an official war artist by the Admiralty. After the war he returned to painting landscapes and taught for many years at the Camberwell School of Art.

Few of the war artists had a more action-packed war than John Worsley. He joined the Navy in 1939, saw action in various warships, and was on the armed merchant cruiser *Laurentic* when she was sunk in the Atlantic in 1942, Having survived this experience, he was appointed an official war artist in July 1943 with the

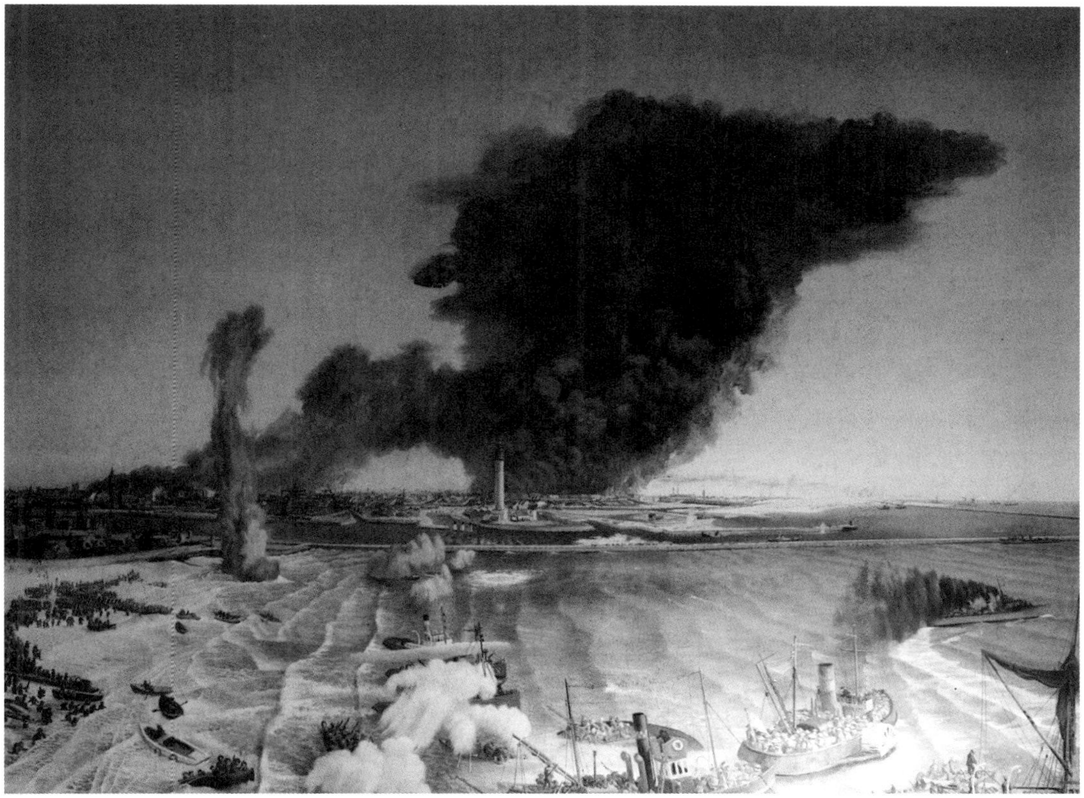

RICHARD EURICH
Withdrawal from Dunkirk, June 1940

A miscellaneous collection of tugboats, paddle-steamers and a Thames barge rescue British troops from the beaches under enemy fire.

Oil on canvas. Signed. National Maritime Museum, London.

task of recording the naval war in the Mediterranean. He witnessed dive-bomb attacks while on board an anti-aircraft landing craft and depicted landings on the beaches of Sicily, but in November 1943 he was captured and spent the rest of the war in a naval prisoner-of-war camp in Germany. Worsley never stopped drawing thoughout the war. He had sent in his pictures to the exhibitions of wartime art organized at the National Gallery, and he continued to make drawings while a prisoner. He was, and is, an accomplished painter, but it is his assured and fluent drawings in pencil, charcoal and pen and ink that provide the most immediate record of his wartime experiences.

POST-WAR DEVELOPMENTS

Paintings of ships and the sea reached a spectacular high point in the 19th century, with the work of Turner, Monet, Winslow Homer and Boudin. In the early part of the 20th century, the artists of the Newlyn School painted some haunting views of fishing boats and fishermen and their families, while professional marine painters such as W.L. Wyllie, Montague Dawson and Charles Pears recorded the warships, merchant ships and yachts of their day. But what of more recent developments?

Obviously, the main thrust of 20th-century art has taken place in other areas. There are no painters of seascapes whose names can be put alongside those of Cezanne, Picasso, Braque, Matisse, Chagall, Paul Klee, Marcel Duchamp, Magritte and those other artists whose pioneering works now hang in the great museums and art galleries of the world. But there is still a demand for pictures of ships, as there is for portraits and landscapes. Shipping companies still want pictures of their ships, yachtsmen want pictures of yachts, and the general public still likes pictures of harbours and beach scenes.

There has also been an increasing demand for pictures that are historical reconstructions of the ships and maritime activities of previous centuries. This has been driven by an increased interest in history and archaeology and by a nostalgia for the great days of sail and particularly for the era of Nelson's navy. Imaginative teaching in schools, enlightened television documentaries, improved museum displays and exhibitions, beautifully illustrated children's books and the historical novels of Patrick O'Brien, Alexander Kent, C.S. Forester and others have contributed to this.

WILLIAM GILKERSON
The Bonhomme Richard *with* Vengeance *and* Pallas *in a gale*

American ships under the command of John Paul Jones are shown in a gale off the Shetland Islands. Gilkerson is an authority on historic ships and on weapons used at sea. This, and his experience as a seaman, enable him to bring an added realism and authenticity to his pictures.

Watercolour. Signed with monogram and dated 1987.

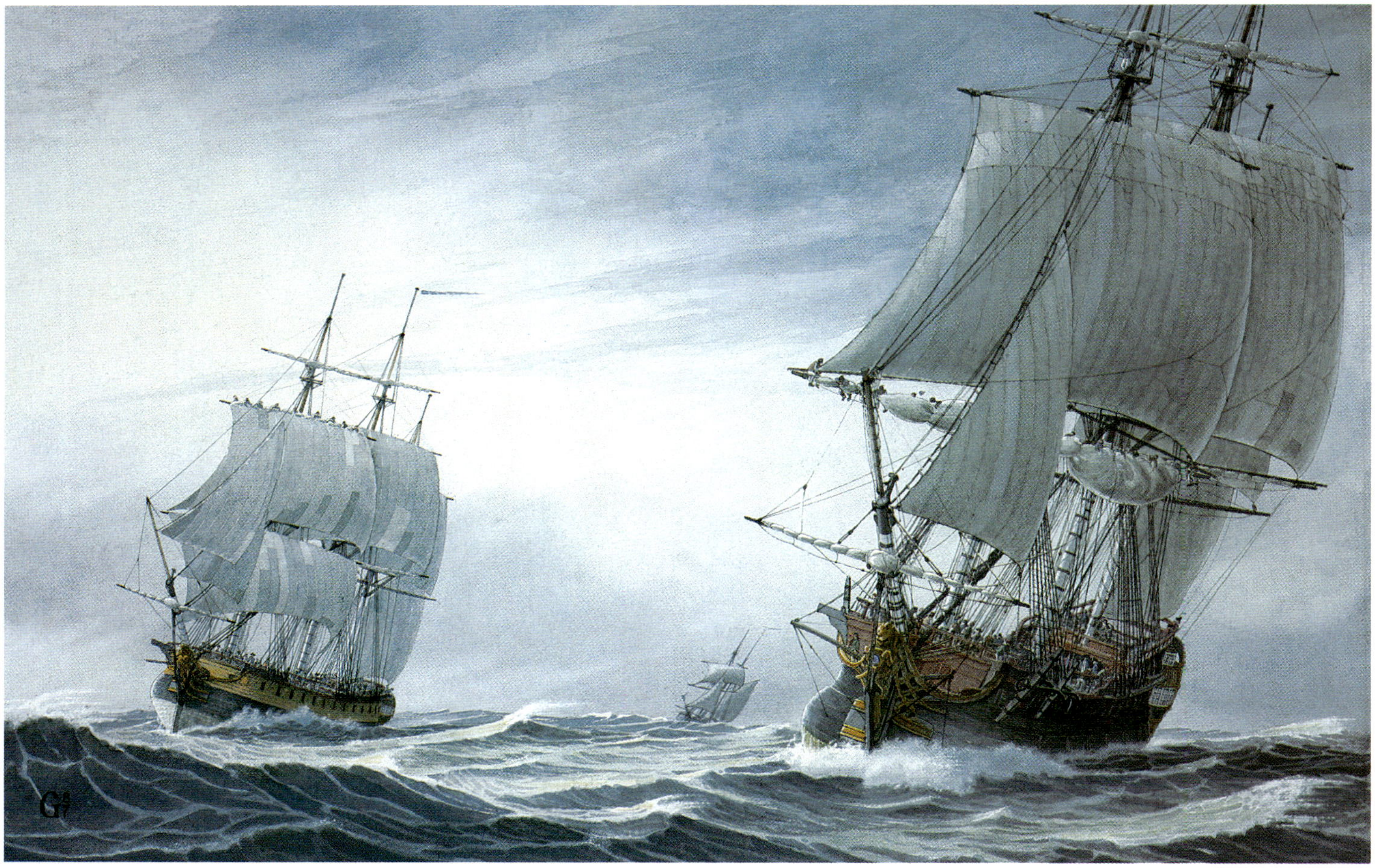

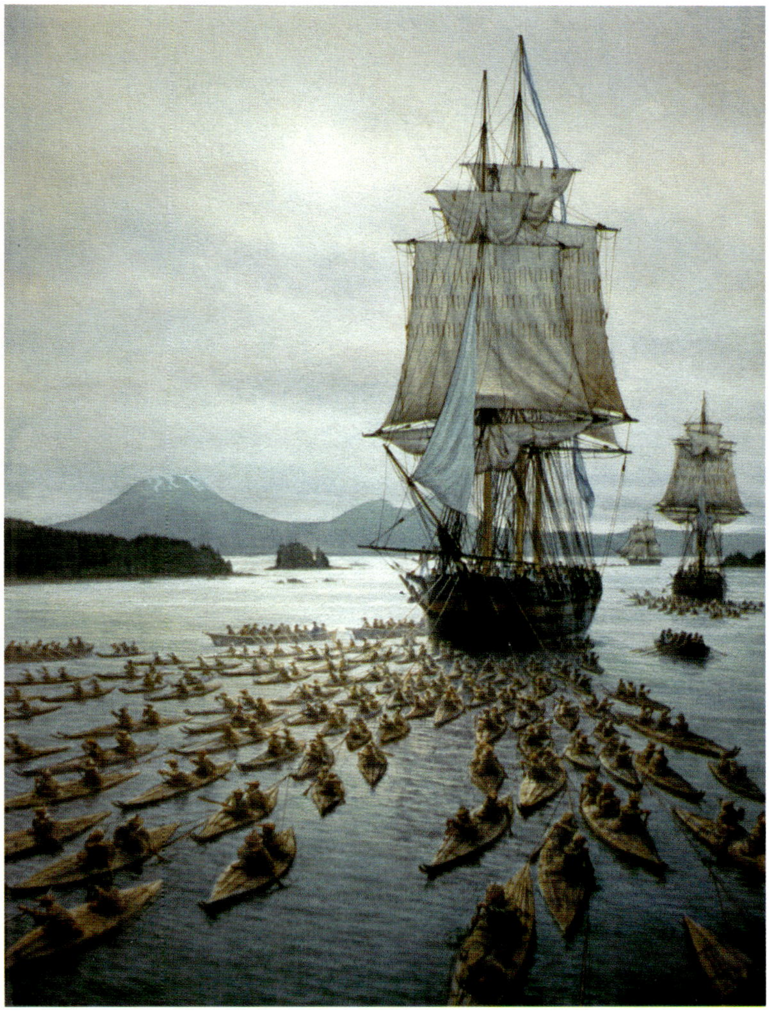

MARK MYERS
The Russian ship Neva being towed across Sitka Sound, September 1804.

The artist here reconstructs the remarkable scene where an invading force of Russian ships was assisted in the calm weather by several hundred local Aleuts in their canoes.

Watercolour. Signed. Artist's collection.

The consequence has been similar to the demand for books of picturesque coastal scenery in the 1820s, and the huge appetite for pictures generated by magazines such as the *Illustrated London News* and *Harper's Monthly*. The publishers of illustrated books, seafaring novels and prints now demand historically accurate pictures of shipping. A number of fine artists have risen to the challenge, with the result that a generation of marine painters has become extremely knowlegeable about the design, construction and rig of historic ships and about ship handling in the days of sail. Their work can be seen in the exhibitions of the Royal Society of Marine Artists in Britain, the American Society of Marine Artists in the United States, and of the *Peintres Officiel de la Marine* in France. It is instructive to compare these with pictures of ships and seascapes made by a long line of marine artists that stretches back beyond Bakhuizen and the Van de Veldes to the earliest woodcuts and engravings, with their tantalizing glimpses of vessels moored along the waterfronts of medieval harbours.

Checklist of artists and their dates

This list is devoted mainly to artists and printmakers mentioned in the text.

ABBREVIATIONS

BI	British Institution
ILN	*Illustrated London News*
RA Schools	The Royal Academy Schools, London
RA	The Royal Academy in London. The earliest and latest dates are given for pictures shown at the Royal Academy. This does not mean that the artists exhibited every year between those dates.
RNVR	Royal Naval Volunteer Reserve

Alexander, William 1767–1816
Born in Maidstone. Admitted to RA Schools in 1784. Artist with Lord Macartney's embassy to China 1792–94. Exhibited at the RA from 1795 to 1804. Became first Keeper of Prints and Drawings at the British Museum. Died in Maidstone.

Anderson, William 1757–1837
Born in Scotland. Trained as a shipwright but moved to London and set up as a marine painter. Exhibited at the RA from 1787 to 1834 and also at the BI. Painted sea battles and estuary scenes with shipping. Died in London.

Atkins, Samuel *fl.*1787–1808
Exhibited at the RA from 1787 to 1796. Is believed to have voyaged to the West Indies and the coast of China. A prolific painter in watercolours of shipyards along the Thames, and of warships and merchantmen at sea in calms and storms.

Bakhuizen, Ludolf 1631–1708
Born at Emden in Germany but moved to Amsterdam, where he made his name with dramatic oil paintings of sea battles and storms. He also produced many pen and wash drawings, a series of engravings, and some pen paintings, or grisailles. Died in Amsterdam.

Bentley, Charles 1806–1854
Born and died in London. Trained as an engraver. Travelled widely in Britain and northern France and painted coastal scenes in watercolours. Exhibited at the BI and the Old and New Water-Colour Societies.

Birch, Thomas 1779–1851
Born in London. His father, an engraver and painter of miniatures, emigrated to America in 1794. Spent some years assisting his father with engravings of views in the Philadelphia area, then set up on his own as a portrait painter. Elected to the Pennsylvania Academy of Fine Arts. Died in Pennsylvania.

Bone, Sir David Muirhead 1876–1953
Born at Partick in Scotland and trained at the Glasgow School of Art. Official war artist 1916–18 and 1939–46. Painter, draughtsman and engraver. Exhibited at the RA. Died in Oxford.

Bonington, Richard Parkes 1802–1828
Born in Nottingham and moved to France in 1817. Visited London and Venice, but most of his watercolours of marine subjects depict the ships and coasts of northern France. Exhibited at the Paris Salon in 1824 and the RA in 1828. Died in London.

Boudin, Louis-Eugène 1824–1898
Born at Honfleur. His father was captain of the local ferry boat. Moved to Le Havre in 1835. In 1844 he set up shop as a stationer and frame-maker. Took up painting and moved to Paris in the 1850s. Moved back to the coast and attained success with his beach scenes. Died at Deauville.

Brangwyn, Sir Frank William 1867–1956
Born at Bruges. Came to London in 1875. Worked in William Morris's workshops 1882–84. Exhibited at the RA from 1885. Produced oil paintings, frescoes and watercolours and many etchings and lithographs. Died in Ditchling, Sussex.

Brett, John 1831–1902
Born near Reigate, Surrey. Entered RA Schools in 1853. His early landscapes were highly praised by Ruskin, but in 1863, following a voyage to the Mediterranean, he took to painting seascapes and beach scenes. Exhibited at RA from 1857 to 1891. Died in London.

Brierley, Sir Oswald Walters 1817–1894
Born in Chester. Made several ocean voyages and between 1841 and 1851 he visited Australia, New Zealand and the Pacific. Appointed Marine Painter to Queen Victoria. Exhibited at the RA 1839–72. Worked mainly in watercolours. Died in London.

Briscoe, Arthur 1873–1943
Born in Birkenhead. Trained at the Slade School of Art and in Paris. Exhibited at the RA and the English Art Club from 1896. He was a keen yachtsman and wrote a book on sailing. Painted ships and seascapes in oils and watercolours and produced many etchings. Died at Chelmsford.

Brooking, Charles 1723–1759
Born in Deptford. Apparently spent some time at sea. Taylor White, Treasurer of the Foundling Hospital, became his patron and rescued him from an unscrupulous picture dealer. He painted warships and merchant ships and calm estuary scenes. Died in London.

Bruegel, Pieter, the Elder *c.*1525–1569
Probably born in Bruegel near Breda. Admitted to Antwerp Painters' Guild as a master in 1551. Travelled in Italy 1551–54. Painted landscapes, seascapes and genre scenes. Numerous prints were made after his drawings including a series devoted to ship types. Died in Brussels.

Bry, Theodore de 1528–1598
Born in Liége, but in about 1560 settled in Strasbourg, where he worked as a goldsmith and engraver. Visited England in 1586 and 1588. Produced engravings for many books of travel and exploration. Moved to Frankfurt in 1590, where he worked on the engravings for his great volumes of *Voyages*.

Burgess, Arthur James Wetherall 1879–1957
Born in Bombala, Australia, and studied art in Sydney. Settled in England in 1901. Exhibited at the RA from 1904. Painted merchant ships and seascapes, and produced many illustrations for the ILN, the *Graphic* and the *Sphere*. Died in London

Buttersworth, James Edward 1817–1894
Born in London, the son (or possibly grandson) of the marine painter Thomas Buttersworth. Emigrated to America about 1847. Lived and worked in the vicinity of New York and painted ship portraits, yacht races and coastal scenes with shipping. Died in West Hoboken.

Buttersworth, Thomas 1768–c 1828
Born in the Isle of Wight. Enlisted in the Royal Navy and after his discharge in 1800 became a professional marine painter of sea battles and ship portraits. Exhibited at the RA in 1813 and at the BI in 1825. There is some confusion between him and another Thomas Buttersworth (who may have been his son) who was born in 1797, lived and worked in London and died at Greenwich in 1842.

Callcot, Sir Augustus Wall 1779–1844
Born and died in London. Studied at the RA Schools. Exhibited at the RA from 1799 to 1843. Painted landscapes and coastal scenes, and views of shipping on the Thames, notably *The Pool of London* of 1816.

Cappelle, Jan van de 1624–1679
Born and died in Amsterdam. He came from a wealthy family, was a friend and patron of many of the Dutch artists of his day and accumulated a large art collection. Celebrated for his calm scenes with shipping and for his winter landscapes.

Carmichael, John Wilson 1800–1868
Born in Newcastle-upon-Tyne. Exhibited at the RA from 1835 to 1859, and at the BI. Moved to London around 1845. Painted a wide variety of maritime subjects in oils and watercolours, produced illustrations for the ILN, and published two books on painting. Died in Scarborough.

Chambers, George 1803–1840
Born in Whitby. Went to sea as a boy but then settled in London, where he painted scenery for the theatre and eventually established himself as a marine painter. Exhibited at the Old Water-Colour Society and received commissions from King William IV and several naval officers. Died in Brighton.

Church, Frederic Edwin 1826–1900
Born in Hartford, Connecticut. Studied with two local painters and then moved to New York where he was a pupil of Thomas Cole. In 1845 he began to exhibit landscapes and in 1849 was elected to the National Academy of Design. In 1853 he painted landscapes in South America and in 1859 voyaged to Labrador. Died in New York.

Cleveley, John, the Elder ***c.*1712–1777**
Born and died in London. Became a shipwright in the Royal dockyard at Deptford and later worked as a ship's carpenter. Painted ship portraits and pictures of shipyards and launching ceremonies.

Cleveley, John, the Younger 1747–1786
Son of John Cleveley the Elder and twin brother of Robert Cleveley. Born in London and trained as a shipwright. Took painting lessons from Paul Sandby. Exhibited at the RA in 1770 and at the Society of Artists. Painted sea battles, ship portraits and coastal views. Died in London.

Cleveley, Robert 1747–1809
Son of John Cleveley the Elder and twin brother of John Cleveley the Younger. Born in London and trained as a ship's caulker. Served in the Royal Navy as a clerk from 1770 to 1777. Took up marine painting and exhibited at the RA in 1780 and 1790. Appointed Marine Painter to the Prince Regent. Died at Dover.

Cole, Thomas 1801–1848
Born at Bolton-le-Moor, Lancashire. Emigrated to America with his family when he was 18 and lived in Pittsburgh and Philadelphia. Took lessons from a portrait painter and studied part-time at Pennsylvania Academy. In 1825 he moved to New York and began painting landscapes. Died in New York.

Cooke, Edward William 1811–1880
Born in London, the son of George Cooke the engraver. Published the first plates of *Fifty Plates of Shipping and Craft* in 1828. Exhibited at the RA from 1835 to 1879, and at the BI. Made numerous visits to Holland and Venice. Died at Groombridge in Kent.

Cotman, John Sell 1782–1842
Born in Norwich. Studied painting in London 1798. Exhibited at the RA from 1800 to 1806. In 1803–05 made sketching tours in Yorkshire and the Greta valley. Lived in Norfolk 1806–34, then moved to London to take up the post of drawing master at King's College. Died in London.

Cotman, Miles Edmund 1810–1858
Born in Norwich, the eldest son of John Sell Cotman. Painted marine subjects and coastal views in watercolours. In 1836 he moved to London to assist his father and took over his position as drawing master at King's College in 1842. Died in Norfolk.

Courbet, Gustave 1819–1877
Born at Ornans in the Franche-Comté. Went to Paris in 1839 and worked in the studio of M. Steuben. After several rejections, he had a picture shown at the Paris Salon in 1844. In 1854 he visited the Mediterranean for the first time and from that date seascapes and beach scenes appear among his other pictures. He died at La Tour de Peilz.

Cox, David 1783–1859
Born and died in Birmingham. After an apprenticeship to a Birmingham locket-painter he moved to London and became a scene-painter. Was a drawing master first at Dulwich and then, from 1814 to 1826, at Hereford. Published several instructional books on landscape painting. Moved back to the vicinity of Birmingham in 1841.

Cuyp, Aelbert 1620–1691
Born and died in Dordrecht in the Netherlands. He was the pupil of his father, the portrait painter Jacob Gerritz Cuyp. Apart from numerous sketching trips around Holland, he lived all his life in Dordrecht. Painted landscapes and river scenes with shipping.

Daniell, William 1769–1837
Born at Kingston-upon-Thames. Accompanied his uncle Thomas on a sketching expedition to India in 1784. They returned to London in 1794 and published *Oriental Scenery.* Began work on *A Voyage Round Great Britain* in 1813. Exhibited at the RA from 1795 to 1838.

Daubigny, Charles François 1817–1878
Born in Paris. Studied with his father, a landscape painter, and with Granet and Delaroche. Painted river views and, following visits to the Normandy coast, seascapes and beach scenes. Visited England in 1866 and 1870 and painted shipping on the Thames. Died at Auvers-sur-Oise.

Dawson, Henry 1811–1878
Born in Hull. Took painting lessons from J.B. Pyne. He moved to Liverpool in 1844 and to London in 1849. Exhibited at the RA from 1841 to 1874 and at the BI. Painted landscapes, coastal views and seascapes. Died in London.

Dawson, Henry Thomas *fl.*1860–1873
Son of Henry Dawson and also a marine painter. He exhibited at the RA from 1866 to 1873.

Dawson, Montague 1895–1973
Born in Chiswick, London. Son of Henry Thomas and grandson of Henry Dawson. Worked as an illustrator in a commercial art studio in London from 1910. Was a naval officer during the First World War and afterwards became a successful marine painter. Exhibited at the RA from 1917 to 1936. Died at Midhurst, Sussex.

Dixon, Charles 1872–1934
Born in Goring-on-Thames. The son of the painter Alfred Dixon, he became an illustrator for the ILN, the *Sphere* and the *Graphic.* Worked mainly in watercolours and painted shipping on the Thames, yacht races, and warships. Exhibited at the RA from 1889. Died at Itchenor, Sussex.

Dodd, Robert 1748–1815
Lived and died in London. Painted sea battles, ship portraits and views of shipping on the Thames. Exhibited at the RA from 1782. Many of his pictures were engraved. His work is often confused with that of his younger brother Ralph (*c.*1756-1817).

Dubbells, Hendrick Jacobz 1621–1707
Born and died in Amsterdam. Apprenticed to Abraham de Verwer. Like Van de Velde the Younger painted calm estuary scenes with shipping and dramatic stormy scenes similar in style to those of Bakhuizen, who was his pupil.

Duncan, Edward 1803–1882
Born and died in London. Trained as an engraver but became an accomplished painter in watercolours. He worked closely with the marine painter William Huggins and engraved many of his pictures. Exhibited at the RA, BI and Old Water-Colour Society.

Dutton, Thomas Goldsworthy *c.*1819–1891
Lived and died in London. Produced lithographs and watercolours of ship portraits and other marine subjects.

Eakins, Thomas 1844–1916
Born in Philadelphia. Trained at Central High School, Philadelphia, and in Paris. From 1879 to 1886 he was a teacher at the Pennsylvania Academy of Fine Arts, and then became a teacher at the Art Students League in New York. Elected to the National Academy of Design in 1902. Died in Philadelphia.

Earle, Augustus 1793–1838
Spent several years living and travelling in South America, Australia and New Zealand, before joining the voyage of HMS *Beagle* as official artist in 1831.

Eurich, Richard 1903–1992
Born in Bradford. Trained at Bradford School of Art and the Slade School. Taught at the Camberwell School of Art. Official war artist to the Admiralty 1941–45. Exhibited at the RA and the New England Art Club.

Fielding, Anthony VanDyke Copley 1787–1855
Born in East Sowerby, Yorkshire, but moved with his family to London. Pupil of his father who was a landscape painter. Exhibited at the RA 1811 to 1842 and the Old Water-Colour Society from 1810. Painted seascapes and coastal views in watercolours. Died in Worthing.

Forbes, Stanhope Alexander 1857–1947
Born in Dublin. Studied at the Lambeth School of Art and RA Schools, and in Paris. Painted in Brittany with La Thangue. He settled in Cornwall in 1884 and became a leading member of the Newlyn School of artists. Exhibited at the RA from 1878.

Foster, Myles Birket 1825–1899
Born in North Shields. Moved to London about 1830. Trained as a wood engraver and spent several years providing illustrations for books and magazines. Took up painting in watercolours about 1859. Exhibited at the RA from 1859 to 1881 and the Old Water-Colour Society.

Francia, Francia Thomas Louis 1772–1839
Born and died in Calais. In about 1790 he arrived in London where he lived for nearly 20 years. Exhibited at the RA from 1795 to 1822. Returned to Calais in 1817 and exhibited regularly at the Paris Salon. Took on Bonington as a pupil. Painted coastal scenes and seascapes in watercolour.

Fraser, John 1858–1927
Went to sea as a young man and spent 20 years travelling all over the world. His two brothers were also seamen. Worked with the marine painter Edouardo de Martino. Exhibited at the RA from 1885 to 1905. Kept a print shop in Westminster. Died in London.

Gore, Charles 1729–1807
Born in Horkstow, Yorkshire into a wealthy family. He was an amateur artist and collector who made numerous copies of Van de Velde drawings. He travelled widely and became an accomplished painter in watercolours. Settled in Weimar in later life and died there.

Goyen, Jan van 1596–1666
Born in Leiden. Studied with Willem Gerritz and Esias van de Velde. He settled in the Hague in 1631, where he became a member of the Painters' Guild. He painted landscapes, river scenes with shipping and seascapes and travelled constantly around the Netherlands in search of subjects. Died in the Hague.

Greaves, Walter 1846–1930
Born in London, the son of a Chelsea boatbuilder. A Thames waterman, he frequently rowed Whistler along the river on sketching expeditions and in about 1863 became Whistler's studio assistant. He painted numerous views of the Thames waterfront and shipping on the river.

Groenewegen, Gerrit 1754–1826
Born and died in Rotterdam. Followed his father's trade as a ship's carpenter but lost part of his right leg in an accident and took up drawing, painting and etching instead, concentrating on topographical views around Rotterdam and pictures of Dutch shipping and craft. He engraved and published 84 prints of ship types between 1786 and 1801.

Hardy, Thomas Bush 1842–1897
Born in Sheffield. Travelled in Holland and Italy. Exhibited at the RA from 1872 to 1897, and at the New Water-Colour Society. He was a prolific painter in watercolours and his coastal scenes and seascapes proved very popular. He died in London.

Heade, Martin Johnson 1819–1904
Born in Lumberville, Bucks County, USA. Worked with local folk-painter Edward Hicks. In 1838–40 he spent two years in Europe. For the rest of his life he moved from city to city. In 1859 he stayed in New York and became friendly with Frederick Church. From 1861 to 1863 he worked in Boston. He died at St Augustine, Florida.

Hemy, Charles Napier 1841–1917
Born in Newcastle-upon-Tyne. In 1852 he emigrated to Australia with his family, but returned to England around 1855. Studied at Newcastle School of Art. Exhibited at the RA from 1869. In 1881 moved from London to Falmouth and painted fishing boats and harbour scenes.

Hodges, William 1744–1797
Born in London. Was a pupil of Richard Wilson, the landscape painter. In 1772 joined Captain Cook's second voyage to the Pacific as official artist, and in 1780 went to India with Warren Hastings. Exhibited at the RA from 1776. Retired to the West Country, where he died.

Hollar, Wenceslaus 1607–1677
Born in Prague. Left Bohemia in 1627 and worked in Stuttgart, Strasbourg and Cologne. In 1634 he was in Holland, and in 1636 entered the service of Earl of Arundel and settled in London. Visited Antwerp in 1644 and Tangier in 1669. Most of his etchings are topographical views, but he also depicted harbours, ships and seascapes. Died in London.

Holman, Francis *fl.*1767–1790
Apparently came from a Cornish family. Lived at Shadwell and Wapping by the Thames in London and painted pictures of shipyards, ship portraits and coastal scenes. Exhibited at the RA from 1774 to 1784.

Hook, James Clarke 1819–1907
Born in London. Entered the RA Schools in 1836. Travelled on a scholarship to France and Italy. Exhibited at the RA from 1839 to 1857. Painted coastal scenes and seascapes.

Huggins, William John 1781–1845
Spent some years at sea on ships of the East India Company. Around 1814 he settled in London and became a marine painter, specializing in ship portraits of East Indiamen. Exhibited at the RA from 1817 to 1835. Worked closely with Edward Duncan, who married his daughter. Died in London.

Isabey, Eugène-Gabriel 1803–1886
Born in Paris. Studied with his father Jean-Baptiste Isabey, a famous painter of miniatures. Appointed as official artist to an expedition to capture Algeria in 1830. Made a *Chevalier* of the *Légion d'Honneur*. Died in Paris.

Joy, John Cantiloe 1806–1866
Born in Great Yarmouth, brother of William Joy. Their father was the guard on the Ipswich Mail Coach. Patronized by Captain Manby, who encouraged the brothers to copy pictures in his collection. Exhibited at the Norwich Society of Artists. They spent some time at Portsmouth as government draughtsmen, then moved to Chichester and back to London.

Joy, William Cantiloe 1806–1866
Born in Great Yarmouth, brother of John Cantiloe Joy. (See above entry for details.) William exhibited at the RA in 1824 and 1832. Both artists painted mainly in watercolours and their subjects included groups of ships at anchor and estuary scenes and coastal views with shipping.

Lane, Fitz Hugh 1804–1865
Born in Gloucester, Massachusetts, the son of a sailmaker. Contracted polio as a child and had to use crutches throughout his life. Trained as a printmaker and from 1832 to 1837 worked in Boston with a lithographic firm. Began painting in the 1840s and exhibited at the Boston Athenaeum from 1841. Moved back to Gloucester in 1849.

Lorrain, Claude 1604/5–1682
Born in the Duchy of Lorraine, France. In 1617 he travelled to Rome where he studied painting with Agostino Tassi. Worked with Goffredo Wals in Naples in 1620 and then returned to France; in 1627 he settled permanently in Rome. The first painting he signed and dated was made in 1629; by 1640 he was the most famous and successful landscape painter in Europe.

Loutherbourg, Philippe Jacques (Philip James) de 1740–1812
Born in Strasbourg. Moved to Paris with his family in 1755. Studied with the painters Carle van Loo and François-Joseph Casanova. Became a member of the French Academy and exhibited at the Paris Salon. Settled in London in 1771 and exhibited at the RA from 1772. Chief designer at Drury Lane Theatre. Died in London.

Luny, Thomas 1759–1837
Born in London. Apparently served as a purser in the Royal Navy under Captain George Tobin. Was a pupil of Francis Holman in London. Exhibited at the RA from 1780 to 1793. He developed rheumatoid arthritis and was confined to a wheelchair. Settled in Teighnmouth around 1807 and died there.

Marin-marie *b.*1901
Born at Fougerolles in France. Has twice sailed the Atlantic single-handed. Self-taught artist. Has regularly exhibited at the Musée de la Marine and at the Beaux-Arts de la Mer annual Salon in Paris. Appointed *Peintre Officiel de la Marine* in 1935.

Mason, Frank Henry 1876–1965
Born in Seaton Carew, County Durham. Educated at the training ship *Conway* and went to sea. During the First World War he served in the RNVR as a lieutenant. Took up marine painting, and exhibited at the RA from 1900. Also produced book illustrations and posters.

Monamy, Peter 1681–1749
Born in London, the son of a merchant from Jersey. Records of the Painter Stainers Company indicate that he was apprenticed in 1696. By 1706 he was established as a marine painter. Apparently self-taught, he was much influenced by the Van de Veldes' work. Died in London.

Monet, Claude 1840–1926
Born in Paris. Brought up in Le Havre in Normandy, where he met Eugène Boudin and Johann Jongkind, who also influenced his work. Studied in Paris. Visited London in 1870. His controversial painting *Impression: sunrise* was exhibited in 1874. Died at Giverny.

Moore, Henry 1831–1895
Born in York, the son of a portrait painter. Studied at the York School of Design. Moved to London in 1853 and entered the RA Schools. Exhibited at the RA from 1853 to 1893. In 1857 he turned from painting landscapes to seascapes. Died in Margate, Kent.

Nibbs, Richard Henry 1816–1893
Born and died in Brighton, Sussex. He was self taught as an artist and divided his time between marine painting, teaching the violin and playing in the orchestra of the Theatre Royal in Brighton. Exhibited at the RA from 1841 to 1888 and at the BI.

Nooms, Reinier (called Zeeman) *c.*1623–1664
Born and died in Amsterdam. The maritime nature of his subjects and his alias 'Zeeman' (seaman) suggest that he spent time at sea as a sailor, but nothing else is known about his life. He painted sea battles and coastal scenes and made more than 160 etchings.

Owen, Samuel 1768/9–1857
A London-based painter of watercolours. He exhibited at the RA from 1794 to 1807. His subjects were port and harbour scenes, coastal views and sea battles. Died at Sunbury-on-Thames.

Ozanne, Pierre 1737–1813
Born and died in Brest. Studied with his elder brother Nicolas-Marie, and when he died in 1811 succeeded him as official draughtsman to the French Navy.

Pears, Charles 1873–1958
Born in Pontefract, Yorkshire. He became an illustrator for the ILN, and *Graphic*. Was an official war artist in the First and Second World Wars. A keen single-handed yachtsman, he wrote and illustrated several books on sailing. He was the founder and first President of the Royal Society of Marine Artists. Died in Truro.

Place, Francis 1647–1728
Born in Dinsdale, County Durham. Moved to London in 1665 where he met Wenceslaus Hollar. From 1670 he travelled widely around Britain making drawings and etchings of landscapes and coastal views. He died in York.

Pocock, Nicholas 1740–1821
Born in Bristol. Apprenticed to his father as a seaman. Between 1766 and 1776 he made 12 voyages across the Atlantic to South Carolina and the West Indies as master of a merchant ship. In 1789 he moved from Bristol to London. Exhibited at the RA from 1782 to 1815. Died at Maidenhead.

Pocock, William Innes 1783–1836
Born in Bristol, son of Nicholas Pocock. Went to sea aged 12 and became a lieutenant in the Royal Navy. He was an accomplished marine painter in watercolours and used his skills while on active service and after he retired from the Navy in 1814. Died in Reading.

Porcellis, Jan *c.*1584–1632
Born in Ghent and brought up in Rotterdam. Studied with Hendrik Vroom. In 1615 he moved with his family to Antwerp where he became Master of the Painters' Guild. Moved to Haarlem in 1622, then to Amsterdam and finally to Zoeterwoude near Leiden. His son Julius was his pupil and so was Simon de Vlieger.

Powell, Charles Martin 1775–1824
Born in Chichester. A self–taught painter, he was heavily influenced by the Dutch artists of the 17th century and many of his paintings depict Dutch ships. Exhibited at the RA from 1807 to 1821 and at the BI.

Prout, Samuel 1783–1852
Born in Plymouth. Moved to London, where he was employed as a topographical draughtsman. Made his first visit to the continent of Europe in 1819 and from that time onward he painted picturesque views of medieval towns. Exhibited at the RA from 1803 to 1827. Died in London.

Ravilious, Eric 1903–1942
Born in London. Attended Eastbourne School of Art, and went on to the Royal College of Art in London. Worked with Edward Bawden for several

years, then moved to Castle Hedingham, Suffolk. Appointed an official war artist in 1940, but was killed on a flight off Iceland.

REDMORE, HENRY 1820–1887
Born and died in Hull. Exhibited at the RA in 1868.

RICHARDSON, THOMAS MILES, Senior 1784–1848
Born in Newcastle. Apprenticed as a cabinet maker. Took up marine painting and exhibited at the BI from 1824 to 1846 and at the RA from 1837 to 1848. Lived and worked in the northeast of England, where he painted landscapes, seascapes and topographical views in watercolours.

ROBINS, THOMAS SEWELL c 1809–1880
Entered the RA Schools in 1829. Travelled extensively on the continent of Europe in the 1850s. Painted marine subjects in watercolours and exhibited at the RA between 1829 and 1874. Died in London.

ROUX, ANGE-JOSEPH ANTOINE (ANTOINE *père*) 1765–1835
Born and died in Marseilles. The father of three sons who all became marine artists. He specialized in ship portraits in watercolours and trained his sons in the same tradition. He is generally regarded as the most accomplished and successful of the family, although the work of father and sons is often very similar.

ROUX, FRANÇOIS GEOFFROI (FRANÇOIS) 1811–1882
Born and died in Marseilles. The youngest of the sons of Ange-Joseph Antoine Roux. Trained by his father and, like him, painted ship portraits in watercolours. Was appointed *Peintre Officiel de la Marine* in 1876.

ROUX, FRANÇOIS JOSEPH FREDERIC (FREDERIC) 1805–1870
Born and died in Marseilles. One of the three sons of Ange-Joseph Antoine Roux. Initially trained by his father but later became a pupil of Horace Vernet in Paris. In 1835 he moved to Le Havre, where his watercolours of the shipping were much admired.

ROUX, MATHIEU-ANTOINE (ANTOINE *fils*) 1799–1872
Born and died in Marseilles. The eldest of the sons of Ange-Joseph Antoine Roux. Trained by his father, he assisted him with the hydrography and cartography business and painted ship portraits in watercolours.

RUISDAEL, JACOB VAN 1628/9–1682
Born in Haarlem, the son of the painter Isaac van Ruisdael, he was probably the pupil of his uncle Salomon van Ruisdael. By 1648 he was a member of the Haarlem Painters' Guild. He travelled in Germany in the early 1650s and in 1656 settled in Amsterdam. In addition to his celebrated landscapes he painted coastal scenes and some memorable seascapes.

RUISDAEL, SALOMON VAN 1600/3–1670
Born at Naarden. Spent most of his life at Haarlem and became a member of the Haarlem Painters' Guild in 1623. Painted landscapes and river scenes with shipping.

SAILMAKER, ISAAC 1633–1721
Born in Scheveningen. The original family name was probably Zeilmaker. He emigrated to London, became a pupil of George Geldorp and painted harbour and coast scenes with shipping and sea battles. He died in London.

SALMON, ROBERT 1775–c 1843
Born in Whitehaven, Cumbria. From 1806 to 1811 he was working in Liverpool and from 1812 was based at Greenock in Scotland. In 1828 he sailed to America and spent the next 12 or 13 years in Boston. He returned to Europe in about 1841.

SCHETKY, JOHN CHRISTIAN 1778–1874
Born in Edinburgh. He was professor of drawing at the Royal Military College, Marlow, Buckinghamshire, then at the Royal Naval College, Portsmouth, and finally at the East India College at Addiscombe. Appointed Marine Painter in Ordinary to King George IV. Died inLondon.

SCOTT, SAMUEL 1701/2–1772
Born in London. In 1732 completed a commission for the East India Company. Settled in Twickenham, near London, in 1758. Painted sea battles, and views of the Thames waterfront and shipping. Died in Bath.

SERRES, DOMINIC 1772–1793
Born at Auch in Gascony. Went to sea and became master of a trading vessel. Captured by a British warship, he was taken to England and after a spell in Northampton settled in London. Was a founder member of the Royal Academy and exhibited there from 1760 to 1792. Died in London.

SERRES, JOHN THOMAS 1759–1825
Born in London. In 1793 he succeeded his father as marine painter to the king, and in 1800 was appointed draughtsman to the Admiralty and sailed on a British warship to make drawings of French harbours. Exhibited at the RA from 1780 to 1825. His wife's extravagances ruined him and he died in a debtors' prison in London.

SOMERSCALES, THOMAS JACQUES 1842–1927
Born in Hull. Served in the Royal Navy as a schoolmaster for 7 years. In about 1874 he was invalided ashore at Valparaiso, Chile, and took up marine painting He returned to Hull in 1892 and exhibited at the RA from 1893. Died in Hull.

STANFIELD, CLARKSON 1793–1867
Born in Sunderland. Went to sea in a collier and in 1812 was pressed into the Royal Navy. In 1815 he sailed to China in an East Indiaman. On his return he left the sea and took up scene painting. Exhibited at the RA from 1820 to 1867. Died in Hampstead, London. (This artist is often wrongly referred to as William Clarkson Stanfield).

STORCK, ABRAHAM JANSZ 1644–1710
Born and died in Amsterdam. He was a prolific painter of sea battles, busy harbour scenes with shipping, and capriccio seaports. His brother Jacobus also painted marine subjects.

Swaine, Francis c.1715–1782
Lived and died in London. Records show that in 1735 he was a messenger employed by the Treasurer and Commissioners of the Royal Navy. Exhibited at the Free Society of Artists from 1761. Painted coastal and estuary scenes with shipping, and sea battles.

Turner, Joseph Mallord William 1775–1851
Born and died in London. Entered the RA Schools in 1789. During the 1790s he made numerous sketching tours around Britain. Made the first of many visits to France and Italy in 1802, and first visited Belgium, Holland and the Rhine in 1817. Exhibited at the RA from 1790 to 1850. Became Professor of Perspective and then Professor of Painting at the RA.

Tuke, Henry Scott 1858–1929
Born in York. Studied at the Slade School of Art. Lived at Falmouth from 1885 onwards. Visited Newlyn in the 1880s and became an associate of the Newlyn School of artists. Painted pictures of fishing boats, ships at sea and nude boys bathing. Exhibited at the RA from 1879.

Velde, Willem van de, the Elder 1611–1693
Born in Leiden. Moved to Amsterdam around 1636. Recorded movements of the Dutch fleet in the 1640s and was present at Battle of Scheveningen in 1653. Emigrated to England in winter of 1672–73 and lived in Greenwich. In 1691 he moved to Westminster. Died in London.

Velde, Willem van de, the Younger 1633–1707
Born in Leiden. The eldest son of Willem van de Velde the Elder. Studied with his father and in about 1648 moved to Weesp to study with Simon de Vlieger. By 1652 he was back in Amsterdam, working closely with his father. He joined his father in England in the winter of 1672–73. Carried out numerous commissions for King Charles II and his brother the Duke of York. In 1694 he joined the English fleet and probably visited the Mediterranean. Died in London.

Vernet, Claude-Joseph 1714–1789
Born in Avignon. His father was a decorative painter. Studied with Jacques Viali in Aix-en-Provence. Moved to Rome in 1734 where his landscapes and marine paintings attracted distinguished patrons. In 1753 he returned to France and died in Paris.

Vlieger, Simon de c.1600–1653
Born in Rotterdam. He was the pupil of Jan Porcellis. By 1653 he was living in Amsterdam. He painted coastal scenes with fishing boats, storms and shipwrecks, and a few sea battles. Dubbells, Van de Cappelle and the younger Van de Velde were his pupils. Died in Weesp.

Vroom, Hendrik Cornelisz 1566–1640
Born and died in Haarlem. Spent three years in Italy in the 1580s, where he met Paul Bril. Travelled to France in 1589 and to Danzig in 1590. He returned to Haarlem

Walters, Samuel 1811-1882
Born at sea on a coastal passage from Bideford to London. His father was Miles Walters, a marine artist. The family settled in Liverpool in the 1820s. He moved to London in 1845 but after 2 years he moved back to Liverpool where he established a thriving business in ship portraits.

Webber, John 1750?-1793
Born in Switzerland. His father was a Swiss sculptor. Studied in Berne and Paris. Came to London in 1771. Accompanied Captain Cook's third voyage to the Pacific as draughtsman, 1776-80. Mostly painted in watercolours. Exhibited at the RA from 1776 to 1793.

Wieringen, Cornelis Claesz. van c 1580-1633
Born and died in Haarlem. Studied with Hendrik Vroom. Many of his pictures of Dutch harbours and river scenes with shipping were engraved and published.

Wilkinson, Norman 1878-1971
Born in Cambridge. Studied at Portsmouth School of Art. Contributed illustrations to ILN from 1898. A lieutenant in the RNVR during the First World War. Painted posters for shipping companies and the railways. One of the leading war artists of both World Wars.

Willaerts, Adam 1577-1664
Born in Antwerp. Moved to Utrecht which was his base for the rest of his life. He painted royal embarkations, arrivals of fleets, coastal views and beach scenes populated with numerous figures.

Willaerts, Abraham 1603-1669
Born and died in Utrecht. He was the eldest son of Adam Willaerts. He studied portrait painting in Utrecht and Paris. Apart from his portraits and genre scenes, he also painted some coast scenes with shipping in a similar style to that of his father.

Whitcombe, Thomas c. 1752-1827
Born in London. He visited Bristol in 1787, toured Wales in 1789 and was in Devon in 1813. Painted ship portraits, sea battles, coastal scenes and harbours. Exhibited at the RA from 1783-1824 and appears to have been based in London for most of his life.

Whistler, James Abbott McNeill 1834-1903
Born in Lowell, Massachusetts. Attended West Point Military Academy. Studied painting in Paris. In 1859 he settled in London and took a house in Chelsea. He visited Britanny in 1861 and Trouville in 1865. In 1866 he spent several months in Chile. He visited Venice in 1879 and stayed for 14 months. Exhibited at RA from 1859 to1879. Died in London.

Wyllie, William Lionel 1851-1931
Born in London. Entered RA Schools in 1866. From 1885 to 1907 he lived by the River Medway, and from 1907 until his death he lived in a house overlooking Portsmouth harbour. He exhibited at the RA from 1868 to 1931. Died in Portsmouth.

Bibliography

BOOKS ON PRINTS AND PROCESSES

BRUNNER, FELIX *A Handbook of Graphic Reproduction Processes* (Teufen 1962)

CHAMBERLAIN, WALTER *The Thames & Hudson Manual of Etching and Engraving* (London 1972, reprinted 1992)

EICHENBERG, FRITZ *The Art of the Print,* (New York and London 1976)

GASCOIGNE, BAMBER *How to Identify Prints: A complete guide to manual and mechanical processes from woodcut to ink jet* (London 1986, reprinted 1995)

GILMOUR, PAT *Artists in Print: An introduction to prints and print-making* (BBC Publications, London 1981)

GRIFFITHS, ANTONY *Prints and Printmaking: An introduction to the history and techniques* (London 1980, 2nd edition 1996)

HIND, A.M. *A Short History of Engraving and Etching* (New York and London 1923, reprinted 1963)

IVINS, W.M. junior, *How Prints Look,* (Metropolitan Museum of Art, New York 1943)

BOOKS ON MARINE PAINTINGS AND WATERCOLOURS

ARCHIBALD, E.H.H. *Dictionary of Sea Painters* (Woodbridge 1980, reprinted 1989)

BERNT, WALTER *The Netherlandish Painters of the Seventeenth Century* (London 1971)

BREWINGTON, DOROTHY *Marine Paintings and Drawings in the Peabody Museum* (Salem, Massachusetts, 1968) *Marine Paintings and Drawings in Mystic Seaport Museum* (Mystic Seaport 1982)

CLARKE, MICHAEL *The Tempting Prospect: A social history of English watercolours* (London 1981)

CORDINGLY, DAVID *Marine painting in England 1700–1900,* (London 1974)

GAUNT, WILLIAM *Marine Painting: an historical survey* (London 1975)

HARDIE, MARTIN *Watercolour Painting in England,* 3 volumes (London 1966)

KEMP, PETER and ORMOND, RICHARD *The Great Age of Sail* (Oxford 1986)

KEYES, GEORGE S. *Mirror of Empire: Dutch marine art of the seventeenth century* (Minneapolis and Cambridge 1990)

LECK, MICHAEL *The Art of Nautical Illustration: A visual tribute to the achievements of the classic marine illustrators* (New Jersey 1991)

MALLALIEU, H.L. *Understanding Watercolours* (Woodbridge 1985)

MYERS, MARK and CREDLAND, ARTHUR and members of the RSMA, *A Celebration of Marine Art: Fifty years of the Royal Society of Marine Artists* (London 1996)

QUARM, ROGER and WILCOX, SCOTT *Masters of the Sea: British MarineWatercolours* (Oxford and New Haven 1987)

ROE, F. GORDON *Sea Painters of Britain,* 2 volumes (Leigh-on-Sea 1947)

RUSSELL, MARGARITA *Visions of the Sea: Hendrick C. Vroom and the origins of Dutch marine painting* (Leiden 1983)

STECHOW, WOLFGANG *Dutch Landscape Painting of the Seventeenth Century* (London 1966, reprinted 1968)

TAYLOR, JAMES *Marine Painting: Images of Sail, Sea and Shore* (London 1996)

VINCENT, ADRIAN *19th Century Maritime Watercolours* (Newton Abbot 1989)

WARNER, OLIVER *An Introduction to British Marine Painting,* (London 1948)

WILMERDING, JOHN *A History of American Marine Painting,* (Boston and Toronto 1968)

WILTON, ANDREW *British Watercolours 1750–1850* (Oxford 1977)

INDEX

References to an artist in the text precede those(in italics) to reproductions of the artists' work.

ABBREVIATIONS AND TERMS USED IN PRINTS

appresso at the house of, i.e. the publisher

aquaforti (a.f., aq., aqua.) made with acid, or etched

aquatinta (aq:tinta) the person who carried out the aquatint process

caelavit (cae., cael.) engraved

delineavit (del., delt., delin.) drew, i.e. the artist on whose drawing the print is based

dessine drawn

designavit (desig.) designed or drew

divulgavit (divulg.) published

effigiavit (effig.) drew

engraved (eng., engd.) usually applies to line engravings

ex archetypis from the original (painting or drawing)

ex officina from the workshop

ex typis from the printing house
excudit (ex., exc., excud.) published

faciebat (fac.) made, i.e. the engraver or etcher

fecit (f., fec., fect.) made

gezeichnet (gez.) drawn

grave engraved

mpressit (imp.) printed

incidebat, incidit (inc.) incised, or engraved

invenit, inventor (in., inv., invt.) invented, i.e. the artist who made the original drawing

lithog (lith., litho.) either the artist who drew the image or the printer of the lithograph

pinxit, pingebat (pinx., pinxt., ping.) painted

sculpsit, sculpebat (sc., sculp., sculpt.) engraved

For a more detailed explanation of printing terms and abbreviations see Antony Griffiths, *Prints and Printmaking* and Bamber Gascoigne, *How to Identify Prints.*